COMMUNITY
&
COMMITMENT

COMMUNITY & COMMITMENT

Religious Plausibility in a Liberal Protestant Church

WADE CLARK ROOF

Elsevier · New York

NEW YORK · OXFORD · SHANNON

ELSEVIER NORTH-HOLLAND, INC.
52 Vanderbilt Avenue, New York, New York 10017

Distributors outside the United States and Canada:
THOMOND BOOKS
(A Division of Elsevier/North-Holland Scientific Publishers, Ltd)
P.O. Box 85
Limerick, Ireland

©1978 by Elsevier North-Holland, Inc.

Library of Congress Cataloging in Publication Data

Roof, Wade Clark,
    Community and commitment; religious plausibility in a
liberal protestant church.

    Bibliography: p.
    Includes index.
    1. Liberalism (Religion)—United States. 2. Commitment
to the church. 3. Protestant Episcopal in the U.S.A.
North Carolina (Diocese) 4. Faith—Psychology. I. Title.
BR526.R66   301.5'8   77-16329
ISBN 0-444-99038-0

Manufactured in the United States

Designed by Loretta Li

TO JENNY AND KATHY,
*in hopes they will appreciate
the best in the American Protestant
heritage, and will discard its worst*

Contents

Acknowledgments

The books that people write usually reflect many influences—their teachers, scholarly works, research opportunities, professional experiences, and the like. All these have borne their imprint on me, but unlike for most professional sociologists the inspiration for this study came in the mid-sixties when I was a parish clergyman in the South. Confronted at the time with parish conflicts over civil rights and right-wing politics, my perceptions of the church's role in society, both in terms of its opportunities and its limitations, were firmly fixed. The matters dealt with in this book may appear academic in character now, but were not so then. Questions about religious commitment, its social influences and consequences, and the tensions between religion and society, were for me at the time acutely real.

While the inspiration came out of such experience, the theoretical concerns dealt with here bear the strong imprint of my educational training. In particular, I am indebted to three very good teachers. Liston Pope and James Gustafson, both at Yale Divinity School in the early sixties, introduced me to the sociology of religion and impressed very deeply upon me the humanness of all religious institutions in their social environment. Later, Gerhard Lenski at the University of North Carolina taught me to appreciate the "religious factor" as a potential if not an actual influence in society. Oddly enough, it was the theologians who influenced my view of the church as a very human, and sometimes frail institution, and a sociologist who helped me to see its possibilities for profound influence in various realms of social life.

With respect to the research itself, I should thank the research offices of the Episcopal Church for initially funding the project. Originally designed as an evaluation of a diocesan exchange program, the Episcopal research headquarters willingly permitted me to include items of interest in their questionnaire study. Robert Stauffer was codirector with me on the project, and I am especially grateful for his assistance in the research design and data collection.

Jay Demerath read an early draft of the manuscript and provided many helpful comments and suggestions. Others who read portions of the manuscript or in one way or another exchanged useful ideas with me about it include Jackson Carroll, Dean Hoge, William Newman, Richard Perkins, David Roozen, and John Seidler. While all have made contributions, none are of course responsible for any defects that remain in the argument put forth. Janet King, Hazel Kirouac, Dianne Pinche, and Lorraine Sylvain all typed portions of the manuscript, for which I am grateful.

Finally, I owe my deepest appreciation to my family. Jenny and Kathy, who were in kindergarten when this project was first begun, are now in junior high, but through it all appear to have adjusted pretty well to their father's seemingly unceasing work on a book. And my wife, Terry, was always there to listen when I needed someone to hear me out, and provided the most pleasant diversions when it was essential to get away from it all.

Amherst, Massachusetts
December 1977

COMMUNITY
&
COMMITMENT

Introduction

The late sixties were traumatic years for most American social institutions, but especially so for the mainline churches. Controversial social issues—civil rights, poverty, and the war in Vietnam, in particular—were hotly debated in every major denomination, often resulting in tensions and conflicts between clergy and laity, and between liberal and conservative laity themselves. Institutionally these strains took many forms, but generally they focused around whether the church should be publicly involved. Should the church as an organization take stands on matters that are divisive to the members? Should churches speak for the members? Should churches concern themselves with social controversies? Questions as these were brought into the open by rank-and-file church members, in response particularly to the participation of clergy in such matters. For by the end of the decade many activist clergy were among the most visible of protestors: they marched for civil rights, joined with the poor on picket lines, and waved banners in antiwar demonstrations. Sizable numbers of lay members, too, though usually with far less display, felt the issues were urgent and morally compelling, and often joined with the clergy in seeking a socially responsive and ethically concerned church.

While all the major religious institutions were riddled with tensions, nowhere were they greater than among the white, liberal Protestant

3

churches. For one thing, these churches—primarily the Congregationalists, Episcopalians, Methodists, and Presbyterians—share a
theological heritage emphasizing social ethics as an integral part of
Christian commitment. Historically these denominations have concerned themselves more with the ethical implications of the Gospel
for society than have evangelical, more conservative Protestants. As
a result, controversies over public involvement and programs of social
action are hardly new to these churches.[1] Second is the fact that these
are established, well-entrenched religious institutions in American
society that draw their memberships primarily from the middle and
upper-middle social classes. As religious institutions they confront a
very serious institutional dilemma in dealing with social controversies.
On the one hand, the churches as a result of their liberal theology are
led to speak to morally compelling issues and to align themselves with
programs of social action. Not to do so would risk compromising
ethical teachings. But on the other hand, if the issues are dealt with
too forthrightly there is danger of alienating the more privileged and
conservative segments of the church. Losing members who support
the status quo means that the church endangers its position of power
among those most capable of exerting influence and bringing about
responsible change in society.

Tensions mounted in the churches, to the point that by the late
sixties severe institutional dilemmas were apparent. Many lay members
protested the church's involvement by leaving the church or with-
holding financial support. Losses in church membership, or at least
lack of growth, were reported by the liberal denominations along with
declines in attendance at worship services and declines in financial
contributions.[2] Opposition to social activism was so widespread that
many of the churches were forced to make large cutbacks in staff
personnel and church programs. These cutbacks had the effect especially
of reducing liberal Protestantism's commitment to interdenominational cooperation and to the pursuit of racial justice in American life.

By the early seventies resistance to an ethically engaged church had
reached such proportions that new priorities were necessary for institutional survival. With a decline in social activism came a decided
turn toward more "spiritual" religion—evangelism, Bible study,
prayer breakfasts, and charismatic renewal. Conservative churches generally were growing and prospering, indicative of the new mood taking

4

hold in the nation at large. Accordingly, the liberal churches accelerated their retreat from public issues and shifted attention away from social concerns to the personal and spiritual needs of their parishioners. Liberal activists who in the previous decade had received a fair amount of support, waging battles against social injustice in the name of the church, now found themselves overcome by conservative sentiments and forced increasingly to relinquish activist views.

Over the course of the past decade, then, there has occurred a phenomenal shift in the outlook of liberal Protestantism: through a phase of social activism into a phase more recently of retrenchment and passive withdrawal. That this shifting occurred when it did indicates not only the close affinity between religion and the secular mood of the country, but perhaps more importantly that the mainline churches are highly heterogeneous, multiclientele organizations sensitive to sentiments arising from many quarters. Such a view is in keeping with the accounts of historians like Sydney Ahlstrom, Martin E. Marty, and Sidney Mead, who describe the deep divisions beginning in the 1920s and lasting into the present over matters of individual gospel versus social gospel.[3] Heavy emphases on *both* types of gospel are found in these churches, varying from time to time in relative influence but always as alternative and opposing ideologies. Marty, in fact, depicts this dynamic in American Protestantism as a "two-party system" of conflicting ideologies:

> One party, which may be called "Private" Protestantism, seized that name "evangelical" which had characterized all Protestants early in the nineteenth century. It accentuated individual salvation out of the world, personal moral life congruent with the ideals of the saved, and fulfillment or its absence in the rewards or punishments in another world in a life to come. The second informal group, which can be called "Public" Protestantism, was public insofar as it was more exposed to the social order and the social destinies of men.[4]

The fact that both types of ideology are firmly rooted in mainline Protestantism probably accounts for much of its growth and spread among many diverse groups in the past and no doubt helps explain why these churches confront institutional strains today. Because of their size and heterogeneity they encompass a broad spectrum of theological and cultural outlook, ideologies, values, and beliefs. Diversity means that often there is little consensus, socially or theologically; and hence, division and discord are quite common in these institutions. Lacking a strong and unified sense of mission as a church, liberal congregations easily fall prey to the shifting forces of opinion and sentiment.

PURPOSE OF THE STUDY

From a sociological perspective, the mainline Protestant churches are an interesting topic of study. They offer social scientists an opportunity to examine various facets of an institution currently undergoing change and experiencing internal tension and conflict. Much research in recent years has focused upon issues such as clergy and social activism,[5] conflicts over church priorities,[6] and reasons why liberal churches are facing institutional crises at a time when conservative churches are apparently growing.[7] All these topics imply a peculiar set of problems confronting the liberal churches, problems perhaps not unique but which are especially paramount at this time.

Whether peculiar or not, the problems facing these churches are, I believe, more serious than are generally assumed. At the bottom of these institutional dilemmas is what I take to be the most serious problem of all—*a crisis of plausibility*. By this is meant not simply the lack of commitment to theological and ethical teachings, but more basically the failure of these churches to fashion a meaningful and compelling faith congruent with modern culture. The problem arises out of the fact that mainline church members, unlike most in the conservative churches, are drawn primarily from those social sectors oriented to the dominant culture of modern, industrial society. Because of their typical middle-class social location, members of these churches find it necessary to relate their belief systems to the contemporary modern world, confronting secular influences that weaken and often undermine basic beliefs and convictions. Confronted as well by an increasingly pluralistic society and growing doubts about themselves as a majority group, not surprisingly many American Protestants view their long-standing religious heritage and way of life as under attack.

This is indeed paradoxical, for it is these very churches that have sought most to modernize Christian faith and to fit it to contemporary

6

life. But despite theological efforts at demythologizing traditional beliefs and doctrines and reconceptualizing them in modern existential terms, church commitment on the part of liberal Protestants is weaker than that of conservatives. This is evident with almost every indicator that social scientists use for measuring institutional commitment. Stark and Glock, for example, in their study of denominational patterns of commitment conclude:

> . . . . the majority of members of liberal bodies are dormant Christians. They have adopted the theology of the new reformation, but at the same time they have stopped attending church, stopped participating in church activities, stopped contributing funds, stopped praying, and are uninformed about religion. Furthermore, only a minority of members of the liberal bodies feel that their religious perspective provides them with the answers to the meaning and purpose of life, while the overwhelming majority of conservatives feel theirs does supply the answers. Finally, the liberal congregations resemble theater audiences, their members are mainly strangers to each other, while conservative congregations resemble primary groups, united by widespread bonds of personal friendship.[8]

But why are the liberal churches in this condition? Often the explanations given are stated in terms of the beliefs held by church members. Stark and Glock themselves take this position, suggesting that the plight of these churches stems from a decline in doctrinal orthodoxy. Presumably traditional Christian beliefs inspire a strong, unswerving commitment, but modernist interpretations and beliefs encourage freedom of thought, critical opinion, and a more detached approach to such matters. And more recently Dean Kelley, in his provocative treatise on the plight of liberal Protestantism, argues the mainline churches are suffering because of a failure to solve problems of personal meaning for individuals.[9] Those churches that offer meaning to ultimate questions of life are the ones, he says, that have demanding standards, strict doctrine, and absolutist teachings. Conservative churches grow because they retain these qualities and recognize their primary task is to lead people to a demanding type of commitment.

My thesis, however, is that this crisis of commitment is largely cultural, not theological, in origin. Tensions in mainline Protestantism today are to a considerable extent the outgrowth of broader tensions in American culture. The difficulties of working out a plausibile and truly meaningful belief system are not simply religious in a narrow

7

sense of the word, but also reflect serious problems of integrating traditional religious conceptions with the scientific and humanistic views that have come to dominate contemporary life. The traditional religious world view rests on an assumption of a supernatural order, compared with secular scientific and humanistic world views which focus only on life in this world; likewise, traditional religious interpretations posit the mysterious forces of a sovereign Deity at work in everyday human affairs whereas scientific, humanist explanations point to the laws of nature as a basis for understanding such matters. While the former leaves room for divine revelation, the latter is concerned with developing objective knowledge and rational explanations. Both of these world views coexist in contemporary American culture, and as alternative approaches to reality they are not always easily reconciled with one another.

With the total culture bifurcated in this way, it should come as no surprise that liberal Protestant churches are today confronting commitment problems. These institutions are caught in between the traditional and secular world views and presently suffer from what Dean R. Hoge calls the "collapse of the middle"—that is, the inability to pull these two competing views together into a single, coherent perspective.[10] As Hoge discusses in some detail, traditional religious world views are firmly rooted in the conservative and evangelical churches, and scientific, humanistic world views in academe; but the mainline Protestant churches are positioned between these two, and find themselves attempting to accommodate both in working out interpretations of social reality that are plausible and convincing. To be sure, for many of the conservatively oriented members of these churches, traditional orthodox beliefs and practices are quite congruent with their accustomed life-styles and values, and hence institutional religion as they know it lends meaning and purpose to their lives. But for a growing number of the members, however, who are scientifically and rationally oriented, conventional church religion is hardly sufficient. They find its beliefs outmoded, its rituals lacking in meaning, and encounter subtle but nonetheless important cognitive strains in trying to link together religious interpretation and everyday life and experiences.

To approach a study of the liberal churches in this way may appear strange, especially coming from a sociologist. Typically sociologists

8

emphasize social class, ethnic, racial, regional, and urban-rural factors, the usual social sources of religious differences. And if there is a predominating perspective on American religious culture over the past twenty years, it is Herberg's description of religious self-identification in terms of Protestant, Catholic, and Jew—the "triple melting pot" of religious communalism.[11] But from the vantage point of the mid-seventies it is clear that the prevailing sociological approaches are insufficient for understanding the religious strains of the last decade, and that new analytic paradigms are called for that take seriously the problems of plausibility *within* the major American socioreligious communities. In an increasingly secular society, cultural meaning systems cannot be taken for granted as if they are equally plausible to all members of the community. Internal cleavages between traditionalists and modernists have intensified not only for Protestants, but very much so for Catholics,[12] and to a lesser extent for Jews as well.[13] That profoundly significant shifts are occurring in the American religious landscape, leading to new lines of division, is evidenced by the types of religious movements that have become so common in the seventies. The rise of Eastern mystical faiths among youth, the growing appeal of the evangelicals and return to forgotten fundamentals, and the spread of charismatic renewal groups across denominational lines—all these, diverse as they are, signal changing realignments in the American people's quest for meaning and belonging.

The basic argument of this book is that *the social basis of liberal Protestantism is currently shifting away from the cultural mainstream and finding increasing support in the traditional, more conservative sectors of the society*. Pressures in this direction were generated out of the controversies over social activism in the late sixties, leading in more recent times to withdrawal and retreat, and a turn to more spiritual matters. In and of itself this is not so striking a thesis in light of all that has been written about the problems facing the liberal churches in recent years.[14] But the sociological implications of this shift in social basis, I believe, have not been fully examined. Consider, for instance, its implications for:

> Cultural cleavages between traditionalists and modernists, and their contrasting styles of religious commitment.

9

> Greater social interaction among the traditionalists, and rein-
forcement of conservative theological beliefs.
> Commitment not only to conservative theology, but to con-
servative social ideologies, values, and ethical views generally.

These are all important issues for the liberal churches and their
future role in American society as mainline religious institutions. The
issues themselves are hardly new to social scientists concerned with
religion, but few attempts have been made to explore systematically
their many ramifications for contemporary Protestant church life. In
so doing we shall find that the changing social location of religion
bears implications not only of a practical sort for churches, but also
for commentators and theorists who seek to understand the dynamics
of belief and participation in these institutions.

THEORETICAL GUIDELINES

In approaching how the social basis of the mainline churches is shifting,
the study focuses upon the social worlds in which people live. More
specifically, it focuses on the social world of the local community in
which people live, and the increasingly close affinities of this world
with traditional, church-oriented religion. While this can hardly provide a total theory of religious change today, it does offer some insights
into the social psychology of religious belief and the way in which
social and religious meanings come to be fused together. We shall
explore these insights in some depth in later chapters, and at this
point, need only sketch the most general features of the approach.

The local community is a significant sphere of social life for many
reasons. In the most fundamental sense, it is the basic residential unit
where people carry out the daily rounds of their lives. Here the vast
majority of Americans are born, grow up, find mates, raise children,
grow old, and finally die, benefiting at each step of the way from
primary-group support structures. From an institutional perspective
the local community is the center of social activity—where people
vote, receive medical care, entertain relatives and friends, and participate in voluntary organizations. To be sure, work is often an exception,
carrying many in a mass society away from the local community and

weakening their ties to community-based institutions. But even so probably for most persons the major structures of social participation and belonging are found within the local community.

Such view has not always held sway in social science. The early theorists, including Töennies, Durkheim, Park, and Wirth, regarded modernization as gradually undermining the communal bonds linking individuals to locality. In their view the local community would be truncated, if not entirely eclipsed. The "eclipse of community" theme emphasizing the increasing scale of societal organization was very prominent in community studies, up until the sixties—as expressed by such well-known writers as the Lynds in Middletown, Warner in Yankee City, and Vidich and Bensman in Springdale.[15] During the fifties and sixties especially, mass society theorists called attention to the rapid dissemination of the national culture, the "massification" of social life, and declining local community bonds. As a result of mass media and other technological advances making possible opportunities for social contacts transcending physical space, a homogenization of cultural life was envisioned that could only result in the loss of locality-specific traditions.

But contrary to such claims, the local community has not withered in rapid dissolution as a primary-group structure. Indeed it persists as a complex system of kinship and friendship networks, formal and informal associations, and symbolic meanings, all very much rooted in family life and ongoing socialization processes. Much recent research underscores the continuing importance of such attachments in all types of residential settings—rural areas, small towns, and even large urban centers—plus the fact that people's local community identification and participation vary widely, depending on their life-style preferences.[16] For individuals oriented to the larger society, lack of attachment to the immediate locale emancipates them from its sanctions and confinements. Yet others, either out of custom or conscious preference, embrace the local community as a world in which they find familiar values, social orientation, and psychic support. The local community is for them, as Benita Luckmann observes, a major "small life-world"— a micro-universe around which social experiences may be structured and interpreted in a complex, anonymous society.[17]

In short, recent studies suggest that local community life persists— less binding now than it once was, but nonetheless organized as a set

11

of social experiences. The critical difference currently is that individuals, now more than ever before, may *choose* whether or not to become involved locally. As the society has increased in scale, so has the individual's range of choices with respect to neighboring, participation in voluntary organizations, and styles of institutional involvement. Symbolically, too, individuals are freer to choose the level of community in which they identify, be it the neighborhood, the local area, the metropolitan center, or the national society. Thus the local community has become, in the words of Morris Janowitz, a "community of limited liability," pointing to the fact that in a highly mobile society people may become very involved in locally based organizations and institutions but still be prepared to sever such ties, and move to other communities, if such participation fails to satisfy their immediate needs or aspirations.[18]

Greater choices on people's part on whether to become involved in local community life bear directly upon their styles of institutional commitment. Individuals with strong attachments to their local primary groups are subject to the approval and censure of neighbors, friends, and close kin. Consequently, these sanctions operate as effective controls over their social values, beliefs, and life-styles. But with the emancipation of such ties, this social control mechanism is significantly altered. Sanctions that were previously powerful become ineffectual, and individuals are left free to pattern their lives largely independent of local community norms.

Whether or not an individual chooses to become involved in local community life, and to subject one's self to its normative constraints, is fundamentally important to traditional, church-oriented religion. For whatever else churches may be, they are as James M. Gustafson points out *natural communities* whose self-perpetuation as institutions rests upon basic social processes, such as the sharing of beliefs in public worship, the socialization of new members into the faith by means of example as well as indoctrination, and regular participation in the common life of the congregation.[19] All these are group-based activities without which cultic, or organized, religion would be impossible. In the Christian tradition especially, congregations have always depended upon drawing a substantial portion of their members from among those with stable social patterns and who regard their social life as opportunity for expressing religious values. In order for churches as

12

we know them to persist, they require a relatively well-established social infrastructure wherein individuals relate to one another regularly and share common beliefs and views.

Once this social fabric begins to pull apart, religious institutions suffer in the process. Without strong social support structures, churches lose many of their qualities as communities in which beliefs, values, and definitions of social reality are shared; and religion becomes instead far more individualized as a personal, private matter. As a result traditional faith can easily lose its plausibility, and it becomes more difficult for church members to maintain commitment, both personally as well as to the established religious institution itself.

THE DATA AND PROCEDURES

Having described the aims of the study, and discussed generally the theoretical framework, next we review briefly the source of data and procedures followed in examining these issues.

The data on which the study is based were collected in 1968, about the time when controversies over social activism in the liberal denominations were at their height. Data are included here for only one denomination—the Episcopalians. The sample consists of 486 white, adult Episcopalians, randomly selected from the North Carolina Diocese. At the time the Episcopal Church was engaged in a large research project and collected questionnaire data on a broad range of topics, both religious and nonreligious. Wherever possible, the research staff sought to use identical questions to those asked in many other surveys. The content of the questionnaire, reproduced in its entirety, is shown in Appendix C.

Admittedly the sample is small compared to those of national surveys, although it is judged to be representative of the diocese under study and, except for its southern character, appears fairly representative of Episcopalians nationally (for further discussion of the sample, see Appendix A). Nevertheless, because of the size and regional quality of the sample, no attempt is made to generalize to some larger population. Rather the intent is more analytic than descriptive. The principal objective in an analytic survey is to explore and unravel underlying relationships among variables, from a given theoretical perspective. The focus is upon substantive issues and less upon descriptive profiles.[20] Hence, our concern throughout will be to look closely at the data and to see what evidence can be mustered in support of the theory put forth.

The kind of analysis carried out here reflects a growing tendency to use survey data for constructing and testing theoretical models in social research. Such approach is sometimes criticized for being overly formal, but it has some distinctive advantages that are often overlooked. By stating clearly on theoretical grounds how variables should be interrelated, a researcher is usually better able to design a research strategy that "controls" for relevant factors, tests for relations among variables in proper causal ordering, and systematizes generally the empirical analysis. For this reason we rely very heavily, although not exclusively, on path models when it is necessary to engage in complex, multivariate analyses. Simple modeling procedures of this kind are increasingly common in social science research. Though obviously not without limiations of their own, they represent a marked improvement over cross-tabular modes of analysis that are still quite customary in research on religion.

PLAN OF THE STUDY

Finally, a word about the plan of the study. There are five parts to the book. Part I raises some analytic issues underlying much of the empirical research on mainline Protestantism. Chapter 1 details these issues, both from methodological and substantive perspectives. Chapter 2 shifts from a critical to a constructive stance, proposing a theory of religious commitment based upon considerations of local community attachment and participation. Part I concludes with Chapter 3 offering a description of the traditionalists and modernists in the churches, looking especially at their social background and life-style characteristics.

There are three major research questions dealt with in the next three parts. Part II turns to the first of these—the social correlates of religious commitment. Chapter 4 examines the basic patterns of belief and practice; and Chapter 5 delves into how the many social correlates are related to the several aspects of religiosity. Part III explores mechanisms by which religious commitment is maintained among the traditional believers. Chapter 6 looks at church commitment in greater depth and investigates some of the subtle ways in which local community ties help to undergird institutional loyalties. Chapter 7 focuses upon more personal, subjective types of commitment, and again ways that local attachments sustain and reinforce religious identity. Part IV is concerned with the consequences of religious belief. Chapter 8 describes various social ideologies, such as racial prejudice, political intolerance, and church activism, and explores the relation of these to doctrinal orthodoxy and cultural influences. Chapter 9 follows up this analysis investigating some of the subtleties of beliefs and their influences.

Finally, Part V sums up the results of the study as a whole and seeks to place them in a broader context of current religious trends in American society. Some speculation is offered about the future of the liberal churches and their changing institutional forms and functions.

[I]

PERSPECTIVES ON LIBERAL PROTESTANTISM

⌈1⌋

Issues in the Empirical Study of Religious Commitment

Social scientists have amassed a considerable body of factual data on the members in the liberal, mainline churches. There is information about their beliefs, attendance at Sunday worship, involvement in parish activities, attitudes on abortion, war, civil rights, and myriad other matters. Despite this storehouse of empirical facts, however, remarkably little is actually known about the *styles* of religious commitment in these churches. Unfortunately, much of the research on religion using surveys and polls is descriptive and only marginally concerned with broader substantive matters. As a result there is far less cumulative knowledge of theoretical significance than might be thought to exist. It is also the case that many of the theories and interpretative schemes used are burdened with institutional assumptions about religion's integrative role in society—assumptions that are highly questionable, if not untenable, in a modern, secular setting. To understand better the changing structures of commitment, we need theories more attuned to the serious problems of plausibility confronted by the mainline churches.

This chapter explores some of the issues, *methodological* and *substantive*, that arise in developing theories of religious commitment. By methodological here, I refer to empirical and analytical matters involved in drawing proper theoretical influences from data; and by substantive, to the broader theoretical considerations about church religion as an institution in contemporary society. As we shall see, discussion of these will lay the groundwork for the theoretical approach proposed in the following chapter.

METHODOLOGICAL CONSIDERATIONS

In developing systematic and testable theories of religious commitment, researchers have to pay close attention to how their choice of analytic procedure affects the interpretations they draw. Greater methodological sophistication in recent years, especially in measurement and data analysis, has led theoretically oriented analysts of religion to become more aware of this than ever before. As a result some theories, which about fifteen years ago were taken as empirically demonstrated, are today under reconsideration in light of more reliable analysis procedures. In the long run this can only lead to theoretical advance, as concepts become better defined and theories better formulated in a logical and testable manner. Indeed, future theoretical contributions arising out of the empirical study of religion rest largely upon further advances of this kind.

The state of affairs at present with respect to studies of religious commitment may be described as healthy confusion. It is healthy in the sense that theories of commitment exist and researchers attempt to test these theories empirically. But at the same time there is a good deal of confusion because there are so many measures of religiosity, conflicting interpretations, and inconsistent research findings. In large part the confusion stems from alternative modes of analysis and varying degrees of rigor in drawing causal inferences.

To illustrate what I mean by healthy confusion, let us examine three very prominent topics currently in the field: multidimensional measurement of religious commitment, the social correlates of religion, and the consequences of religious belief. Each of these is important in understanding mainline church religion today, and all have received considerable attention in empirical research. For this reason we shall examine each of the topics in some detail.

Multidimensional Commitment

In the past twenty years, empirical researchers have concerned themselves increasingly with defining and measuring individual religiosity. Following World War II it became evident to many that no single measure of religiosity could accurately describe the quality of American religious life. While some observers pointed to increases in church attendance and affiliation as indicative of a postwar revival, others detected an erosion of orthodox beliefs as the society became more secular. Recognition of this apparent paradox led Will Herberg to conclude in the early sixties that "America is at once the most religious and the most secularistic of nations."[1] Religion was clearly of social significance in America, but what aspects and just how were matters calling for more precise formulation.

Largely as a result of the landmark studies by Gerhard Lenski and Charles Y. Glock, multidimensional approaches to religion are commonplace today. In the 1958 Detroit-area study, Lenski distinguished between associational and communal types of religious participation and between doctrinal orthodoxy and devotionalism, and was able to document distinct influences of each in the political, economic, and family realms.[2] About that time Glock proposed that religious commitment should be defined along five dimensions: belief, ritual, knowledge, experience, and consequences.[3] His schema was more systematic than Lenski's. Whereas Lenski was concerned primarily with religion's impact on other social institutions, Glock's efforts were devoted more specifically to defining the many aspects of religious commitment itself. But more importantly, both helped to establish the necessity of multidimensional approaches to religion in empirical research.

Since then researchers have continued to explore the multidimensionality question, although there is little agreement today as to the number of dimensions or their proper labels.[4] Studies generally show that dimensions not only vary independently of each other, but that the use of any single measure may be a poor predictor of others. Dimensions concerned with belief and feelings usually cluster together as do the dimensions in which religious behavior and participation predominate. Knowing this has helped to advance our understanding of the individual's patterns of religiosity, and to recognize that commitment is a complex, multifaceted phenomenon not easily reduced to any single notion or operational measure.

But judging from its potential, this line of research has resulted in fewer theoretical advances than might have been expected. By and large the research is exploratory and descriptive, aimed more at unraveling the many dimensions of belief and behavior than at explaining why such patterns exist. Seldom do investigators inquire into the logical interrelationships among dimensions or offer explanations for dimensional variations in styles of religious commitment. In fact, questions about the *meaningfulness of the dimensions themselves and why they hang together as a total system of commitment* have received relatively little attention. In this respect there have been few advances beyond Lenski and Glock, who were both concerned with broader conceptual matters.

In part, the lack of advance reflects the heavy reliance upon *factor analysis* in these studies. Factor analysis as a procedure is often used for extracting from a large number of empirical indicators a smaller number of factors that presumably explain the relationships among the measured variables. The procedure is designed to elicit constructs from the data rather than impose them, and to generate factors that maximize the reduction of residual variance for a total set of indicators. While very useful as an exploratory technique, its application to the multidimensionality question raises some thorny conceptual questions.

The most serious of these has to do with *causal* relationships among the many dimensions themselves. In principle, factor analysis is most appropriate where there are no direct causal links among the empirical indicators; the latter are taken as "caused" by the extracted factors, thus making the observed correlations among indicators presumably spurious.[5] Following this logic religious indicators should not be causally interrelated, but instead should reflect underlying factors. But can we expect this to be the case with religiosity? If by religiosity we refer simply to its subjective forms, i.e., beliefs and meanings, then we might properly assume that these can be accounted for by one or more psychological factors. Personal beliefs and meanings may be manifestations of underlying internal predispositions and may themselves be functionally unrelated. That is to say, religious identity may be thought of in some sense as a unitary phenomenon.

But if religious commitment also refers to institutional belonging and group participation, then the causal issue becomes far more problematic. Social belonging and participation are different from religious meanings, so different that questions immediately come to mind about how the two types of commitment are logically interrelated. For example, many studies report a positive association between orthodox belief and church attendance among church members. This makes good intuitive sense, but does this mean that socioreligious group participation is essential to maintaining a religious belief system? Or is it the case that doctrinal beliefs prescribe whether an individual participates in a religious institution? Both views are found in the theoretical literature, and the two imply alternative causal ordering.[6] Of course, reality may not be so simple that we can say it is one or the other, but the logical issue remains to be dealt with from a theoretical standpoint.

From a theory-building perspective, it makes little sense to apply a method that treats the "meaning" and "belonging" indicators as unrelated if indeed they are. If one does proceed in this way and applies factor analysis, significant intercorrelations are likely to remain after all factors have been extracted. Thus, on both theoretical and empirical grounds, it would seem more reasonable to take into consideration the causal assumptions from the very start. Not that factor analysis is necessarily or always inappropriate, but simply that causal relations among religious dimensions cannot be overlooked if one is interested in developing systematic, empirically based theories.

Another problem concerns generalizability. Because factor analysis yield factors directly from the data, the results are particularly sensitive to sample characteristics. Thus we may give similar questionnaire items to two different groups, find that four factors account for, say, 70 percent of the variance, and yet discover that the item loadings on these factors differ so much that it is untenable to regard the multidimensional structure of commitment as equivalent from one group to another. In other words, factor analysis helps to uncover dimensional patterns within a specific sample but does not give direct tests of any single pattern of loadings across groups. Again for exploratory analysis this is not a serious problem, but for testing theories it is less than ideal.

Essentially it means that the number and types of dimensions observed in one denominational group are unlikely to hold in another.[7] Denominational groups vary considerably in religious and cultural traditions, to such an extent that we would hardly expect to find uniform systems of commitment. Depending upon theological heritage, groups differ significantly in their interpretations of ritual obligations, fundamental beliefs, and personal and social ethics. Given the fact that religious teachings are transmitted by socioreligious group subcultures, norms of commitment in any denomination will reflect social and cultural influences as much as, if not more than, theological tradition.

In conclusion, it would seem important in developing a better understanding of individual commitment (a) to explore, in depth, patterns within a single denomination, or families of denominations such as liberal Protestants who share similar theological and cultural backgrounds; and (b) to focus primarily on the *basic* forms of religiosity common to, say, the mainline Protestant churches, delving deeply into how these are interrelated with one another. Rather than to search endlessly for refinements in dimensional structures, what I am suggesting is a more theoretical approach placing emphasis on a few, but highly important, types of commitment thought to be causally significant. In this respect, Andrew Greeley's "meaning" and "belonging" framework would seem to offer a good starting point.[8] Not only does it help in grouping the basic types, such a framework promises as well to shed some light on the conceptual linkages among them. Later in the study we will have opportunity to explore this possibility.

Social Correlates of Religion

Another source of confusion concerns the social correlates of religious commitment. By this I refer to the relationships among independent variables that presumably influence religious commitment and the possibility that these are causally interrelated themselves. Our use of the nebulous term *correlate* is itself an indication that relatively little is known about such matters.

Studies on religiosity have uncovered numerous social psychological correlates, such as extrinsic and intrinsic orientation, dogmatism, conventionalism, and authoritarianism. In addition, much attention has been given to social background factors like social class, education, sex, family cycle, rural-urban residence, generation, region, and age. Typically what happens is that researchers concentrate upon a single factor, or variable, in formulating a theoretical explanation, often with little or no consideration of how the other variables may be causally connected. If spuriousness is dealt with at all, all too often it is by means of looking only at a few, haphazardly selected control variables, and one at a time at that. All too seldom does one find simultaneous controls for variables that, on the basis of some explicit theoretical rationale, logically follow as antecedent or intervening factors in a given explanatory scheme.

Thus we know there are many social influences on religious commitment, but often all we know is that the many influences are somehow related to one another and to religiosity. The precise form and relative importance of such relationships remain unknown. While mystery of this sort is perhaps appreciated by some mystics and religious enthusiasts, it is hardly a virtue to the analyst. In fact, empirical mysteries of this kind, as Hubert M. Blalock points out in another context, can result in fruitless debates over the significance of one or another type of variable.[9] If there are no serious causal connections among the variables, then relative importance can be assessed easily in terms of the variance explained in religiosity. But if there are causal influences of one independent variable upon another, including the possibility that the various religious dimensions may themselves be interrelated, then the rationale for using simple correlational procedures breaks down. Unless replaced by simultaneous-equation methods, it is easy to make biased inferences about the importance of any, or all, of the explanatory factors.

In order to avoid this as much as possible, it is helpful to postulate multivariate models of the social influence on religion. Such models not only aid in clarifying the linkages among variables, but help to determine which factors should be controlled, thereby increasing the chances of drawing more reliable conclusions. Where variables are related in a linear, additive fashion, multiple regression procedures such as path analysis offer a means of obtaining estimates of the relative importance of factors, including direct and indirect effects. Assuming one-way causation, simple recursive path models permit a researcher to judge the impact of an explanatory factor while controlling simultaneously for other factors. Such procedures are useful particularly in resolving theoretical disputes or differences of opinion about the types of factors, religious or nonreligious, which may be operative.

In many instances, of course, more complex models are required to represent social reality adequately. Lacking information about the subtleties of relationships, specification analysis is often a useful first step in developing such models, especially if there is reason to believe some factor operates as a conditioning influence inflating or deflating the associations between an independent variable and a dependent variable. This makes it possible to formulate more precise relationships and prepares the way for developing more elaborate interaction models.[10] We shall proceed in this fashion in later chapters where our concern is with specifying the decline of religious plausibility and its consequences. Among church members whose belief systems are highly plausible, we would expect to find patterns of meaning and belonging in the religious institution that very likely do not hold, or hold to a lesser degree, for those whose beliefs are otherwise. Assuming that we are correct in thinking that the liberal Protestant churches today confront serious cultural and ideological conflicts between traditionalists and modernists, it follows that analyses "specifying" conditions under which religious patterns hold, or fail to hold, are essential to our understanding of the contemporary religous situation.

Consequences of Orthodox Belief

Few topics in the sociology of religion have provoked as much attention and controversy as the consequences of religious belief. Following in the intellectual tradition of Max Weber and Ernst Troeltsch, many have argued that the social implications of orthodox Christian dogma are conservative and have sought to defend this thesis by amassing data on a wide range of attitudes and behaviors. The exact logical connections are often left unstated, or if stated, only vaguely so; but the basic assumption is that orthodox doctrines foster conservative social ideologies, prejudicial attitudes, reactionary political views, and the like. Often such claims are made even when there is little more than correlational evidence on which to base the argument.

Perhaps the most widely discussed work of this sort recently is

26

Glock and Stark's *Christian Beliefs and Anti-Semitism*.[11] Using cross-tabular analysis of responses from a San Francisco Bay area sample, they argue that orthodox religious faith induces Christians to adopt a particularistic stance regarding the possession of religious truth, which in turn prompts hostilities toward religious outsiders, especially Jews because of their alleged crucifixion of Christ. Because of this negative historical image of the Jew, Christian belief is thought to perpetuate stereotypes resulting in secular anti-Semitism. Thus a theological explanation is put forth to explain the anti-Semitic attitudes of church members, the majority of which are from the liberal Protestant denominations. Others of similar persuasion have suggested that religious dogma plays an important part in explaining prejudice toward minorities generally,[12] conservative politics,[13] and conservative views about the church's role in public affairs.[14] None of these researchers make charges against the mainline Protestants in quite the way as do Glock and Stark, but theological factors are taken to be of paramount importance in accounting for conservative responses. Typically what is assumed is that church members experience internal pressures leading them to fashion attitudes and behaviors consonant with their beliefs, and it is the beliefs that have predominating influence.

Obviously there is much truth in the basic thesis that religious beliefs are influential in shaping people's views. Much of the "Protestant ethic" research tradition, indeed, bears support in its favor. But methodologically speaking, this research often suffers serious defects. One is that cross-tabular modes of analysis, so common in these studies, fail to provide a sufficient empirical test of the hypothesis. In the Bay Area study, for example, Glock and Stark offer table after table of bivariate statistics consistent with portions of their argument, but never do they present the simultaneous relationships among all the variables. Without the latter it is impossible to check fully their theoretical model for internal consistency. Recent reanalysis of their data, in fact, shows that the empirical patterns do not hold in the way they say.[15] Another problem, not only in Glock and Stark's work but in this line of research generally, is lack of attention to other explanatory factors that are perhaps as important, if not more than, religious belief itself. Spuriousness is a serious problem in many theories of creedal influence, and unfortunately one cannot easily dismiss the possibility unless all the relevant control variables and explanatory factors are brought into the study design. Numerous critics in recent years have alerted us that this may well be the case, on the grounds that *both* religious orthodoxy and consequential attitudes and ideologies may covary in relation to a common antecedent factor—a particular cognitive style, cultural tradition, or some other social psychological or sociological correlate.

This is best illustrated in Russell Middleton's reappraisal of the relationship between Christian faith and anti-Semitism.[16] Using path analytic techniques, he examined the impact of five different facets of religious belief as mentioned by Glock and Stark (orthodoxy, libertarianism, particularism, religious hostility to the historical Jew, and religious hostility to the modern Jew) and found that their effects on anti-Semitism do not conform to the hypotheses advanced. Although the five facets combined account for 15 percent of the total variance in anti-Semitism, when other important background and social psychological intervening variables are held constant the 15 percent reduces to 2 percent. Despite their apparent importance, upon closer scrutiny it becomes clear that religious beliefs are not as predictive of the consequences as often thought and that beliefs are themselves anchored within larger constellations of cognitive, culturally based response patterns.

Again as with the social correlates, there is simply no substitute for well-formulated research designs and systematic testing of hypotheses. As more sophisticated methodological techniques come into use, we can expect to find more defensible empirical conclusions and hopefully some resolution of substantive issues such as this one. The present research seeks to make some advances along this line in readdressing the issue of religious consequences, looking at orthodox beliefs in their larger traditional cultural context. As we shall see later, lifting religious beliefs out of the total cultural setting in which they are found and treating them as if they can be analyzed apart from their cultural meanings can be quite misleading.

THEORETICAL CONSIDERATIONS

Next we turn to some broader substantive concerns, more interpretive and speculative but no less perplexing to the study of religion. It is necessary to place recent changes within the liberal Protestant churches into proper perspective, and to do this we have to look at trends generally for religion in modern, secular society. Our fundamental argument, it should be recalled, is that the social basis for institutionalized church religion is shifting generally away from the more modernized sectors of industrial society and toward traditional-oriented social strata and groups. We have assumed this to be the case though we have not as yet explored its implications.

Few people would insist today that church religion can be what Emile Durkheim and, to a lesser extent, Max Weber regarded as its very essence—namely, the glue that holds society together. It is evident that church-linked beliefs and values are less and less a part of the cultural mainstream in modern, industrial society. Whatever its functions in the past, one would hardly argue that church religion is a major source of cultural integration in contemporary society. The reasons for this are not hard to understand. In a democratic, pluralist society such as the United States, no single religious group controls a monopoly of authority over the entire society. Even those with large mass followings lack the power to enforce common beliefs and sanctions. Consequently, the churches' role as custodian of cultural values has been preempted to a very great extent by other institutions. Insofar as religion at all fulfills such integrative functions for the total society, it is America's "civil religion" that does so rather than the churches themselves. To be sure, the churches participate in the celebration of the country's democratic values and beliefs, but the latter as a national faith transcends the religious denominations and is closely aligned with the political institutions of modern society.[17]

Furthermore, advanced social differentiation in contemporary society makes it unlikely, if not impossible, that church religion can provide a basis for cultural unity. For as society becomes more complex, the religious sphere becomes increasingly segregated from other institutional sectors, and hence what takes place in the occupational and political realms tends to be secluded from direct religious influence. The result is not merely institutional specialization, or further separation of the religious and secular spheres; but religious values come to have little, if any, demonstrable relationship to what people actually do in the everyday world of work and politics. Secularization in this sense is, of course, much greater in Western, modernized societies, although there are important variations. For example, in Europe church

29

religion is strongest among marginal groups that have been least affected by modernizing influences; but in America churches enjoy greater middle-class credibility and still occupy, relatively speaking, positions of power and symbolic significance. As Thomas Luckmann observes, in Europe historically church religion has maintained its traditional posture and has become restricted to a minor part of the population, but in America the churches have sought instead to hold on to their members by accommodating beliefs and practices to a more secular clientele.[18]

But even so there has occurred in all modern societies a shifting in religious meanings, as Peter Berger points out, away from the "public" sectors of contemporary life, and greater concern with the "private sphere." Although religion may have lost influence in the society at large, it has considerable force in the individual's private life—that is, as a source of personal values, self-identity, and cognitive meaning. Essentially this means, however, that churches are less and less capable of providing a common set of meanings, values, and definitions of reality that can be shared throughout society. Greater privatization of beliefs and commitments generally can only mean that religion loses its traditional function of providing a religiously based moral order for the society. Berger comments on this as follows:

> . . . . privatized religion is a matter of the "choice" or "preference" of the individual or the nuclear family, *ipso facto* lacking in common, binding quality. Such private religiosity, however "real" it may be to the individuals who adopt it, cannot any longer fulfill the classical task of religion, that of constructing a common world within which all of social life receives ultimate meaning binding on everybody. Instead, this religiosity is limited to specific enclaves of social life that may be effectively segregated from the secularized sectors of modern society.[19]

The privatization of religion is especially pronounced among liberal Protestants. Because they tend to be more highly educated, more middle-class, and highly mobile socially and geographically, members of these churches typically espouse a high degree of individualism. This in turn fosters tolerance for the views of others, and together these two encourage free thought in religious matters. Individualism also breeds distaste for group conformity and thus undercuts a person's willingness to submit to group norms and sanctions. All these are described by Dean Kelley as traits of a "weak" religion because they fail to nurture strong commitments to *organized* religion.[20] Even if we do not accept Kelley's argument in full, certainly it is the case that such traits intensify problems of plausibility for the liberal churches. They signify a highly personalized form of religion and one that suffers, institutionally speaking, from a lack of consensus over such vital matters as doctrinal belief, authority, and the nature and purpose of the church. In this respect we can extend Luckmann's observation by noting that in America, unlike in Europe where traditional church religion has been pushed to the periphery of modern society, churches in trying to accommodate the secular culture have opened themselves up to severe internal strains.

These changing conditions for religion bear profound implications for personal commitment. Three concerns that seem especially pertinent to liberal Protestants are (1) the social reinforcement of commitment, (2) religious reality construction, and (3) religious plausibility as it bears upon people's styles of commitment. We look at each of these in turn.

Social Bases of Commitment

As was mentioned earlier, churches are natural communities whose survival as institutions depends upon organized, group-based activities. Commitment to church religion on the part of an individual does not occur in a social vacuum but instead takes place in a sociocommunal context in which believers come to know one another, share their faith as well as other sentiments, and develop close bonds of unity. Of course not all church members develop close attachments, but because institutional religion is a collective enterprise it generally fosters strong group loyalties and identities among the deeply committed.

We can go even further and observe that the social context of the believer plays a crucial part in helping create and maintain a plausible belief system. Individuals who are well integrated into a believing community are better able to believe themselves, for out of the group they receive social support and reinforcement in their definitions of reality. Such a social base is described by Berger as a "plausibility structure"—that is, networks of interaction among those sharing common beliefs and views about reality.[21] Its functions are especially important in contemporary society, considering that religious meanings are not generally shared in the public sectors. As traditional religion has lost its hold in the wider realms, socioreligious group involvement has become increasingly important to believers as a means of reinforcing religious loyalties.

Implicit in the notion of a shifting social basis for church religion is a view of secularization, essentially as a process in which the plausibility structure for religion *diminishes in scope—from society as a whole to smaller, more fragmented social spheres*. Envisioned in this way secularization does not eliminate religion from the modern scene but rather implies that its plausibility is increasingly restricted to the traditionally oriented sectors of the society. To assert this is not to dismiss churches as unimportant to the believers or even to suggest they are socially insignificant. A religious world view may not prevail in society generally but still inspire commitment among members from within certain social strata and sectors. Its declining plausibility in society at large may actually signal new and alternative social forms for religion, thus making them quite important as social phenomena.

It seems reasonable to suggest that considerations of plausibility structure are increasingly pertinent to the liberal Protestant churches. Historically traditionalists have outnumbered modernists in these churches; and if present trends continue in the direction they have been going over the past ten years, we can only expect these institutions to become more closely identified with traditional cultural styles. If indeed this is the case, then we need to know more about the cultural traditionalists in these institutions—who they are, their values and outlook, and styles of institutional commitment. It is conceivable if the mainline churches continue to lose members and support, the remnants of the faithful might at some point best be regarded as "cognitive minorities" perpetuating a deviant set of beliefs and values in an otherwise secular context. Accordingly, we can expect that processes of social interaction among members will take on added significance as a means of maintaining commitment. Sectarians have long depended upon group interaction as a reality-maintaining mechanism, and it is very likely that in this sense churches are becoming like sects. In either instance, those individuals integrated into social networks supportive of the faith are the ones most likely to hold on to personal faith and commitment.

To know more about such processes, we have to locate and describe the sociocommunal substructures that nurture religion today. Considerable attention has been given to the family and the ethnic group as contexts of meaning and support. Undoubtedly there are other substructures that play a part in aiding traditionalists in a secular setting to construct and to maintain shared meanings for religion. We must not only identify these but understand more about the way they function as plausibility structures for religion in the modern world.

Religious Reality Construction

Already we have seen that religion's shifting basis in society bears directly upon plausibility. Now we need to look further into the cognitive aspects of religious reality construction in order to draw out the social psychological implications of these changes.

Broadly speaking, the privatization of religion in the modern world implies that individuals themselves must play a larger part in constructing their personal belief systems. Greater individual autonomy enhances the possibility that people will exercise choice in the selection and interpretation of ultimate beliefs and values, especially considering there is so little consensus in the society as a whole. This means they may draw selectively from the Judeo-Christian heritage as well as from other religious traditions, thus increasing the chances of syncretistic, highly individualized systems of meaning fashioned around personal needs and preferences. While this implies some important qualitative changes, the basic point is that such meaning systems are largely a product of the individual's own creation. To a greater extent than in the past, modern life confronts the individual with the need to work out one's own convictions about ultimate reality.

The construction of religious meaning is probably more engaging for members of the liberal, mainline churches than for conservatives and sectarians. Unlike the latter whose beliefs are rigorously enforced, mainline church members are allowed more freedom to fashion their own. Liberal churches admit people into membership without strict tests of doctrinal belief; in addition, these denominations encourage members to exercise more freedom of thought and behavior. Consequently, members often form beliefs with relatively little guidance from others and without benefit of rigidly prescribed doctrinal stan-

33

dards. Thus it is not surprising that they share so little in the way of consensus about the nature of Christian faith and the demands of commitment it places upon them.

Greater individual autonomy also means that people's belief systems, potentially at least, may bear the strong imprint of their own cultural values and world view. Believers are not simply socialized into models of reality handed down through religious tradition. Instead they bring to their religion their own life experiences and perspectives, and out of the interaction of these two—*both* religious and cultural elements— emerge the symbolic worlds by which people order and interpret their lives. This means formal religious doctrines are always filtered through culturally based experiences, leading to a good deal of variation in people's conceptions of religious reality, even within a congregation. For this reason theorists like Geertz, Bellah, and others have emphasized the necessity of interpreting religion as an expression of an individual's world view and value system.[22]

In keeping with our general interpretation, we would expect that increasing numbers of mainline Protestant church members are finding within religion support for, and legitimation of, traditional values and outlooks. This helps explain not only the retreat from social action and turn to personal religion but also the social ideologies held by many of the mainline members. Conservative traditionalists tend to be parochially minded when it comes to matters of racial and ethnic prejudice, tolerance of civil liberties for others, and attitudes toward the church's involvement in controversial issues. Thus, religious faith can easily become intermingled in such ideologies, and it is essential in establishing the sources of these views to ferret out the many strands of influence, both theological and cultural.

Plausibility and Commitment

By now it should be clear that problems of plausibility—both in terms of support structures and cognitive meanings—are of paramount importance for contemporary church religion. In this final section, we review several major theoretical approaches to commitment in recent research and offer some suggestions about developing theories more pertinent to the religious situation in modern society. It is very important that we do this because theoretical paradigms generally in the sociology of religion, not unlike those found more broadly in sociology, bear the strong imprint of structural-functional thinking. One important outgrowth of this functionalist legacy, unfortunately, has been the tendency for commentators simply to assume that a religiously based moral order persists in modern society and that all individuals regardless of social location are exposed to, and informed by, this set of teachings and values. Such assumption is usually implicit rather than explicit and often subtle in its implications.

Two themes are especially prominent in sociological interpretations of religious commitment: *socialization* and *deprivation-compensation*. The first is very common in discussions on social roles and the way they influence an individual's "style" of religiosity. Women are thought to be more religious than men, for example, because of differential sex roles. Wife and mother roles are expressive and thus are presumably more congruent with religious values such as love, compassion, and human concern.[23] Age as a role-related factor is implied when it is asserted that beyond age thirty-five there is a steady increase in religious activity until old age. Adulthood usually involves family responsibilities which, when combined with maturation, favor religious commitment.[24] Members of differing social classes, it is likewise argued, are socialized into contrasting life-styles and vary somewhat in levels of participation in voluntary organizations. Middle-class people are characterized by greater associational activity and thus tend to become more affiliated with and involved in religious groups.[25] Finally, generation is judged important among white ethnics as an index of assimilation, calling attention to the tendency for Americans to become socialized into religious, and especially churchgoing, norms.[26]

Of the two, however, deprivation-compensation is probably the predominant view. Not only for early nineteenth-century theorists but among recent writers, deprivation-compensation as a framework has received considerable attention. To cite an example, Glock, Ringer, and Babbie argue that women, older people, and the lower socioeconomic classes—those most deprived socially in American society—find alternative gratification through religious involvement.[27] Others holding on to deprivation as a general theme have sought to refine it somewhat by means of multidimensional considerations. Demerath, Goode, and others reason that the lower classes, for example, are more likely to "feel" and "believe" their religion as compared to the upper and middle classes who place greater stress on the "doing" aspects.[28] By distinguishing between types of commitment, they are able to show that social class is inversely related to orthodox belief and devotionalism but positively associated with religious participation such as church attendance and parish activities. In other words, the deprived are sectlike in style, but the socially and economically privileged are churchlike.

Various criticisms have been raised against deprivation theories. For our purposes here, the crucial point is that both the socialization and deprivation interpretations assume that religious values are widely shared throughout the society and are generally plausible to the populace. It is simply taken for granted that one's role or status positions embody opportunities for expressing commitment—in varying styles— to the religiously based moral values of American culture. But as we have seen, it is this fundamental assumption that is questionable in a highly differentiated society where religious norms are segregated from the other institutional sectors. Increasingly in modern society, obligations associated with age, sex, and class roles can be fulfilled without serious attention to religious norms. Individuals not having been exposed to religious culture cannot be expected to express such value commitments in their everyday roles. Moreover, it is unlikely in a secular culture that deprived persons will find sufficient compensation in otherworldly rewards. As the plausibility of traditional religion declines, so does the likelihood that people will turn to it as a source of gratification.

Rodney Stark underscores this point in a reappraisal of deprivation theory. After reviewing the best evidence available, he concludes that economic deprivation predicts differences in religiosity better for church members than for the American population as a whole. For the latter—that is, people with only *minimal* religious affiliations— social class differences simply do not hold as deprivation theory predicts. Even in the realm of religious ideology, often cited as a haven for the dispossessed, the survey evidence shows that the lower classes are less committed than the middle and upper classes. Commenting upon this, Stark writes:

> In order for economic deprivation to result in certain kinds of religious commitment it is necessary first that a religious perspective is a *plausible*

option for the deprived persons in question. If they have retained some minimal connection with religious perspectives, then it seems to follow that poverty and failure will motivate persons to seek the comforts of faith. But the fact remains that the economically deprived are those for whom religious options are least likely to be relevant. In society generally, economic deprivation operates mainly to shut persons off from religion rather than to drive them into faith as a means of compensation.[29]

In other words, there is no reason to expect that people in secular society will necessarily offer religious interpretations—either for worldly fortunes or misfortunes. Where a strong religiously based moral order is lacking, interpretations in terms of socialization or deprivation must be qualified depending on whether religious perspectives are a *plausible option*. What this means is that plausibility of belief has to be treated as problematic, rather than taken for granted.

Accordingly, it makes sense to develop theories of commitment that take into consideration such options. Obviously there are varied sources of religious involvement, and certainly no single theory can fully explain why people initiate and/or maintain such commitment. But theories of religious socialization would be improved if rather than assuming this occurs universally, more attention were given to those social sectors in which traditional religious culture is found and persists as meaningful. Religious socialization occurs with some groups far more so than with others even within the mainline denominations. Indeed, for many in the mainline churches whose ties to the institutions are weak, there is relatively little socialization of the young into religious doctrines and values. Likewise, deprivation theories would be improved, if as Stark mentions, they were cast more specifically for those who opt for the compensations of faith. Among people who so choose, such explanations are perhaps fitting, but they are not applicable for many others today, both outside of and inside the mainline churches.

In conclusion, it would seem that greater attention should be given to cognitive considerations or the ways in which a religious world view makes sense in a person's life. Max Weber emphasized this point when he wrote that a religious person may be "driven not by material need but by an inner compulsion to understand the world as a meaningful cosmos and take up a position toward it."[30] For Weber, of course, cognition was only one consideration among many and as such did not preempt other factors in his own analytical scheme. But given the problems of plausibility confronting the churches today, it is essential to stress more than ever before perhaps how conceptions of reality are constructed in both a personal and collective sense. Church religion's stronger hold among the traditionally oriented invites questions of how world views are maintained as meaningful in a secular milieu and of how beliefs lend interpretation, and perhaps legitimation, to a particular group's outlook and way of life.

CONCLUSIONS

This chapter has reviewed the existing literature on religious commitment, from a methodological as well as a substantive point of view. Methodologically, we have seen that research on commitment often suffers from a lack of attention to *causal* relations among variables. In discussions on the dimensions of religion, the social correlates of religion, and the consequences of religious belief, it is clear there is a good deal of confusion over the social and religious characteristics of American church members. From a broader theoretical perspective, we have seen that most sociological explanations presuppose a religiously based moral order. Theories of commitment derived from a structural-functional perspective are especially vulnerable to this charge, and thus fail to consider adequately problems of plausibility confronting many believers in modern, secular society.

In sum, the review suggests the need for more satisfactory, multidimensional models of commitment based upon realistic assumptions about traditional religion's role in contemporary society. With this in mind, we turn to Chapter 2, where we attempt to develop such an approach.

⌐2⌐

A Theory of
Religious Plausibility

Our concern in this study is to advance a theory of religious commitment, building upon the guidelines of the previous chapter. As should be clear by now, such a theory must deal with the problem of plausibility and provide insight into the shifting social bases of religion in contemporary society. This chapter gets to the heart of the matter and outlines a perspective particularly fitting to the liberal Protestant churches. Major emphasis is given to developing a theoretical framework for the empirical analysis that follows in subsequent chapters. Hence at this juncture we switch from critical commentary about issues and perspectives, and turn to the formulation of an alternative explanation.

LOCALS AND COSMOPOLITANS

Earlier we said that traditional church religion is less and less capable of providing a unified set of meanings for people in the society as a whole. Too many individuals in modern society have abandoned faith, or perhaps more accurately privatized its meanings, for these commitments to carry broad social significance. Privatization generally implies a process by which religion's influence diminishes in scope—

from public to more limited social realms. In terms of groups and collectivities, this means that though religious meanings have lost much of their binding quality in the larger society, they still retain symbolic significance in smaller, more circumscribed social spheres. Religion's integrative power is not lost, but rather the social contexts in which it functions are changing.

Proceeding from this vantage point, the question then becomes: What are the pertinent social spheres in which religion is located today? Certainly there are many, but one not to be overlooked is the *local residential community*. Even though religious definitions of reality play less of a role in the society at large, they hold greater power in the more restricted social world of the local community. By the latter is meant the phenomenal world of the geographically bounded community, characterized by close social bonds with family and kin, friends, and neighbors—that is, the world of primary relations developed on the basis of residential propinquity. This is a realm of the familiar and the intimate, set aside and distinguished from the more public, rationally based aspects of everyday life. This is a realm of strong communal identity, distinct from the more individualistic, role-specific experiences of modern society. In a highly differentiated society, local communities are for many important, though voluntary, foci of belonging and meaning, if for no other reason than that they provide a refuge from the anonymity and impersonalism of the larger mass society.

Why the local community as the social basis for traditional church religion? Essentially because local social bonds are an important locus of *Gemeinschaft* in modern society. Or to borrow Peter Berger's term, the local community is important because it serves as a *plausibility structure* undergirding religious beliefs and definitions of reality. A plausibility structure involves an ongoing social context in which people interact on the basis of shared meanings. Residential communities function well in this respect because they are relatively stable as structures of interaction over time and because strong symbolic meanings are attached to them. Consequently, even in a secular world the local residential community persists for many as a sphere of shared religious views.

Of course, not simply religious, but also traditional values of all kinds are symbolically identified with local community life in modern

40

society. A fundamental fact of community life in a mass world is the conflict of local and translocal forces, the clash between the old ideals of the autonomous, self-sufficient community and the influences of the wider culture. Values associated with the former—for example, inner-directedness, free enterprise, thrift, and traditional morality—directly clash with new ideas and views imparted through the mass media and from distant power centers. For many traditionalists the influences from outside are viewed as severe threats to the stability of the local community and to a way of life that is highly valued.

The clash over cultural styles is felt in all the institutions of contemporary life, but in none more so than the institutions of socialization. Because they deal with the transmission of people's basic values and beliefs, such institutions as those concerned with education, religion, health, and welfare are especially vulnerable to internal conflict. These are the institutions in which many traditionally oriented persons seek to exert influence and to preserve and protect a cultural heritage thought to be endangered. It is here that broad segments of the community often become embroiled in controversies over very basic issues, such as control over neighborhood institutions, goals and priorities of community organizations, and "new" versus "old" beliefs and views.

So deep and widespread are those cleavages in American society today that social scientists have found it useful to distinguish character types on the basis of local community involvement. Such a distinction is that between *locals* and *cosmopolitans*. Locals are more attached to their immediate social locale and are quite sensitive to the primary groups in which they interact, such as the family, neighborhood cliques, and community organizations. In contrast, cosmopolitans have their commitments centered outside the residential community and tend to identify more with abstract, generalized groups that may be spatially remote, such as their profession or the corporation in which they work. Robert K. Merton describes the two character types in his Rovere study:

> . . . the localite largely confines his interests to this community. Rovere is essentially his world. Devoting little thought or energy to the great society, he is preoccupied with local problems, to the virtual exclusion of the national and international scene. He is, strickly speaking, parochial.

41

Contrariwise with the cosmopolitan type. He has some interests in Rovere and must of course maintain a minimum of relations with the community since he, too, exerts influence here. But he is also oriented significantly to the world outside Rovere, and regards himself as an integral part of that world. He resides in Rovere but lives in the great society. If the local type is parochial, the cosmopolitan is ecumenical.[1]

As Merton's description implies, locals and cosmopolitans differ in two fundamental ways: their patterns of social participation, and their orientations to the world around them. The first pertains to styles of social belonging, and the second to differences of world view and meaning. So important are these, we must explore in some depth their relevance to religious commitment.

LOCALS—THEIR PARTICIPATION AND BELONGING

Contrasting styles of social participation are a recurrent feature of locals and cosmopolitans. Differences in social belonging between the two in fact are probably the most salient of all. Locals are more attached to the social life of their immediate communities, and consequently this is reflected in both the extent of their participation and in the types of organizations in which they are involved.

These contrasting styles are nowhere better documented than in Merton's original study. Locals in "Rovere," Merton discovered, favored social activities that permitted them to know and interact with as many people as possible. They preferred to participate in voluntary organizations suited to making contacts and maintaining old friendships. Compared with the cosmopolitans, they were much more likely to be involved in fraternal organizations (e.g., Elks), secret societies (e.g., Masons), and service clubs (e.g., Lions, Kiwanis); and less likely to affilate with professional associations or hobby clubs. Even in public leadership roles, a similar tendency was evident: local influentials gravitated toward elected political posts obtained through personal contacts, and cosmopolitan leaders preferred those positions calling for special skills and expertise.

Merton found that these life-style differences persisted even when controls were introduced for level of education and occupational status. Ruling out social class as the basis of such differences, it would appear that locals, more than cosmopolitans, tend to have their social commitments reinforced through primary-group interaction. They rely very much upon the normative expectations of real, concrete groups of people who interact directly with one another. As a result, the influences of family, work group, neighborhood, and community play a big part in shaping their social life—in effect, they are major reference groups whose norms and outlook are persuasive.

It is not surprising, then, that locals should be more involved than cosmopolitans in religious groups. Because of their strong primary-groups ties, they are more exposed to the norms and sanctions favoring religious participation that exist in most American communities. Family, kinship, and ethnic groups have always been important carriers of religious norms, and in a secular society they become even more crucial as structures in which religious socialization takes place. For locals, this means that much of their social interaction with relatives, friends, and neighbors involves people sharing a common religious tradition. To the extent that it does, the local's primary-group ties serve to reinforce the norms and values of the more inclusive religious community.

For those attracted to developing close friendships and informal, communal relations, churches are an obvious place to turn. They provide opportunities for individuals to share common interests and develop close bonds of affection—among small subgroups of members at least. The degree to which informal, primary relations exist varies from one congregation to another, but the best available data indicate that friendship patterns are fairly extensive across American denominations. Among Protestant and Catholic groups in the United States, according to Stark and Glock, about a third of the parishioners have most of their friends in their congregations, a third have some friends, and about a third have none.[2] Even though for many members churches are little more than Sunday morning rituals with few communal ties, still for many others they function as close intimate fellowships.

Many people obtain from their congregations, satisfactions not only for their religious impulses but for social needs as well. Among these are group identification and a sense of social location—needs that are perhaps not religious in any ultimate sense, but that are easily fulfilled by religious groups. As in other normative organizations, church members are typically characterized by strong moral commitments that encourage the formation of primary relations. Drawn together on the basis of common values, they often develop intimate and personal bonds with fellow members. This is especially true in American society where, for historical and social reasons, religious groups have long played, as Greeley says, a "quasi-ethnic" role in providing a sense of belonging.[3]

For locals the belonging functions of religion manifest themselves particularly in the realm of religious participation. Attendance at worship services and involvement in church organizations (e.g., young couples clubs, choirs, study groups) are highly visible activities in many communities. Because of their public character they are subject to strict scrutiny and sanctions by those who deem the behavior as proper. Among those sharing common values, one's absence from public ritual is conspicuous and easily interpreted as indifference toward, or even the rejection of, group values. Given that locals are especially sensitive to primary-group expectations, their tendency toward conformist behavior is not surprising. No doubt this explains the observation of many researchers that church attendance and parish activity vary depending on the level of people's social integration within suburban communities and small towns.[4] In both types of settings, public religious rituals are prone to become defined as collective affirmations of group values, especially among those sharing a strong sense of communal identity. And considering that locals attach considerable significance to traditional, community-based values, their churchgoing easily becomes bound up with, and expressive of, these commitments.

LOCALS—THEIR IDEOLOGIES AND MEANINGS

Important, also, is the fact that locals and cosmopolitans differ widely in the social worlds in which they live. Given their contrasting lifestyles and social experiences, they are inclined to view the world through different eyes—to develop distinctive interpretations of life and distinctive systems of meaning. Thielbar, for example, found in his research that locals were prone to *personalize* their interpretations of social experience. That is, they preferred to interpret experiences in concrete terms that were meaningful in their own lives: to view international relations as interpersonal relations, and the national debt as similar to an individual's personal debt.[5] Probably this reflects their greater reliance upon interpersonal norms for interpreting social experiences. By comparison, cosmopolitans are cognitively oriented to a world of structural relations in the larger society and more predisposed toward impersonal, universalistic values and interpretations.

With respect to religious beliefs, the implication here is clear. Locals tend to personalize their conceptions of reality in such way that they probably find literal, otherworldly beliefs about the Deity far more acceptable than do cosmopolitans. They are predisposed to rely more upon anthropomorphic conceptions of God and to hold to simple, unsophisticated supernatural beliefs. For this reason literal orthodox doctrines and beliefs should possess a plausibility of meaning among locals unknown to those oriented to a broader, more secular world.

Religious doctrines and beliefs, however, do not exist in a cultural vacuum. Locals who in matters of religious conviction are highly traditional in outlook, adhere generally to conservative social ideologies. This conservative, and often defensive, posture on the part of locals is reflected in a range of attitudes and views: antichange ideologies, prejudice toward minorities, political intolerance, and conventional notions about morality. In a limited social world, both religious and nonreligious beliefs very strongly reflect the cultural setting of which they are a part. Religious and nonreligious beliefs covary together as part of a larger constellation of cultural ideology.

Recent studies of the dynamics of belief systems help to explain why conservative ideologies are so pronounced among locals. Converse's work on political belief systems is especially insightful and directly relevant to our concern.[6] Converse defines a *belief system* as "a configuration of ideas and attitudes in which the elements are bound together by some form of constraint or functional interdependence". He goes on to postulate as two major characteristics of belief systems, the centrality of certain of their idea-elements and the range of subjects encompassed by them. The first indicates that some beliefs are more consequential in the system than others and that changes in these more central beliefs will lead to more widespread repercussions in the rest of the related set. The second suggests that belief systems may be very narrow or broad, referring to the idea-elements that are included within a particular set of beliefs. For belief systems generally, this formulation offers insights into their structural properties and how they become modified or resist change.

Converse's primary concern was to examine what happens to political belief systems as one moves down the information scale from political elites to the masses. He observed that two significant changes were likely to occur: first, the degree of constraint among idea-elements in the belief system weakens; second, objects central to the belief system tend to shift from the "remote, generic, and abstract to the increasingly simple, concrete, or 'close to home'."[7] Extending this same logic to our character types, we would expect similar psychodynamic processes to occur with increasing localism. For those whose breadth of perspective is limited, their belief systems are less abstract and sophisticated in content; and hence their belief systems are governed less by internal consistency among the idea-elements and tend to reflect instead a composite of particularistic and "close to home" values.

Cast in somewhat different terms, we can say that individuals with limited perspectives tend not only to hold inconsistent views but to reify them. Though the term is somewhat ambiguous, *reification* as used here implies a belief on the part of an individual that his or her views are endowed with superordinate meaning and justification. Berger and Luckmann describe a reified belief system as resulting in a conception of social reality as fixed instead of in process, absolute instead of relative, natural instead of conventional, and in general as a product of forces that are more than human.[8] Thus the term connotes many of the ideological characteristics of authoritarianism and non-economic conservatism: strong normative commitments, ethnocentrism, rejection of outgroups, and obedience to external authorities.

Although little research has been given to the matter, empirical study documents a relationship between breadth of perspective and reification. Kohn's research demonstrates that individuals with narrow, parochial outlooks tend to view the world in fixed, absolute terms.[9] Individuals with broader perspectives, on the other hand, are less prone to such rigidities and are more capable of transcending fixed social boundaries in their outlook. Commenting on this in his essay on "Authoritarianism as World View," Howard Gabennesch notes:

46

The broader one's outlook on the social world, the more likely he is to perceive the imperfections and immorality which can characterize institutions and their human representatives. As the "sacred canopy" of cultural axioms begins to be regarded with a more skeptical eye, the locus of moral decisions tends to become less extrinsic to human actors. . . . Individuality and human differences become more understandable and acceptable in the absence of rigid, absolute standards. Moral ambiguity is likely to be more recognized and accepted. There is less tendency to believe that moral value necessarily resides in conventionality and unquestioning obedience to external authorities.[10]

Reification functions, Gabennesch argues, as a psychological mechanism explaining why people with very little education are often authoritarian in outlook. People with little education, and narrow perspectives generally, tend to conceive of social reality in fixed, absolute terms. But with broadened perspectives individuals usually gain in intellectual flexibility which in turn results in a more conscious awareness that the sociocultural order is essentially human in origin and character, and not simply an extension of one's own group norms. Stated in Converse's terms, greater breadth results in a shift in the objects central to the belief system toward the more generic and abstract and away from the simple and concrete. Whatever the choice of terms, the basic point is that breadth of perspective is a liberalizing influence, resulting in belief systems that are open and flexible, and less bound by the constraints of cultural conditioning.

CENTRAL QUESTIONS FOR INVESTIGATION

Up to this point, the discussion has centered around the broad implications of local versus cosmopolitan orientations for religious belonging and meaning. Essentially the argument was that an individual's social involvements in, and attachments to, the local community function to sustain traditional religious commitment. In effect, the local community with its strong primary group bonds of kinship, family tradition, and friendship serves as a plausibility structure for church religion in contemporary society. What all this means insofar as specific hypotheses are concerned, however, remains to be discussed.

In turning to the hypotheses, it will be helpful to keep in mind the schematic diagram shown in figure 2.1. This describes local-cosmopolitan community orientations: first, as dependent on several background influences; and second, as intervening between these background influences and the religiosity and "consequential" variables. What the diagram shows is that community attachments must be studied as part of a larger nexus of relationships. Solid lines suggest hypothesized causal relations derived from local-cosmopolitan theory; broken lines indicate weaker linkages, yet important to the explanatory model. Intended only as a sensitizing scheme, the diagram provides an overview of the theoretical matters that will be of concern to us.

Specifically, there are three major questions to which the research is addressed:

1. How do the basic patterns of religious commitment differ for locals and cosmopolitans, controlling for background variables like social class and community size?
2. In what ways does local community involvement help the individual believer to maintain a plausible faith?

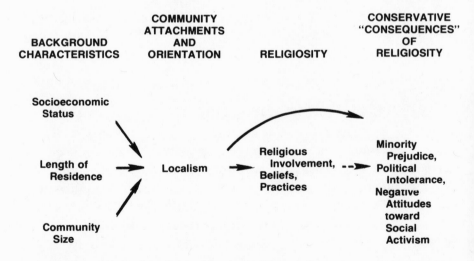

FIGURE 2.1 Conceptual Model for a Local-Cosmopolitan Theory of Religion

_____ Basic causal relations.

_ _ _ _ _ Weak, questionable relations.

3. Are the conservative "consequences" often alleged to religion derived from religious belief or from influences external to commitment such as breadth of perspective?

Each of these requires further elaboration in order to spell out the significance of local community attachments and to pose issues for empirical investigation that are of concern to the liberal Protestant churches at present.

Patterns of Commitment

The first question is the most basic: just exactly how do locals and cosmopolitans within religious groups differ in their styles of commitment? Until we know more about this we can hardly proceed to the other questions.

Quite clearly, locals are more committed generally to the institutional life of the church. Differences between the two in religious belonging are especially evident in liberal Protestant denominations. Even though the Gallup polls indicate that around 40 percent of Americans attend religious services in a typical week, this figure masks a great deal of diversity among Protestant groups. The highest levels of attendance are found among the theologically conservative sects and churches where norms of institutional loyalty are strongly emphasized. But in the more liberal mainline denominations there is a wide percentage spread between active and infrequent attenders. Regular weekly attenders may number, in fact, no more than 25 to 30 percent for liberal denominations such as Methodists, Congregationalists, and Episcopalians.[11] No doubt for these active participants the belonging aspects of religion are highly important, and hence we would expect to find a disproportionate number of locals among them.

In the realm of religious beliefs, or religious meaning, there is probably even more diversity among liberal church members. Studies report that on many orthodox doctrines, the range of beliefs professed varies from one denomination to another as much as seventy percentage points.[12] Even within the same Protestant congregations there are wide differences in what people believe, in literal versus symbolic conceptions of God, and degree of personal doubt. The full range of dissensus is probably greater than church members recognize, considering that members are often uninformed about the beliefs of others within the same congregation. This probably reflects, as Demerath and Hammond point out, a response on the part of many in religious institutions to adjust to a secular setting by leaving "traditional doctrine understated and, wherever possible, unmentioned."[13] At the very least we know that, for Americans generally, growing numbers are expressing uncertainty about traditional beliefs even though they continue to say they "believe" in religious doctrines.[14]

Given the diversity of belief, the local-cosmopolitan distinction again is helpful. As already noted locals tend to personalize beliefs and are more likely to accept literal interpretations of God, heaven and hell, and other such doctrines. These are the members who resist efforts at demythologizing the faith, or in any way substituting contemporary meaning systems for traditional orthodoxies. Literal and rigid views on their part may reflect a lack of capacity for complex symbolization; but because such beliefs are congruent with their traditional life-styles, locals probably experience fewer cognitive strains than do cosmopolitans. Fewer strains should manifest themselves in adherence to orthodox beliefs, greater personal religiosity, and less doubt.

The local-cosmopolitan dimension, thus, promises to tap diversities in both belonging and meaning in liberal Protestant congregations. It should predict levels of religious commitment within these denominations equally as well as, if not better than, more customary social correlates like social class. Because of its sensitivity to levels of religious plausibility, the distinction is well suited to predicting styles of religious commitment in the mainline churches.

But more is involved in developing a theory of local-cosmopolitan religious plausibility than simply empirical predictability. How are these community orientations related to other independent variables? And what are their logical status as social psychological orientations—independent explanatory variables, or intervening variables in some broader theory? The previous theoretical discussion on belonging and meaning makes clear our conviction about its independent significance. Nevertheless, we cannot escape the fact that the relation of these community orientations to religion is complex, and possibly even spurious owing to other causally antecedent influences. That is, breadth of perspective and religious commitment may covary simply because *both* depend upon some antecedent factor.

In this respect, two sets of factors particularly deserve consideration: social class and community size. It is conceivable that people's local versus cosmopolitan orientations are a reflection of their social class. The greater a person's education or experience in a white-collar occupation the less likely the ties to the local community. Previous research on locals and cosmopolitans has shown this to be the case, although none of the researchers investigating this issue has concluded that the orientations are simply an outgrowth of one's level of education or occupational status. "Educational and occupational differences," writes Merton, "may *contribute* to the differences . . . but they are not the *source* of these differences."[15] Merton's own choice of words for emphasis is suggestive of why we should examine systematically these relationships. Assuming that the orientations vary independently as social psychological dimensions, they may still partly reflect social class influence and may indeed help to interpret how such influence operates. Considering the attention given to social class in previous studies of religiosity, it is essential that we look carefully at this issue.

Community size is a contextual variable, quite different but nonetheless important. Its significance arises out of theories of urbanism—such as those of Georg Simmel and Louis Wirth—which assert that urban life encourages norms of tolerance, the weakening of primary group attachments, and anonymous, impersonal relations generally.[16] That urban dwellers should be more cosmopolitan in outlook would seem to follow. Dobriner, in fact, argues that community size is an extremely important correlate of cosmopolitanism for this reason.[17] Yet more critical assessment of urbanism suggests this need not necessarily be so: large numbers of urban dwellers remain isolated from the hypothesized consequences, as implied by the notion of *urban villagers* in American cities.[18] Thus we are left in a quandary, uncertain as to the relation of urban life to localism-cosmopolitanism, and forced in the absence of a convincing argument one way or the other to examine the issue empirically. The decision to turn to data as the arbiter is urged on, further, by the interest expressed recently in "urbanism as a subculture"[19]—a view that suggests that urban mentality is far from uniform in contemporary America, but depends instead very strongly on the types of social networks of which an individual is a part.

Maintaining Religious Commitment

In addition to describing the religious profile of locals and cosmopolitans, we are interested in the question: how is traditional religious faith maintained? The question becomes pertinent in a secular setting where we cannot assume a strong, societal-based plausibility structure. Belief systems always rest upon a social base wherein they are confirmed and acted upon, and in modern society the social structures undergirding commitment have shifted away from the larger society to smaller, more circumscribed enclaves of social experience. As this has happened the social base for church religion has dwindled to the traditional-oriented social strata and groups.

These changes are crucially important for the manner in which religious identities are socially maintained in the mainline churches. Unlike sectarians, the established churches do not attempt to isolate or insulate their members from nonbelievers; they do not view themselves as separate from the society and hence have not established institutional mechanisms prescribing proper social contacts for their followers. This means that normal, everyday processes of social interaction are crucially important in determining if beliefs are reinforced. Individuals having strong bonds with fellow believers can find support in their beliefs and convictions; those who do not are more vulnerable to secularizing influences. People's ordinary social networks and attachments thus assume for church members a significance more subtle perhaps than often realized.

Group attachments are significant for mainline Protestants in America today especially. Compared with Catholics and Jews, the ethnic and religious life is more separate for Protestants.[20] Many lack a strong ethnic communal structure, and up until quite recently have not thought of themselves in any way as a minority. Lacking these natural support structures, other types of mechanisms come into play. One of these is the individual believer's psychological bonds with significant religious others. If an individual holds a strong positive orientation toward the religious community, his or her own identity is reinforced. But without this, especially considering that for many nominal Protestants there are often few social ties binding them to the religious community, religious identities and loyalties easily erode.

Following this reasoning, primary-group orientations should serve to reinforce religious commitment. But since not all individuals conform uniformly to primary-group loyalties, again the local-cosmopolitan distinction is insightful. By comparison with their cosmopolitan counterparts, locals are known to be highly responsive to primary-group norms and sanctions and are more likely to conform to what significant others in their immediate environment expect. This being the case, there are two issues where the community orientation distinction should prove helpful: (1) for determining whether commitment to the church as an institution follows essentially from theological belief or from local, primary-group attachments; and (2) for determining the extent to which the belonging and meaning functions of religion hang together. These are discussed in depth in subsequent chapters, but brief mention here is in order.

If local, primary-group attachments are increasingly important for church religion in contemporary society, then perhaps they better explain why people are belongers in the religious institution than do the doctrinal beliefs held by church members. Theological explanations for church commitment are often given, the basic argument being that orthodox beliefs nurture participation in, and support for, religious institutions.[21] Without denying the fact that beliefs are important to many church members, nevertheless local, primary-group ties probably play just as important a part in undergirding institutional commitment. Churches survive as social institutions because dependable individuals and groups support them on a regular, week-by-week basis. The social bonds and solidarities that develop out of such voluntary commitment cannot be discounted, recognizing of course that sorting out the social and purely theological sources of institutional support is exceedingly difficult to do.

The second issue has do to with the relation of *religious meaning* to *socioreligious group belonging*. Religious meaning entails the personal, subjective aspects of commitment: beliefs, private devotional practices, and the importance, or salience, of faith to the believer. On the other hand, socioreligious group belonging includes a person's associational and communal ties, such as attendance at worship services, participation in religious activities, and friendships within the group. Establishing the relation of these two basic aspects of commitment to one another is not easy, for as was noted in Chapter 1 some theorists argue that beliefs lead to church belonging, and others that belonging sustains beliefs and meanings.

Of course both processes occur in reality, but from our perspective it makes sense to stress the primacy of the belonging aspects.[22] Participation in the religious community exposes the believer to others sharing the faith, which, in turn, helps to reinforce personal commitments. Especially in a pluralist society where, as Greeley says, religion fulfills a quasi-ethnic role in providing a sense of belonging, the meaning aspects of religion should be intimately rooted in the belonging. Given this perspective we would expect the belonging-meaning relationship will be stronger for locals than for cosmopolitans. Their religious commitments should be more generally integrated, the assumption being that local, primary-group attachments help to maintain a strong plausible faith. If this is correct, such attachments would then appear to play an important part in undergirding not only institutional, or church-centered, commitment, but strong religious identities as well.

Breadth of Perspective, Orthodoxy, and the "Consequential" Dimension

The schematic model raises a final and more controversial issue calling for study: whether the conservative social ideologies—the so-called consequences of religion—are primarily a result of faith or of factors external to belief. We have already reviewed in Chapter 1 empirical literature claiming that religious faith is a major source of conservative and prejudicial attitudes as well as some of the methodological problems inherent in these arguments. The task here is to show how the local-cosmopolitan distinction sheds additional insights into this important issue.

In the discussion on religious ideology, it was observed that nonreligious factors can play a significant part in shaping belief systems. Socioreligious groups themselves are the carriers of distinctive and often provincial social and political norms that have little to do with theology. Social interaction within these groups results in the exposure of believers not only to religious but to *nonreligious* sentiments as well. Thus it becomes extremely difficult, if not finally impossible, to sort out fully the sources of all the belief system elements. Richard H. White summarizes the situation very pointedly:

> . . . . any given religious group has a history of its own—a history that is affected by the cultural location of its members, by their relative economic positions, and a host of other "so called" ethnic factors. The point to be made is that insofar as religious groups are characterized by group-specific norms, these norms constitute the "religious factor" regardless of whether they have been logically derived from theology or picked up somewhere on the Italian countryside.[23]

White's lucid description is consistent with the more analytic interpretation given by Converse. Recall that he postulated the crucial importance of level of information: the greater the information, the more constrained the idea-elements in the belief system and the more likely that universal and abstract principles will function as central, organizing motifs. In other words, *the relative weighting of theological and cultural factors varies depending on degree of constraint in the individual's belief system*.

Harold E. Quinley interprets from this perspective the wide gulf in views between the clergy and the laity in liberal Protestant churches.[24] Theological convictions play a central role in the belief systems of liberal ministers and extend over a wide range of issues, resulting in major attitudinal and behavioral implications. Especially in the realm of social ethics, religious faith seems to be a much more potent prod to action and concern among ministers than among lay members. Liberal ministers who reject literal orthodoxies tend to hold to a demythologized faith, resulting in strong ethical commitments to justice, brotherhood, and equality. But among laity, relations between religious and ethical beliefs are considerably weaker. By comparison, rank-and-file lay members typically lack a religiously integrated set of social attitudes at the level of constraint that characterizes most clergy.

There would seem to be no reason why we cannot extend the principle of constraint to apply generally to lay members' belief systems. By so doing we have a basis for expecting that among cosmopolitans there will be greater ethical commitment. Much the same as with the clergy, cosmopolitan church members are more likely to have discarded traditional orthodoxies in favor of a this-worldly, activist faith that stresses

55

involvement in social and political issues. Events in the 1960s led progressive, liberal-minded church members to seek a more active role for the church in public affairs. But as was noted in the Introduction, these involvements were soon to provoke strong conservative reaction and resistance among many rank-and-file laity. The result in the late sixties and early seventies was a polarized church, strongly divided over priorities, and suffering severe institutional strains. And if the hypothesis of attitudinal constraint among cosmopolitans is correct, we can infer that an important basis for these strains were differences between traditionalists and modernists in their religious belief systems.

Quinley describes such differences between traditionalists and modernists as follows:

> . . . religious "traditionalism" represents, in brief, a continuation of the nineteenth-century Protestant emphasis upon doctrinal orthodoxy and a miraculous, soul-saving God. Its adherents are concerned largely with bringing the Word of God to others so that they may receive salvation in the afterlife, and have tended to be individualistic and moralistic in their ethical orientations. The churches' role in public affairs, they believe, should be an indirect one. By bringing others to Christ, the churches change the hearts of men and thereby contribute to the betterment of society; they have no business, however, becoming embroiled in the day-to-day issues of politics.
>
> Religious "modernism"—the term we will use to cover the liberal wing of Protestantism—represents in the broadest sense an accommodation of religion to secular and scientific thought. Clergymen of this persuasion have demythologized religion and have accepted science, not religious or Biblical authority, as the source of objective knowledge about the physical universe. God is seen as "immanent" in the everyday affairs of men, and religion is grounded in the human condition itself rather than in some conception of the supernatural.[25]

Whatever the sources of these belief systems originally, they are perpetuated today by cultural traditionlists and modernists who find affinities between their religious and social ideologies. Traditional Protestants, or "Private Protestants" as Marty calls them, tend to align themselves with conservative political, economic, and social views, which encourage an individualistic conception of redemption and religious responsibility. Modernists, or "Public Protestants," on the contrary, have largely replaced supernaturalism and otherworldliness with an ethical concern about human relations is society, and advocate the need for social reform as well as accommodation of religion to contemporary thought and concerns.[26] These ideological differences not only persist in the mainline churches, they are probably intensifying because of the growing cleavages between the two in life-style and outlook in contemporary America.

This raises questions about two issues, both of which are of interest to the study of religious commitment: (1) the sources of conservative sentiment in the churches, and (2) the complexity of influences, religious and nonreligious, shaping the ideologies of church members.

First, the fact that cultural influences predominate in intrachurch conflicts suggests that religious beliefs may exert far *less* of an influence on church members' attitudes than often assumed. In matters of cultural attitudes—such as racial and ethnic group prejudice, civil liberties and political intolerance, and view of the church's proper role in society—traditional norms play a big part in defining people's responses. Those church members with strong primary-group attachments to the socioreligious group tend to be more parochial and narrow-minded, and hence are probably the prime carriers of conservative religious ideology. As viewed from this vantage point, the "consequences" of religion are more likely to be cultural rather than religious in origin.

Second, even though cultural factors perhaps predominate, we should not lose sight of the fact that there are many types of religious meanings and diverse consequences that flow from personal faith. For example, to cite Allport's important distinction, there are *intrinsic* and *extrinsic* religious meanings: intrinsic referring to an orientation in which commitment is an end in itself, adhered to because it is deemed worthy of personal loyalty; extrinsic referring to a motivation for religion on the basis of what it can provide, such as security, comfort, or status.[27] That these two motivations to religion result in widely differing consequences is amply demonstrated, especially in the realms of prejudice and intolerance. Intrinsic commitment is conducive of tolerance, concern, and respect for others. On the contrary, extrinsic commitment motivated out of a desire to use religion for instrumental purposes, is often associated with intergroup prejudices and authoritarian political attitudes.[28] As this distinction in personal religious orientation indicates, religious meanings are quite subtle and varied in their consequences to individual believers.

Knowing this, plus the fact mentioned earlier that cosmopolitans should tend toward more constrained and integrated belief systems, we are led to expect that with greater breadth of perspective there should follow more intense concern over intrinsic religious principles and values. In other words, a broadened outlook on the cosmopolitan's part should help in transcending the cultural trappings of religion and to develop a more consistent, ethically oriented belief system. Not that locals are incapable of similar concerns, but rather because of their narrow, reified perspectives, their religious values are probably more easily overshadowed by parochial interests. This might help to explain not only the diversity of religious sentiments, but also why the liberal Protestant churches are riddled with strains and conflicts in the modern world.

SUMMARY

These, then, are the predictions we seek to examine, all of which follow from the theory of local-cosmopolitan religious plausibility. Certainly this is not a total theory of commitment, yet it offers important insights into changes in mainline Protestantism in modern, industrial society. This chapter has sought to spell out in detail these changes looking at three aspects of religious commitment: basic patterns of belonging and meaning, social network mechanisms supporting traditional belief systems, and the relevance of the believer's breadth of perspective for the "consequences" of religious commitment. Plausibility is a key consideration for all three aspects, and in each instance the local-cosmopolitan distinction offers some light on what we might expect in a changing, secular society.

Having sketched the theoretical predictions, we now turn to the data. Any study that seeks to examine empirically the local-cosmopolitan theory must satisfy two conditions: first, establish valid measures of the independent variable itself, and second, explore fully its relation to the various dimensions of religious commitment. The next chapter focuses on the first, and subsequent chapters turn more specifically to the religious considerations.

⌐3⌐

Locals and Cosmopolitans as Character Types

In developing a framework for our analysis, it is necessary that we pay close attention not only to the religious changes adrift in the liberal denominations but also to the concepts we propose to use in analyzing these changes. Normally this would not require so much attention, but because the local-cosmopolitan distinction is new to the study of religious commitment we must examine it carefully. Rather than apply the distinction in an ad hoc manner, without much concern either for its substantive meaning or its empirical measurement, this chapter sets forth in some detail the concepts, the measures, and social correlates of the character types. With this background of information, we can then turn to the religious issues before us with a good deal more clarity and understanding.

THE CONCEPTS

Distinctions between locals and cosmopolitans are commonplace in many writings on industrialization, urbanization, and modernization. Like many other typologies, this one can be traced to Töennies's fundamental distinction between *Gemeinschaft* (communal) and *Gesellschaft* (associational) relationships.[1] The terms as used in the social change literature imply about what Töennies intended—the polar extremes in social relations between the close and intimate, on the one hand, and the distant and formalized, on the other. Carle Zimmerman, in 1938, was the first to use the terms in this manner in an analysis of rural communities.[2] But more than anyone else, Robert K. Merton established their usage as explanatory attributes.[3] He was the first to suggest a local-cosmopolitan theory, in which the terms were used to describe an individual's alternative modes of social participation within a community. His Rovere study was concerned with community influentials and the manner in which they exerted personal influence. Locals exercised influence by means of their community-based networks of personal ties and friendships, whereas cosmopolitans relied upon the prestige, skills, and experience that their corporate or professional position conferred upon them. Thus the two modes of social participation emerged as quite different styles of influence.

Interestingly, the relevance of the distinction was something of a serendipitous discovery. In the course of the Rovere study, several seemingly unrelated characteristics became interpretable in these terms. Styles of participation in voluntary organizations, alternative interaction patterns, and variations in geographic mobility, could all be seen as stemming from basic differences in a person's orientation to the community. In this respect localism-cosmopolitanism may be thought of a general dimension of social differentiation tapping orientational and behavioral components.[4] Psychologically, it refers to an individual's reference orientation, either to a geographically bounded community or to the larger social world; and behaviorally, it encompasses a pattern of social participation consonant with the individual's level of community identity.[5]

Since Merton introduced the polarity, others have found it useful in studying not only community leaders but many other populations as well. Alvin Gouldner, in his study of college professors, proposes that localism and cosmopolitanism are "latent identities" that predispose academicians to differing patterns of participation—locals more loyal to the employing school, and cosmopolitans more committed to professional activities outside the college or university.[6] Herbert Gans uses the concepts for describing people's preferences about community needs and policies. In Levittown, New Jersey, cosmopolitan residents were especially concerned with the quality of the community's schools for preparing children to attend the best colleges and for entering professional careers. Compared with their local counterparts, they favored higher school budgets, long-range educational planning, and decision making by experts rather than by local politicians.[7] Ritchie Lowry, in a study of community ideology, links the local-cosmopolitan polarity to "two cultural orientations," one which he calls Conservative, the other Utopian.[8] And finally, Everett C. Ladd, Jr., argues that cosmopolitanism-parochialism is replacing liberalism and conservatism today as the primary axis of political ideology in the United States. He examines political ideologies in the Hartford metropolitan area—including the downtown city, an outlying suburb, and a nearby small town—concluding that local community versus metropolitanwide outlook subsumes much of the conflict over regional planning, approaches to urban problems, and degree of cooperation with federal government agencies.[9]

All these studies imply a fundamental difference between locals and cosmopolitans in their *scale* of social participation and orientation—thereby pointing to the advanced levels of differentiation in modern society. As opportunities for social interaction transcending the barriers of physical space increase, people have greater choice in deciding between national and local references in outlook and value commitment. Owing to modern developments in mass communication and transportation, no longer are people as geographically bounded as they once were. Consequently, the range of choices available in matters of cultural style, reference groups, and even sense of community is greater than ever before.[10]

A conception of scale is essential for understanding contemporary status differentiation. Systems of social prestige in local communities often differ from those of the larger society. Even among individuals with similar economic standing within the same community, there are often marked differences in life-style as, for example, between the old and new middle classes and between "old-timers" and "newcomers."[11] Individuals holding the same occupations may view themselves in different status systems—in either a local status order or a national socioeconomic order. Status distinctions cut across social classes and other groupings, and for this reason local versus cosmopolitan contrasts figure very prominently in studies of life-styles,[12] bureaucratic commitments,[13] political ideology,[14] and community

61

conflict.[15] These contrasts compare favorably with if not exceed those of social class, especially in the realm of values and ideologies where individuals today exercise a considerable amount of personal choice.

In sum, locals and cosmopolitans can be considered as major character types in contemporary American life. In the past several decades these two have come to characterize very pointedly the split in American culture between traditionalists and modernists. One group is committed to the older, traditional values and outlook identified with the old middle classes of the nineteenth century. The other regards the modern as the normative order to be followed, as found among the new middle classes of salaried professionals, corporate managers, and skilled workers. Joseph R. Gusfield describes these value differences in terms very similar to our character types. He writes:

> The cultural fundamentalist is the defender of tradition. Although he is identified with rural doctrines, he is found in both city and country. The fundamentalist is attuned to the traditional patterns as they are transmitted within family, neighborhood, and local organizations. His stance is inward, toward his immediate environment. The cultural modernist looks outward, to the media of mass communications, the national organizations, the colleges and universities, and the influences which originate outside of the local community. Each sees the other as a contrast. The modernist reveres the future and change as good. The fundamentalist reveres the past and sees change as damaging and upsetting.[16]

MEASURING LOCAL-COSMOPOLITAN ORIENTATIONS

Next we turn from describing the concepts to considerations of empirical measurement. Distinguishing between the two character types is relatively straightforward, in the sense that the terms refer to an individual's orientation either to the immediate social environment or the larger society. The basis for the difference lies in the scale of social reference and participation. Operationally, however, the empirical referents for "local" and "cosmopolitan" are by no means obvious. In fact, two differing research traditions have developed with alternative approaches, one focusing upon the residential community as the unit of social participation and the other upon the work setting.

The first emphasizes the community in which one lives and people's tendency to develop social attachments—some more strongly to a specific locality than others. In contrast, the second treats localism-cosmopolitanism in the organization of work, pointing out that employing organizations (for example, colleges, hospitals) compete with outside professional interests for workers' loyalties. As would be expected, the more general approach has been taken in community studies and the vocational-specific in organizational studies.

In this study we rely upon a communal conception, in keeping with Merton and others interested generally in local-cosmopolitan patterns. The fundamental assumption here is that the locality (usually a named residential place) is for some people the fundamental sphere of social participation, and for others is secondary in terms of participation and involvement in the larger society. As Roland Warren phrases it, within any local community in contemporary society there will be individuals more strongly oriented "horizontally" in social participation, and others who are more strongly oriented "vertically."[17] Not that one necessarily excludes the other but rather that individuals will tend to attach relatively more significance to one or the other modes of social participation.

Several complexities emerge in trying to arrive at valid measures of these orientations. A quick review of the more important of these will be helpful for understanding the procedures followed in the current study.[18] One problem is that localism is often defined in terms of a specific locality but cosmopolitanism lacks a precise empirical referent. What defines a cosmopolitan? Absence of local community attachments, or commitments and social involvements outside the community in the larger society? Because of this ambiguity, it seemed wise in a survey study to rule out behavioral indicators as measures. Lack of social participation in the local community does not necessarily imply an extralocal, or cosmopolitan, mode of social involvement. Some people may be physically present in a community but yet attached to other localities, and thus not very involved in voluntary organizations. Instead, it was determined that a proper measure would have to contrast, sharply as possible, local versus extralocal *orientations*, and thereby force even community nonparticipants into discriminating between the two reference alternatives.

Another problem concerns the local communities and whether they themselves vary in degree of localism or cosmopolitanism. That is, do locals in one place differ from locals in another because the communities differ? Obviously communities do vary in cultural milieu, especially if one thinks of the most extreme cases (for example, college towns versus rural communities). Yet in the context of contemporary society, such contrasts would seem to be overshadowed by the broad cultural changes brought about by the "massification" of values and life-styles generally. As the society has increased in scale, intercommunity differences have declined relative to the growing divergence of national and local cultures. Nevertheless, because people's styles of social participation are sometimes affected by distinctive community traditions, again it seemed wise to rely upon orientational rather than behavioral measures of localism-cosmopolitanism. This choice was reinforced by Thielbar's findings showing that a single orientation measure discriminates quite effectively between locals and cosmopolitans across several, very diverse college settings. Looking at five college and university populations—ranging in educational and cultural characteristics—he found a moderately high average correlation ($r = .69$) between community orientations and life-styles, indicating that the predictive power of the orientational measure holds up quite well across the several populations.[19]

Following the leads of Dobriner, Dye, and Thielbar, the following items were used as measures of local community reference:

1. Despite all the newspaper and TV coverage, national and international happenings rarely seem as interesting as events that occur in the local community in which one lives.
2. Big cities may have their place, but the local community is the backbone of America.
3. When it comes to choosing someone for a responsible public office in my community, I prefer a person whose family is known and well-established.
4. The most rewarding organizations a person can belong to are the large, state and nationwide associations rather than local community clubs and activities.

These have all been used, singly or in combination, in previous studies as well as in my own research.[20] Each of the items taps some feature of local community reference, such as community events, family standing, sentiment in favor of the small residential community, and associational preferences. The second item was somewhat risky in that it taps an antiurban bias as well, but preliminary analysis indicated that the responses that it evoked were not out of line with those of the other three. Taken as a whole, the items appear to tap major components of an individual's community orientation and identification.

These items were randomly distributed in the mail questionnaire used for collecting data for the Episcopal study. Responses to the four separate items are shown in table 3.1. Although there are too few

TABLE 3.1

Distribution of Responses by Category for Each of the Local-Cosmopolitan Items, in Percentages

ITEMS	PERCENTAGE OF RESPONDENTS GIVING EACH ANSWER (N=486)				TOTAL
	Strongly Agree	Agree	Dis-agree	Strongly Disagree	
1. Despite all the newspaper and TV coverage, national and international happenings rarely seem as interesting as events that occur in the local community in which one lives.	12.8	27.4	34.1	25.7	100.0
2. Big cities may have their place but the local community is the backbone of America.	29.1	35.0	20.7	15.2	100.0
3. When it comes to choosing someone for a responsible public office in my community, I prefer a person whose family is known and well-established.	25.7	29.9	28.4	16.0	100.0
4. The most rewarding organizations a person can belong to are the large, state and nationwide associations rather than local community clubs and activities.	21.5	36.4	24.2	17.9	100.0

response categories to make meaningful comparisons, quite clearly the distributions of responses for all four approximate the normal curve. About 60 percent of the cases fall in the middle two response categories, except for the second item which is a little lower. Agree responses to the first three items were interpreted as tapping localistic orientations, as were disagreements to the fourth. To obtain a summary scale, responses were summated without weights or other manipulations, following an item analysis indicating reasonable internal consistency (Cronbach's *alpha* = .81).[21] Scale scores range from 4 to 16, with the distribution slightly skewed in the upper direction as reflected by a mean value of 9.21. The item analysis failed to uncover any serious evidence of acquiescence, or any other systematic bias, in the responses.[22] Even though the scale is quite simple, the inter-item consistencies suggest that it should prove reliable as a predictor.

Table 3.2 shows the actual and percentaged distribution of scale scores. In the analysis these scores are treated in one of two ways: (1) either as a basis for a typology, in a twofold (locals versus cosmopolitans) or fourfold manner (locals, moderate locals, moderate cosmopolitans, cosmopolitans); (2) or for carrying out correlation and regression analyses. The fourfold typology is largely a convenience for analytic purposes. Because it is somewhat cumbersome, however, simple local-cosmopolitan comparisons are usually made. Using the summary localism scores in regression analyses, of course, stretchs assumptions since the orientational measure is at best ordinal. But considering the greater range of analytic techniques which interval data permit, plus the fact that treatment of ordinal data as interval usually results in negligible measurement error,[23] the gains should compensate for any biases or violations that are introduced. Wherever possible, we shall

TABLE 3.2

Actual and Percentaged Distribution of Local-Cosmopolitan Scale Scores

	SCALE SCORES			
	4–5 COSMOPOLITAN	6–8 MODERATELY COSMOPOLITAN	9–13 MODERATELY LOCAL	14–16 LOCAL
%	18	30	32	20
N	88	146	155	97

rely upon more than a single type of analysis in order to minimize the possibilities of misguided inferences.

SOCIAL CORRELATES OF LOCALS AND COSMOPOLITANS

Having described the measurement procedures, we turn next to a description of locals and cosmopolitans. This will provide us with a better understanding of these as major character types in contemporary society and, in addition, serve as a basis for comparing our findings with those of others. In any empirical study, and especially one such as this which relies upon a new, exploratory variable, it is essential to know if the measures used are sufficiently valid and reliable to predict social correlates known to exist. If not, it will hardly be possible to test empirically the local-cosmopolitan theory of religious plausibility. But should we find that the scale does predict reasonably well, we can then proceed with greater confidence in our results. At least we will have some assurance our data—which are admittedly based on a small southern survey—are not grossly peculiar or different from others.

To check this, we shall examine three important sets of correlates for locals and cosmopolitans: their work settings and socioeconomic status, regional and community residence, and life-styles. Along each of these lines previous research offers some evidence against which we can compare our findings.

Work and Socioeconomic Status

Many researchers including Merton, Stone and Form, Dobriner, and others underscore differences between locals and cosmopolitans in occupational characteristics. These studies have shown that locals generally are less educated, less likely to hold professional jobs, and are typically found in more traditional work settings. By and large, these signal status rather than purely economic, or class, differences. Status distinctions of this kind are quite common in a complex, highly differentiated society wherein the more traditional economic sectors persist along with the modern. Operators of small businesses and home-owned independent stores, for example, may command salaries commensurate with corporation managers, but their status is hardly comparable in any American community. Stone and Form's research suggests, in fact, that small businessmen and "organization men" are likely to engage in status struggles, even to the point of each emphasizing their own distinctive claims to respect and emulation.[24]

Table 3.3 presents our data on the work settings for locals and cosmopolitans. Consistent with our expectations, locals are more likely to be self-employed than cosmopolitans. The overall proportion of self-employed types for the sample is small, but locals are disproportionately represented among them. Relatively speaking, they are more inclined to work in small retail stores, small industrial shops, factory assembly shops, and small clerical pools. By contrast, cosmopolitans are well represented in schools and in managerial positions of large firms.

Is it the case also that locals and cosmopolitans vary in level of

TABLE 3.3

Work Situations of Locals and Cosmopolitans, in Percentages

WORK SITUATION VARIABLES	LOCALS (N=249)	COSMOPOLITANS (N=231)
Employment Status*		
Self-employed	31	12
Employed by someone else	69	88
	100	100
Work Settings**		
Small retail store	4	1
Large retail store	4	4
Small industrial shop	8	2
Factory assembly shop	9	0
Small clerical pool	9	0
Large clerical pool	3	9
Manager in small firm	13	12
Manager in large firm	14	27
School	10	22

*Significant at .05 level.
**Ns do not add to 100 percent

68

education, occupational type, and income? Previous evidence supports the view they should differ in education and occupation but not necessarily in income.[25] Our data reveal differences in all three, although they are somewhat stronger with education and occupation. General socioeconomic characteristics for the two are displayed in table 3.4.

The cosmopolitans have had considerably more years of formal education. More than 70 percent of the cosmopolitans are college graduates as compared with about 34 percent of the locals. Impressive as this may be, these percentages do not fully convey the significance of completing college for the cosmopolitans. When the comparisons are computed within educational categories, there are striking differ-

TABLE 3.4

*Socioeconomic Characteristics of Locals and Cosmopolitans,
in Percentages*

SOCIOECONOMIC CHARACTERISTICS		LOCALS		COSMOPOLITANS	
Education*					
Less than high school		19		2	
High school		10		3	
Technical, trade		11		6	
Some college		30		18	
College		20		35	
Professional, graduate		10		36	
	Total	100	(N=240)	100	(N=231)
Occupation*					
Professional, technical		24		32	
Managers, officials, proprietors		29		34	
Clerical, sales		24		25	
Craftsmen, operatives, service, laborers		23		9	
	Total	100	(N=238)	100	(N=232)
Income					
Less than $7,500		31		21	
$7,500 to $15,000		31		39	
$15,000 plus		38		40	
	Total	100	(N=232)	100	(N=231)

*Statistically significant at .05 level. In this and subsequent tables percentages are rounded off to add to unity.

ences between those who have finished college and those who attended but did not graduate. Among these latter almost three-fourths are locally oriented in outlook; but among college graduates this figure drops to about one-third. Possessing a college or university diploma, thus, appears to make a critical impact on one's breadth of perspective. Perhaps this suggests it is the social opportunities resulting from a college education, and not years of education per se, which makes the big difference in outlook. No doubt the social role experiences of the college educated play a considerable part in helping to sustain broadened references and outlook.

Cosmopolitans, as expected, are more represented than locals in professional and managerial jobs. Differences are evident particularly at the professional level. Even more so there are differences at the blue-collar level—with only 9 percent of the cosmopolitans involved in manual occupations as compared with 23 percent of the locals. Income differentials are minor at the upper end of the salary scale, but differ by about 10 percentage points at the lower end.

One final observation is that of the three socioeconomic status indicators, education is the best predictor of cosmopolitan reference. Relative to occupation and income, education better differentiates between the two orientational possibilities. Education brings about broadened experiences—what Howard Becker termed *mental mobility*[26]—permitting people to move beyond the microcosmic social worlds that confine their values and standards of judgment. Especially if new mental horizons result in subsequent social experiences that reinforce the broadened perspectives, education can be a major determinant of cosmopolitanism. All previous research points to this conclusion, and in this respect the present findings are no different.

Region and Community Residence

Next we examine a very different kind of correlate—geographical location of residence. Very little is actually known about whether region is related to people's local versus cosmopolitan proclivities. Despite the stereotypes of southerners as parochial and narrow-minded, it is easy to exaggerate regional differences; studies outside the South, too, have uncovered large numbers of people with localistic inclinations. Southern-born background, thus, may not be as strong a correlate

70

as popular wisdom would suggest. In addition to region, there are other residential variables that are probably better predictors. Dobriner singles out the importance of community size, although the presence of urban villagers within the largest of American cities cautions us against expecting too strong a relationship.[27] Still others, such as Hunter and Kasarda and Janowitz, emphasize length of residence within a community as a significant factor shaping people's local attachments.[28]

Southern background turns out not to be very helpful for distinguishing between locals and cosmopolitans. The distributions shown in table 3.5 differ by not more than 5 percentage points, indicating that the proportions of the two types are almost the same among southerners. Such findings lend support to the view that localism is not simply a regional subculture, but instead characterizes individuals from all areas of the United States. Local versus cosmopolitan contrasts are probably becoming relatively uniform across the society, and if so, regional differences may be less and less salient in the future. Unfortunately, we have too few nonsoutherners in the sample for extensive regional comparisons.

The distributions by community size are presented in table 3.6. It is reasonable to expect disproportionate numbers of locals in the smaller communities, and indeed this is what we find. About 50 percent of the locals come from communities smaller than 50,000 people as compared with about 35 percent of the cosmopolitans. Taken as a whole, however, these differences are not very large. People with both orientations are found in every type of community—from rural areas to large cities with a quarter of a million or more inhabitants.

TABLE 3.5

*Locals and Cosmopolitans with Southern and Nonsouthern Background, in Percentages**

REGION	LOCALS (N=240)	COSMOPOLITANS (N=233)
South	75	70
Non-South	25	30
Total	100	100

*Not significant at .05 level.

TABLE 3.6
Locals and Cosmopolitans by Community Size, in Percentages*

COMMUNITY SIZE	LOCALS (N=244)	COSMOPOLITANS (N=229)
Less than 15,000	32	21
15,000 to 50,000	18	13
50,000 to 100,000	21	14
100,000 to 250,000	22	41
More than 250,000	7	11
Total	100	100

*Statistically significant at .05 level.

In an industrial society where nationally shared life-styles and perspectives develop and diffuse through the mass media, physical boundaries are less and less important in determining people's outlook and affiliations. Indeed, it is this very fact which makes the community orientation differences so interesting, and potentially very insightful.

Of greater importance than community is a respondent's length of residence within a given community. The longer the stay, the greater the chances of developing strong community attachments. Table 3.7 shows the mean localism scores by length of residence for three age categories. Because local community attachments are likely to increase with age, it was important to hold age constant so as to sort out the effects of length of residence per se. Doing so we still find that the localism scores are positively associated with the number of years a

TABLE 3.7
Mean Localism Scores by Length of Residence in Present Community, Controlling for Respondent's Age

| LENGTH OF RESIDENCE | RESPONDENT'S AGE | | |
	20–34	35–49	50+
Less than 1 year	4.91 (35)	5.21 (22)	6.04 (10)
1–2 years	7.96 (35)	8.02 (22)	11.31 (11)
3–10 years	9.07 (22)	10.09 (32)	12.08 (14)
11–30 years	10.34 (56)	11.22 (70)	11.73 (18)
More than 30 years	— (2)	11.39 (52)	12.04 (55)

person has lived within a community. Except for minor inversions in the 50+ category, the pattern is strikingly consistent. In addition, the data confirm the fact that levels of localism increase across age categories. People develop localistic attachments and perspectives as they increase both in years of stable residence and in age. The product-moment correlation between age and localism is .15, and between length of residence and localism .33. Controlling for age the latter coefficient reduces only to .28, thus suggesting that length of residence is an important correlate.

Quite clearly, length of residence is a stronger correlate of localism than either region or community size. In this respect the North Carolina findings are consistent with those obtained in other studies. In Hunter's Chicago study and Kasarda and Janowitz's Great Britain survey, length of residence emerged as a major predictor of friendships and communal bonds within a community. Such results indicate that distinctions between newcomers and old-timers are very real in communities everywhere and that with time many new residents will attach themselves to, and identify symbolically with, the social life of the area in which they live.

Life-Styles

Finally we look at two life-style characteristics: organizational affiliations and reading preferences. Many observers, including Merton, Stone and Form, and Thielbar, have reported qualitative differences between locals and cosmopolitans in the organizations in which they are involved as well as in their choice of magazines. Similar differences are also found in this sample.

Table 3.8 shows that locals are more involved in fraternal, veteran and military, and service and civic organizations. Cosmopolitans, on the other hand, hold greater affiliations with political, civil rights, literary, and professional groups. The percentage differences are not huge, but the styles of organizational activity are similar to those reported elsewhere. Locals generally prefer organizations with strong communal bonds, whereas cosmopolitans tend to align themselves with groups organized around specific interests and needs. Pertinent here also is the fact there are no significant differences between locals and cosmopolitans in the actual number of organizations regularly

TABLE 3.8

Locals and Cosmopolitans Having One or More Organizational Memberships by Type of Organization, in Percentages

TYPE OF ORGANIZATION	LOCALS (N=248)	COSMO-POLITANS (N=236)	SIGNIFICANCE LEVEL
Fraternal	26	12	.05
Veteran and Military	11	7	N.S.
Political	18	25	N.S.
Civil Rights	2	8	N.S.
Literary and Study	21	34	.05
Professional	23	40	.05
Service and Civic	46	32	.05

attended (excluding religious). As a whole the observations suggest that it is not organizational involvement as such, but rather contrasting styles of organizational participation which distinguish the two. This is not surprising considering that status, rather than class, differences are expressed in the local-cosmopolitan patterns.

Of the several types of magazines respondents were able to choose, fraternal magazines are the only ones for which locals indicate a greater preference than do cosmopolitans (see table 3.9). Cosmopolitans express definite preferences for news, news analysis and commentary, literary, and professional magazines. Merton observed in his study, more than

TABLE 3.9

Locals and Cosmopolitans Who Regularly Read Magazines by Type of Magazine, in Percentages

TYPE OF MAGAZINE	LOCALS (N=241)	COSMO-POLITANS (N=234)	SIGNIFICANCE LEVEL
Fraternal	10	3	N.S.
News*	43	71	.05
News Analysis and Commentary**	2	7	N.S.
Literary	9	22	.05
Professional	9	16	N.S.

*Time, Newsweek, U.S. News and World Report.
**New Republic, National Review.

two decades ago, the strongest differences between the two in reading habits were with national news magazines. This reflects of course the cosmopolitan's strong orientation to national and international events, and interest generally in concerns of the larger society. The fact that such readership continues to distinguish these two character types from the time of Merton's Rovere study to the present is itself an indication of the reliability of the distinction.

SUMMARY

This chapter has reviewed in some depth the local-cosmopolitan concepts, their measurement, and empirical correlates. Proceeding with essentially a Mertonian conception of the two orientations as anchored in a community context, a scale was developed using community reference items. Though quite simple as a scale, it was shown that the measure predicts social correlates as expected—from the realms of work and socioeconomic status, region and community residence, and life-styles. Not shown but deserving comment is the fact, also, that scale scores were not associated with sex differences. On the basis of other studies, especially Hunter's Chicago research, it was expected that the respondent's sex would be unrelated to the orientations. What emerges are the following character-type profiles: locals, as lower-status, older, stable small-town residents, and participants in fraternal, service, and civic activities; and cosmopolitans, as higher-status, younger, urban and geographically mobile, and involved in professional and interest organizations. But these are only profiles and should not be construed as rigid determinants of the alternative styles. The significance of the distinction lies, to a large extent, in the fact that it cuts across many of the conventional lines of social class and community size.

Taken as a whole, the results give assurance that our measure is a valid and reliable predictor. Lack of contrary, or inconsistent, findings when compared with studies from such diverse settings as Chicago and Great Britain, is itself quite striking. Also the results indicate that the North Carolina Episcopal sample is not fundamentally different from others in its empirical parameters. With confidence then in both the scale and the data, we turn to the substance of the study and begin analysis of the religious patterns.

[II]

SOURCES
OF
RELIGIOUS
COMMITMENT

[4]

Patterns of Commitment

Our first concern with religious commitment is to explore its social correlates. Who are the actively involved in the church? Who are the traditional believers? What are the social characteristics of these committed members? Answers to these very basic matters are a prerequisite to any further investigation. But rather than assemble data on as many correlates as possible, we shall examine in depth only one—local community orientations. This strategy makes sense for several reasons: one, because we know so little about the religiosity of locals and cosmopolitans a thorough and comprehensive analysis is required; and two, an intensive, systematic inquiry into a single correlate, or small set of closely interrelated correlates, promises to yield more insight than a general overview. With these guidelines in mind, we are ready then to submit the local-cosmopolitan hypothesis to its first empirical test.

In this and the following chapters, the components of religious commitment fall under one or the other of the two basic types: *belonging* and *meaning*. Of course not all aspects of religion can be so neatly categorized, but for explanatory purposes this scheme is highly useful. Recall that we are concerned less to deal with every conceivable religious dimension possible than to arrive at a better understanding of the basic patterns themselves. The discussion in Part II is thus extremely important since it raises the most fundamental question in our study: how do locals and cosmopolitans differ in religious styles? In search of an answer, this chapter will describe the general patterns of commitment, and chapter 5 will attempt to place the findings into broader theoretical context.

SOCIORELIGIOUS GROUP BELONGING

In any religious group, people come together to worship, share their common faith, and enter into fellowship with one another. That is to say, church religion is fundamentally a social phenomenon. Obvious as this may be, yet it is this very fact that makes it possible to understand not only why religious systems are highly organized, but how it is that people's social and communal bonds give shape to their religious life. In religion, as in other phases of human activity, people are social beings whose predispositions to participate depend in large part upon their ties of friendship and affection with others. The stronger these bonds and the primary group satisfactions obtained from them the greater the likelihood of religious involvement.

Turning to table 4.1, we can see how people's local social bonds affect their religious involvement. Shown are data for three different measures of socioreligious group involvement: church attendance, church activities, and parish friendships.

Church Attendance

The data leave no doubt about differences in church attendance among locals and cosmopolitans. Sixty-five percent of those scoring high on localism can be classified as regular attenders, that is, attendance weekly or nearly every week. This proportion falls as one reads across the table to a low of 34 percent among the most cosmopolitan. Small differences are observed among those who attend a couple of times each month, but the local-cosmopolitan proportions are much more striking in the case of irregular attenders. Forty-two percent of the high-scoring cosmopolitans rate their attendance as once a month or less, as contrasted with less than 20 percent of the locals.

TABLE 4.1

*Socioreligious Group Involvement by Degree of Localism,
in Percentages (N Varies from 471 to 475)*

MEASURE OF RELIGIOSITY	LOCAL	MODER-ATELY LOCAL	MODER-ATELY COSMO-POLITAN	COSMO-POLITAN
Church Attendance				
Every week	37	28	21	11
Nearly every week	28	30	33	23
Percentage Regular Attenders	65	58	54	34
Two, three times a month	18	21	22	24
Once a month or less	17	21	24	42
Total	100	100	100	100
Church Activities				
Three or more	22	19	16	10
Two	24	19	17	13
Percentage Highly Involved	46	38	33	23
One	21	27	22	30
None	33	35	45	47
Total	100	100	100	100
Congregational Friendships				
Four	17	7	12	7
Three	17	11	9	10
Two	18	27	21	12
Percentage Highly Communal	52	45	42	29
One	17	20	22	24
None	31	35	36	47
Total	100	100	100	100

Statistically significant at .05 level in each instance.

Such differences are especially evident with attendance at Sunday worship services. No other ritual activity is as important in the Christian tradition as Sunday services; nor is there a more public expression of the meaning and sacredness of religion. This symbolism in American church life, however, is most meaningful to those with strong social ties in their communities. Public worship affirms group solidarity for those whose social bonds unite them in a common life and helps to establish a close identity of religious and community concerns. No doubt that as communal attachments and sentiments decline, so does the significance of church belongingness.[1]

Church Activities

Sunday worship may be the single most important ritual celebration, but many other religious activities take place within the typical American church. In fact, for many devoted members more time and energy are actually invested in activities such as choirs, missionary societies, and Bible-study groups than in Sunday worship services. Small groups as these permit people to get to know one another and to engage in specific activities of interest; also they offer opportunities for group leadership, thus making it possible for many individuals to assume positions of responsibility who otherwise would find little to do in the institutional life of the church.

Given the local's attachments to primary groups, one would very reasonably expect that such ties should help to maintain an interest in congregational activities. The data in table 4.1 show that indeed they do. Looking at the number of church-related activities, it is clear once again that locals participate more than cosmopolitans. The pattern is especially pronounced when percentages are combined for the upper categories of organizations, groups, or activities in which members participate. For example, 46 percent of those with strong local community attachments take part in two or more group activities. But among those with fewer local attachments the percentages who are highly involved decline predictably: from 38 percent to 33 percent to finally 23 percent among the most cosmopolitan. While about 20 percent of the locals claim participation in three or more activities, only 10 percent of the most cosmopolitan do. Note also that among those reporting no involvement in church organizations, 46 percent of the cosmopolitans fit this category as compared with about 34 percent of the locals.

Clearly there is a relationship with the number of church activities.

Yet it is evident that the association is not as strong as was previously found with church attendance. Why this should be is not obvious, although the finding is not uncommon in other research.[2] Perhaps the explanation lies in the gross character of the measure. The number of religious activities within the church tells us nothing about the frequency of involvement or the level of a person's commitment to them. By comparison it is less informative than church attendance as a measure of associational involvement.

Congregational Friendships

Are locals also more likely to have close friendships within churches? It is reasonable to predict that they would. Church members having strong local community attachments should know more fellow congregants because of social contacts both inside and outside of the religious institution. Usually locals know more people in the community, plus they tend to have greater appreciation for longstanding ties with friends and kin. Their networks of relations within the community often overlap those of the congregation, with the result being that involvement in one reinforces the other.

Table 4.1 also reports these findings, showing that locals do have more close friends in their church congregations. To appreciate these differences, it should be noted first that more than a third of the entire sample report they have no close friends in their congregations. This is in keeping with Stark and Glock's observation that 39 percent of Episcopalians have no parish friends.[3] Among liberal Protestant churches generally this figure is quite high compared against the more conservative churches. Of interest here, however, is the variation within the denomination. The percentages of those with no parish friends range from 31 percent to 47 percent depending upon degree of localism. Within an established denomination such as the Episcopal church, there are discernable contrasts in the extent to which people are tied to their churches by bonds of friendship. Variation *within* congregations is probably as great, if not greater, than between denominations.

Using Stark and Glock's criterion that a person is imbedded in a religious community if he or she has at least *two* out of five friends in the church, the contrasting styles become even clearer. More than half of the locals in the extreme category, or 52 percent, meet this standard of two church friends as compared with only 29 percent of the highly cosmopolitan. In short, to the extent that people claim to have close friends within congregations, such friendships are more characteristic of those who are highly integrated into local community networks of interaction. In Stark and Glock's terms, locals tend to develop "religious communities" wherein people know one another and relate to one another as friends and acquaintances. On the other hand, cosmopolitans create "religious audiences," or gatherings which meet for religious purposes but are lacking in close ties of friendship and affection. Both are found in mainline protestant churches, again indicating that there is considerable variation in style of participation in a given congregation.

Subjective Measures of Church Involvement

In addition, the Episcopal Survey included questions that asked the respondents how well they fit into their congregations and how important church membership was to them. These more subjective measures provide a check on the behavioral indexes plus yield additional insight. As table 4.2 shows, locals consistently give more affirmative replies than cosmopolitans when asked, "How well do you think you fit in with the group of people who make up your church congregation?" While 51 percent of those most locally oriented replied "very well," not more than 20 percent of the cosmopolitans replied in this way. Likewise, in response to the question about the importance of church membership, 40 percent of these same locals reported "extremely important" as compared with 27 percent of the highly cosmopolitan. To the local, "fitting in" is an essential part of religious involvement. Belonging is important because of the primary group satisfactions that it offers.

In brief, we arrive at similar conclusions whether using the subjective measures or the more customary indicators of socioreligious group involvement: *locals participate in traditional, church-type activities more than cosmopolitans*. Because they are highly involved in networks of social interaction within their communities of residence, locals probably experience greater pressures to belong in religious communities. Very likely their participation is more meaningful also, given their

TABLE 4.2

*Subjective Measures of Church Involvement by Degree of
Localism, in Percentages (N= 466 and 472, Respectively)*

SUBJECTIVE MEASURES OF CHURCH INVOLVEMENT	LOCAL	MODER- ATELY LOCAL	MODERATELY COSMOPOLI- TAN	COSMOPOLI- TAN
How well do you think you fit in with the group of people who make up your church congregation?*				
Don't	1	7	6	25
Not too well	8	10	14	15
Fairly well	40	38	47	40
Very well	51	45	33	20
Total	100	100	100	100
All in all, how important would you say your church membership is to you?				
Fairly unimportant	3	3	4	5
Not too important	5	5	7	8
Fairly important	14	14	21	23
Quite important	38	39	37	37
Extremely important	40	39	31	27
Total	100	100	100	100

*Significant statistically at .05 level.

traditional values and life-styles. Whatever the reasons, the patterns
seem clear enough. Religious participation in a congregation is intimately bound up with the social dynamics of local community life.
Attachments to, and psychic identification with, residential locality
are closely linked to the levels of solidarity found within established
religious institutions. In a very real sense, the community is the setting
in which traditional religious symbols and values become meaningful
since it is here that many people's fundamental patterns of social
interaction and social roots are located.

PERSONAL BELIEFS AND PRACTICES

Next we turn to personal, more private types of religious meaning. These include people's beliefs, sentiments, and devotional practices, which are distinguished from socioreligious group participation by their more solitary and individualistic character. Unlike the organized, more public aspects of church life, the private religious life is highly subjective and spontaneous, involving as William James put it, the "feelings, acts, and experiences of individual men in their solitude . . . in relation to whatsoever they consider the divine."[4] Compared with some religious traditions liberal Protestant denominations place less stress on the experiential aspects of commitment, but they do emphasize the importance of historic doctrines along with personal faith and piety. It is these latter beliefs and practices we are interested in here.

Whereas there is good reason to expect locals and cosmopolitans to differ in religious belonging, it is less clear they should in the subjective aspects of religiosity. At the cognitive level, certainly we would expect differences: locals will more likely find traditional beliefs acceptable and regard personal piety as the essence of religious commitment. Yet the social pressures of belonging and conforming, so important in understanding why locals are highly involved in religious institutions, should play less of a role in shaping personal religious styles. People may be encouraged to participate in religious activities due to social pressure, but this should be less so with personal faith and practices. In what follows we shall see if indeed similar differences do exist, this time looking at three measures of personal commitment: type of belief, the importance of faith, and devotional practices.

Literal versus Symbolic Beliefs

Among church members, religious beliefs are central to personal faith. Doctrines such as belief in a personal God, Jesus Christ as Saviour, and heaven and hell as supernatural realms, are basic to historic Christian teachings and vital parts of the prescribed creeds that have been handed down through the centuries. Yet probably no aspect of the Christian heritage is more vulnerable to the secularizing influences

86

of modern society. Supernatural conceptions inherited from the past often erode when confronted with the views of modern science, and consequently many people both within and outside the churches find traditional orthodox doctrines incongruent with contemporary life. That such doctrines are no longer central in the thinking of many liberal church members is of concern for traditionalists and a source of considerable latent conflict within mainline Protestantism. For our purposes here, the historic doctrines provide a measure of the acceptance or rejection of traditional teachings and offer an opportunity for examining the changing conceptions of ultimate reality.

We look first at the most universal tenet of Christian faith—the doctrine of God. Table 4.3 shows that the majority of respondents hold to beliefs characterized by the first three statements, which depict God in traditional, anthropomorphic imageries. But as would be expected, the cosmopolitans do not endorse orthodox conceptions as do the locals. Cosmopolitans consistently reject beliefs describing the Deity in personal, supernatural terms. While more than half (52 percent) of the highly cosmopolitan respondents reject notions of God as "wrathful judge," "personal Being," and "creator and ruler," fully 85 percent of the extreme locals hold to these beliefs. Of the three orthodox statements, the "creator and ruler" image evokes the most discriminating endorsements: from 29 percent of the cosmopolitans, to about 41 percent of the moderates in the combined categories, up to a high of 54 percent among the locals.

The fourth possible response, describing God in terms of the beauty and majesty of nature, did not receive much support. Nor are the patterns for locals and cosmopolitans very meaningful. The fifth response is more discriminating, for it taps a conception of God about which there is far less consensus. An humanistic image here replaces a naturalistic, one which is somewhat more attractive to the more liberally minded cosmopolitans. Almost 10 percent of the highly cosmopolitan prefer it over the traditional, supernatural views as compared with about 3 percent of the other respondents. These percentage differences are small, but they are in keeping with our expectations.

By far the most interesting contrasts have to do with the conceptions of God cast as "higher power or force" and "ultimate or unconditional love." These latter represent *impersonal* images of Deity, quite distinct from the anthropomorphic views usually associated with traditional

TABLE 4.3

Belief in God by Degree of Localism, in Percentages (N=470)

CATEGORIES OF BELIEF IN GOD	LOCAL	MODERATELY LOCAL	MODERATELY COSMOPOLITAN	COSMOPOLITAN
God is:				
1. a powerful and sometimes wrathful judge of man's behavior	4	2	2	1
2. a personal Being who watches over and cares for our lives	27	25	19	18
3. the creator and ruler of the universe	54	42	40	29
Percentage with Anthropomorphic Conceptions (1,2,3)	*85*	*69*	*61*	*48*
4. the beauty and majesty of nature	2	5	3	3
5. that part of each person which is basically good	3	2	3	10
6. a kind of higher power or force in the world	5	14	15	15
7. ultimate or unconditional love	5	10	16	21
8. I do not believe God exists	—	—	2	3
Total	100	100	100	100

Statistically significant at .05 level.

orthodoxy. By comparison, the cosmopolitans are far more inclined to endorse these modernist conceptions. For example, 21 percent of those least attached to the local community conceptualize God not in personal terms but as "ultimate or unconditional love." Among those whose ties to the community are stronger, the impersonal, more abstract beliefs are less acceptable. These results describe probably the most salient difference in their beliefs: whereas the locals hold to traditional, anthropomorphic conceptions, cosmopolitans prefer to think in more abstract terms. Rather than personalize their beliefs the latter adhere more to impersonal, demythologized religious principles.

Finally, it should be noted that nearly 3 percent of the highly cosmopolitan-oriented do not believe God exists. Differences between cosmopolitans and locals are not as great here as perhaps would be expected. The relatively small number of respondents claiming nonbelief is consistent, however, with national surveys showing that very few Americans are willing to acknowledge lack of belief in the existence of God.[5] What is interesting is that cosmopolitans within a religious population continue to acknowledge belief in God but tend to reconceptualize their convictions. The content of their beliefs is more likely to change than belief itself suggesting that in future research more attention should be given to alternative theistic conceptions.

Three other orthodox doctrines were examined as well; belief in the divinity of Jesus, beliefs about heaven and hell, and beliefs concerning the Bible. Similar variations in these are displayed in table 4.4.

TABLE 4.4

Beliefs About Jesus, Heaven and Hell, and the Bible, by Degree of Localism, in Percentages (N varies from 452 to 473)

CATEGORIES OF BELIEF	LOCAL	MODERATELY LOCAL	MODERATELY COSMOPOLITAN	COSMOPOLITAN
Jesus:				
1. " . . . God living among men"	57	53	45	22
2. " . . . a man called to reveal God's purpose"	38	31	37	39
Percentage Traditional (1,2)	95	84	82	61
3. "embodied the best that is in all men"	3	9	10	16
4. " . . . great man and teacher"	1	5	5	17
5. " . . . not sure there was such a person"	1	2	3	6
Total	100	100	100	100

TABLE 4.4 (*Continued*)

Beliefs About Jesus, Heaven and Hell, and the Bible, by Degree of Localism, in Percentages (N varies from 452 to 473)

CATEGORIES OF BELIEF	LOCAL	MODERATELY LOCAL	MODERATELY COSMOPOLITAN	COSMOPOLITAN
Heaven and Hell:				
1: "these words have no meaning"	0	2	8	9
2. "ways of speaking about acceptance of, or separation from, God"	6	10	13	36
3. " . . . words used to express final reward or punishment"	21	25	33	31
Percentage Symbolic (1,2,3)	*27*	*37*	*54*	*76*
4. "physical places"	73	63	46	24
Total	100	100	100	100
Bible:				
1. "written by wise and good men, but God had no more to ,do with it than he did with other great literature"	5	10	19	32
2. "written by men inspired by God, but it contains factual errors"	39	60	70	58
Percentage Symbolic	*44*	*70*	*89*	*90*
3. "God's Word and all that it says is factually true"	56	30	11	10
Total	100	100	100	100

Statistically significant at .05 level in each instance.

Looking at the statements about Jesus, we find contrasting beliefs similar to those concerning God. Well over half of the locals hold the view that Jesus was indeed the Incarnate God living in the presence of his contemporaries. Among the highly cosmopolitan the modal conception is slightly different: Jesus is a *man*, called to reveal God's purpose to men. However important or unimportant the distinction theologically, it is of interest from our perspective. The image of Jesus as a man, albeit a unique one, conveys fewer supernatural trappings than does the doctrine of the Incarnation, and probably for this reason it is more acceptable to the cosmopolitans. If, however, we treat both responses as indicative of an orthodox conception of Christ, clearly the vast majority of all respondents—cosmopolitans and locals—are traditional in their views on Jesus. The cosmopolitan's propensity to modernist beliefs is shown better in the responses to the third, fourth, and fifth statements about Jesus. In all three instances the patterns are clear and consistent: cosmopolitanism is associated with either unorthodox views of Jesus as "great man and teacher" and as embodying "the best that is in all men" or disbelief in the historical figure. Thirty-nine percent of the highly cosmopolitan respondents endorse such views, in contrast to 5 percent of the extreme locals.

Finally, the patterns are very similar with beliefs about heaven and hell and the Bible. Locals favor literal orthodox meanings, whereas cosmopolitans more readily accept symbolic interpretations. This is particularly apparent where localism is strongly associated with the proportion interpreting heaven and hell to mean "physical places." Cosmopolitans, on the other hand, prefer to view these as images describing a person's relation with, or estrangement from, the Deity. These percentage spreads are among the highest in the study as shown by the proportion accepting symbolic interpretations—from 27 percent up to 76 percent among the most cosmopolitan. In the case of the Bible, 56 percent of the locals as compared with 10 percent of the cosmopolitans view it in the fundamentalist terms as factually true and without error. Combining responses to the first and second statements (both of which are taken as symbolic, nonliteral responses), we see that only 44 percent of the locals hold to more liberal views about the Bible. This proportion increases significantly with cosmopolitanism, up to an impressive high of 90 percent.

Thus we find that breadth of perspective is related to traditional versus modernist beliefs. In one doctrine after another, we find substantial and consistent variations. Locals are far more inclined to hold literal, anthropomorphic conceptions and to dismiss symbolic interpretations of the kind which cosmopolitans find more acceptable. Quite clearly, the two character types discriminate very effectively between literal and nonliteral imageries in supernatural conceptions. People having limited social experiences favor anthropomorphic beliefs probably because of their lower levels of cognitive sophistication. But with increasing conceptual sophistication they reformulate their imageries in a more symbolic mode, bringing them into line with their experiences and outlook.

Importance of Faith

A second measure of religious meaning concerns the importance, or salience, of faith in a person's life. Rather than supernatural conception, this has to do with the significance the believer attaches to religious conviction in everyday life and the extent to which beliefs and values enhance personal experience. Following King and Hunt's lead, the measure is better described not so much as a way of being religious as an orientation to religion or a type of motivation for commitment.[6] As such it is very much akin to Allport's notion of intrinsic religion.

Table 4.5 displays the responses of locals and cosmopolitans to three items on the importance of faith. Locals disproportionately report that their religious faith is salient in their lives, but the differences are not huge. The spread is greatest with the agree-disagree item, with 93

TABLE 4.5

Responses to Measures of Religious Importance by Degree of Localism, in Percentages (N=478)

MEASURES OF RELIGIOUS IMPORTANCE	LOCAL	MODERATELY LOCAL	MODERATELY COSMOPOLITAN	COSMOPOLITAN
My religious faith is:				
1. "of central importance. . . ."	54	39	34	40
2. "important for my life. . . ."	42	54	59	49
3. "only of minor importance. . . ."	4	7	7	11
Total	100	100	100	100

TABLE 4.5 (*Continued*)

Responses to Measures of Religious Importance by Degree of Localism, in Percentages (N=478)

MEASURES OF RELIGIOUS IMPORTANCE	LOCAL	MODERATELY LOCAL	MODERATELY COSMOPOLITAN	COSMOPOLITAN
Making decisions on the basis of religious faith:				
1. "Seldom . . . "	8	9	7	12
2. "Sometimes . . . "	11	10	12	8
3. "Most are . . . but in general, unconscious way"	46	55	59	57
4. "Most are . . . consciously attempt to make them so"	35	26	22	23
Total	100	100	100	100
Without my religious faith, the rest of my life would not have much meaning to it.*				
1. Agree strongly	61	61	56	46
2. Agree somewhat	32	22	25	27
3. Disagree somewhat	4	10	12	14
4. Disagree strongly	3	7	7	13
Total	100	100	100	100

*Significant at .05 level.

percent of the highly local agreeing to faith's significance compared with 73 percent of the highly cosmopolitan. Lack of greater differences here, plus statistical insignificance for the other two items, suggests that religious meaning is probably important to many cosmopolitans as well. Compared with the percentage spreads observed with the belief items, or with church attendance, the importance measure quite clearly taps an alternative dimension of commitment. Or possibly the differences are blurred because of *indiscriminate proreligious* responses on the part of the locals.[7] It is difficult to assess the latter with the data at hand, but we do look further at intrinsic religious meanings and their implications later in the study.

Devotionalism

Yet another important type of personal religious commitment is *devotionalism*. By this is meant a style of commitment emphasizing the importance of close, personal communion with God. Included here are individual acts of contemplation, study, and worship that are relatively spontaneous, informal, and private. They are similar to an individual's beliefs in the sense that they are personally meaningful. But unlike beliefs, devotionalism is a behavioral expression of commitment.

Table 4.6 shows the local-cosmopolitan contrasts for three devotional activities: personal prayer, Bible reading, and the reading of religious literature. Locals are more likely to report regular prayer than are cosmopolitans although, again, the differences are not large. About 81 percent of all locals pray at least once a week compared with slightly less than 70 percent of the combined cosmopolitan types. The greatest difference occurs among those who say they seldom or never pray. Greater proportions of cosmopolitans have abandoned prayer altogether than have locals.

In Bible reading, the pattern of differences is somewhat stronger. Forty-one percent of the highly local respondents are regular Bible readers, i.e., report reading every day or more than once a week. Among cosmopolitans the figures are 19 and 14 percent for the moderates and strongly oriented types, respectively. Again, cosmopolitans are more likely not to engage in this form of devotional practice. Much the same holds with the reading of religious literature. This activity is more common among locals than among cosmopolitans, especially if comparisons are restricted to those reporting to do so on a regular basis. Whereas 39 percent of the locally oriented respondents report frequent reading, 24 percent of the highly cosmopolitan respondents claim this type of religious commitment. Unlike with prayer and Bible reading, however, this difference is not statistically significant.

Obviously the locals evidence greater religiosity on all three of the devotional items. Traditional piety of this kind would appear more congruent with their life-style and outlook. But two observations should be made.

TABLE 4.6

Devotional Practices by Degree of Localism,
in Percentages (N=458)

DEVOTIONAL PRACTICES	LOCAL	MODERATELY LOCAL	MODERATELY COSMOPOLITAN	COSMOPOLITAN
Personal Prayer*				
Every day	66	61	48	47
More than once a week	15	19	24	20
Percentage Praying Regularly	*81*	*80*	*72*	*67*
More than once a month	7	6	11	5
Several times a year	7	6	9	8
Seldom or never	5	8	8	20
Total	100	100	100	100
Read the Bible*				
Every day	18	7	5	3
More than once a week	23	19	14	11
Percentage Bible Readers	*41*	*26*	*19*	*14*
More than once a month	17	20	21	19
Several times a year	21	27	26	33
Seldom or never	21	27	34	34
Total	100	100	100	100
Read Religious Literature				
Every day	20	14	6	4
More than once a week	19	14	18	20
Percentage Reading Regularly	*39*	*28*	*24*	*24*
More than once a month	27	28	31	26
Several times a year	22	31	30	29
Seldom or never	12	13	15	21
Total	100	100	100	100

*Statistically significant at .05 level.

First is the fact that, overall, the percentage of respondents scoring high on devotionalism is quite large. This is most evident with personal prayer where 55 percent of the total sample reports daily prayers. High rates of devotionalism are very common in American religious surveys, and in this respect the current findings support Stark and Glock's conclusion that private devotions are more often practiced in liberal Protestant denominations than public religious rituals.[8] Even though church members may not attend worship services regularly, still they tend to be religious in their private lives. This substantiates the point that religion in contemporary society is very much a privatized phenomenon, and that the public and private dimensions of religiosity vary somewhat independently of one another. The extent to which they vary and the conditions under which they do so are topics for further exploration in Part III.

And second, in matters of devotionalism and saliency, locals and cosmopolitans simply do not differ as much as they do in other types of religious commitment. Perhaps this is because inspirational literature is widely disseminated and read today by active as well as inactive church members. For many individuals as Luckmann points out, inspirational writings are the medium through which a religious identity is self-constructed and self-maintained.[9] Those who otherwise might not be religious find such literature useful in clarifying their own values and ultimate concerns. Inspirational literature is instrumental in the quest for personal meaning and identity, and we would expect that cosmopolitans, too, engage in such efforts.[10] Whereas locals may be devotional out of habit and custom, cosmopolitans may consciously engage in such practices in order to fulfill specific needs and obtain psychological rewards.

In brief, we find local-cosmopolitan differences in the several types of personal religiosity—traditional belief, importance of faith, and devotionalism. Of these the relationships are stronger in the realms of belief and supernatural imagery, prompting the speculation that belief systems are more sensitive than are other aspects of religious meaning to contrasting cognitive styles. In other words, it would appear that cosmopolitan life-experiences are associated with greater secularization in beliefs than in personal piety. That this should be true is not too surprising considering that religious identity is increasingly privatized in the modern world, both inside and out of established churches.

SOCIOECONOMIC STATUS, COMMUNITY SIZE, AND AGE AS TEST FACTORS

Up to this point, the analysis has concerned only two variables without any checks to see if other social factors are operating. This was done for purposes of highlighting the local-cosmopolitan contrasts but is hardly sufficient analytically. It is well known, for example, that the higher one's social standing in American society the more likely a person will take part in religious activity. So it is possible that social class, and not community attachments, is the actual explanation for why locals are belongers in religious organizations. Also, how does a respondent's age affect the patterns? And what about the size of the community in which the respondent lives? Until we know more about these influences we can hardly rest contented with the foregoing results on either the belonging or meaning dimensions.

This section delves further into these matters by examining other independent variables. The strategy will be to look at test factors one at a time, saving the combined simultaneous effects of all variables for consideration in the next chapter. Choice of test factors is limited here to those known to be relevant to both level of community orientation and religious commitment. Thus, our concern is with those variables that have already come up as potentially significant in previous discussions, either on religion or localism as an orientation.

Socioeconomic Status and Its Effects

More attention has been given to socioeconomic status as a factor shaping religious commitment in empirical research than any other single correlate. As was pointed out in Chapter 1, numerous scholars have shown that complex, multidimensional religious patterns exist among the social classes. What they argue generally is that socioeconomic differences in religion are primarily of kind, not degree, and that such differences must be ferreted out by means of multidimensional measures. Middle-class church members, for example, are more likely than working-class ones to participate in religious group activities, as reflected in their higher rates of church attendance and greater involvement in parish organizations. Contrariwise, lower-status members score higher on the creedal and devotional aspects of religious commitment. Such individuals presumably "believe" and "feel" more than "do" their religion. Based upon such observations, Demerath concludes that the two classes favor alternative styles of *churchlike* and *sectlike* religiosity and that both are often found within a single religious institution.[11]

More recently studies have questioned the extensiveness of social class patterns, suggesting that socioeconomic differences are probably exaggerated. Whether true or not, we can hardly avoid the issue here since social class is a correlate of some importance to religion.

Moreover, there is another reason why social class comes into play: people's ties to local communities are themselves often affected by their level of education, or by their experiences within white-collar occupations. Thus it is conceivable that local-cosmopolitan effects on religion are simply spurious, owing to the fact that socioeconomic status factors account for variation in either one or the other, or both, the independent and dependent variables.

Table 4.7 provides a first test, looking at local-cosmopolitan patterns of religiosity among occupational groups. Here the sample is divided according to four occupational (census) categories: professionals, managers and officials, clerical and sales, and craftsmen, operatives, and laborers. The data are shown only for church attendance and orthodoxy, since these are probably the two most important dimensions under consideration. The orthodoxy index is a composite of the four belief items discussed earlier: imageries of God, Jesus Christ, Heaven and Hell, and the Bible (see Appendix B for index construction).

The analysis here focuses on those with "high" literal orthodoxy scores, i.e., respondents holding traditional views on all four doctrines, and "regular" church attenders, i.e., respondents who say they attend weekly or nearly every week. By inspection we see that the data support our hypothesis even with occupation held constant. In all four occupational groups, locals are more likely than cosmopolitans to be regular attenders at worship services and to adhere to orthodox beliefs. The

TABLE 4.7

Religiosity of Locals and Cosmopolitans Within Occupational Groups,
in Percentages

OCCUPATIONAL GROUP	PERCENTAGE REGULAR CHURCH ATTENDERS	PERCENTAGE HIGH ON ORTHODOXY
Professionals		
Locals (N= 57)	67*	41*
Cosmopolitans (N= 74)	42	10
Managers and Officials		
Locals (N= 70)	59*	48*
Cosmopolitans (N= 79)	44	19
Clerical and Sales		
Locals (N= 57)	61	38
Cosmopolitans (N= 58)	52	21
Craftsmen, Operatives, Laborers		
Locals (N= 55)	59*	46*
Cosmopolitans (N= 21)	32	22

*Significant at .05 level.

pattern is remarkably consistent, even if the differences are not always statistically significant, and demonstrates that the local-cosmopolitan plausibility theory predicts these two aspects of religiosity reasonably well. It is noteworthy, also, that the differences are fairly constant, among blue-collar craftsmen about the same as among white-collar professionals. Differences as these lead to greater confidence in the hypothesis and support the view that localism-cosmopolitanism and socioeconomic status represent two, quite different, axes of social differentiation. Controlling for social class reduces slightly the local-cosmopolitan differences but does not fully explain the relationship. As hypothesized, the religious patterns reflect what Merton's earlier theorizing would predict generally.

But to substantiate the claim more fully, we must look more systematically at the several socioeconomic status variables in relation to religiosity. These results are reported in table 4.8, summarized in the form of zero-order and partial correlation coefficients. The zero-order, or total, coefficients describe the original relationships with the religious commitment measures. Partial coefficients, on the other hand,

TABLE 4.8

Zero-Order and Partial Correlation Coefficients Between Localism and Religiosity Measures, Controlling for Socioeconomic Status
(N varies from 452 to 471)

MEASURE OF RELIGIOSITY	ZERO-ORDER CORRELATION	CONTROLLING FOR:		
		EDUCATION	OCCUPATIONAL PRESTIGE	INCOME
Church attendance	.42*	.38*	.40*	.41*
Church activities	.21*	.19*	.20*	.20*
Congregational friendships	.25*	.20*	.22*	.24*
Orthodoxy	.29*	.22*	.27*	.28*
Importance of faith	.16	.12	.14	.14
Devotionalism	.13	.05	.10	.11

*Statistically significant at .05 level.

describe the same associations once the effects of the test factor have been statistically controlled. They offer a summary measure of how well the associations hold up after removing the other influences.

This analysis shows the partials to be only slightly smaller than the zero-order coefficients. Beyond this, two other observations are worth noting. First, it is clear that controlling for years of education, occupational prestige,[12] and income has relatively little effect. In no instance does a control for these variables reduce the correlations between localism and religiosity below statistical significance. Importance of faith and devotionalism are weakly related to begin with, as we would expect from the previous analysis. Second, of the three status variables education produces the strongest effects. Partialing for education reduces the correlations more so than for either occupational prestige or income, especially with orthodoxy and devotionalism. Apparently education has a greater impact on the subjective aspects of local-cosmopolitan religious styles. Such patterns prompt the speculation that education is closely bound to an individual's breadth of perspective and that education's effect upon religion may depend upon *intervening* local-cosmopolitan orientations. This possibility is examined in the next chapter, but for now it seems safe to rule out spuriousness as a serious problem. Whatever the complex interrelationships among these variables, we can be assured the differences between locals and cosmopolitans in religiosity are not accounted for by education or social status more generally. Socioeconomic position may contribute to these differences but does not explain them.

Community Size and Its Effects

Community size is another important correlate of institutional religion. Compared with life in rural areas and small towns, urban existence fosters innovative life-styles. Evidence on a wide range of behaviors—for example, political dissent, divorce, alcoholism, smoking marijuana—underscores an association between urbanism and deviation from dominant cultural standards. Theories of urbanism have typically emphasized, following Louis Wirth and the "Chicago School," the importance of ecological variables such as a city's size, its density, and heterogeneity. The experience of living among large numbers, in close association with others of diverse background, encourages norms of tolerance, the weakening of primary-group restraints, and loosening of traditional moral values. All things considered, the consequences of urban residence are greater individualism, impersonalism, and secularism. More recent views on urbanism have cast some doubt upon so simple an explanation, but clearly urban life is less supportive of traditional religion than rural and small-town life. Because of their size, urban centers attract innovators who espouse and disseminate new perspectives and values. Cities generate deviant subcultures and expose people to new and alternative ways of living. Following this line of reasoning, we should not be surprised to find community size related to local and cosmopolitan differences in religion.[13]

Already we have seen that community size is related to localism-cosmopolitanism. The larger the community of residence, the greater the chances that individuals will be cosmopolitan in outlook. With regard to religion, the conclusions are somewhat mixed. Orthodox beliefs are generally found to decrease as community size increases, but measures of religious practice appear to be less affected.[14] That is, urbanites adhere to traditional beliefs less than people in rural and small-town settings but attend religious services about equally, or only slightly less. In North America at least, this is the pattern that seems to hold.[15]

Table 4.9 displays roughly similar results. The percentages indicating high scores of religiosity are generally lower within the larger communities. Unfortunately the cell sizes are in some instances quite small, which makes it easy to overextend the findings. But as a whole, it appears that urban life and experiences are less conducive to traditional beliefs and personal religious practice than to associational and communal types of involvement within the socioreligious group. As Herberg, Lenski, Greeley and others have suggested, urban conditions may generate in individuals needs for communal identification

TABLE 4.9

Religiosity of Locals and Cosmopolitans by Community Size, in Percentages

MEASURES OF RELIGIOSITY	COMMUNITY SIZE CATEGORIES							
	Rural to 15,000		Less than 100,000		100,000 to 250,000		250,000 or Larger	
Attendance at church every week, or nearly every week								
Locals	80	(62)	76	(72)	59	(32)	61	(11)
Cosmopolitans	52	(25)	61	(37)	52	(48)	50	(12)
Involvement in two or more church activities								
Locals	46	(36)	49	(46)	32	(17)	41	(9)
Cosmopolitans	31	(16)	31	(22)	38	(35)	33	(8)
Possession of two or more congregational friends								
Locals	63	(49)	54	(51)	53	(28)	57	(8)
Cosmopolitans	50	(24)	37	(21)	33	(31)	39	(9)
High score on orthodoxy								
Locals	59	(46)	47	(45)	24	(13)	35	(7)
Cosmopolitans	13	(5)	18	(10)	13	(10)	19	(7)
High score on importance of faith								
Locals	62	(51)	58	(56)	49	(26)	41	(7)
Cosmopolitans	44	(21)	47	(29)	42	(39)	41	(10)

Statistically significant at .05 level in each instance.

and belongingness that offset any striking declines in church attendance and congregational activitivies among urbanites.

Again we see that the predicted patterns for locals and cosmopolitans hold. No matter which of the conventional religiosity measures is used, locals are more religious than cosmopolitans in communities of all sizes. The differences are somewhat greater in the smaller communities, but are found in the large urban areas as well. This is consistent with our expectation that the two character types differ in traditional religious commitment no matter the type of community in which they live. Locals can be found in rural areas, small towns, and large cities; and wherever they are, they are generally more religious than their cosmopolitan counterparts.

Age and Its Effects

Finally we turn to another type of control variable—the respondent's age. Age is critically important in the present study since, as has already been shown in Chapter 3, a respondent's degree of localism varies directly with his or her age. With age individuals become more settled in their communities and hence more likely to have strong ties binding them to relatives and friends. Not surprisingly, then, localistic perspectives are especially pronounced among the older, well-established residents of a community.

Studies examining the relation between age and religiosity yield inconsistent results. To summarize, briefly, points on which there is some consensus, most research shows that (a) people become more religious creedally and devotionally as they move through the life-cycle,[16] and (b) after a period of decline in religious participation during the early adult years, there is a steady increase up until at least about age sixty.[17] The latter point borders upon controversy in that there is dispute over what happens in the years beyond sixty. One interpretation offered by Glock and others emphasized steady increases in religious activity until old age. Essentially age is seem as leading to decreasing involvement in secular pursuits and inspiring individuals to greater religious participation as an alternative source of gratification. Another interpretation is that aging involves a more general process of disengagement or withdrawal from society. This latter suggests a pattern of decreasing involvement following middle age in

103

organizations of all kinds, both religious and nonreligious. Rather than turn to religion, disengagement theory predicts that an aging person in the middle to elderly years gradually severs ties with the religious institution.[18]

In the present study the data support the conventional interpretation of steady increases in religiosity with age. This holds generally for all six measures, but is especially true in the case of church attendance (see table 4.10). Socioreligious group involvement tends, on the whole, to increase with age, as do orthodoxy, importance of faith, and devotionalism.

Of greater interest, however, is the support Table 4.10 provides

TABLE 4.10

Religiosity of Locals and Cosmopolitans by Age, in Percentages

MEASURE OF RELIGIOSITY	AGE CATEGORIES							
	Less than 30		35–49		50–69		70 and over	
Attendance at church every week, or nearly every week*								
Locals	57	(16)	65	(27)	66	(38)	73	(17)
Cosmopolitans	45	(13)	56	(30)	55	(29)	61	(16)
Involvement in two or more church activities*								
Locals	40	(10)	37	(24)	40	(21)	57	(9)
Cosmopolitans	33	(8)	35	(15)	37	(21)	31	(8)
Possession of two or more congregational friends*								
Locals	28	(10)	51	(28)	50	(29)	52	(15)
Cosmopolitans	13	(9)	39	(22)	38	(20)	43	(14)
High score on orthodoxy*								
Locals	35	(9)	28	(35)	24	(40)	39	(11)
Cosmopolitans	20	(6)	21	(33)	21	(33)	13	(6)
High score on importance of faith								
Locals	27	(10)	29	(30)	34	(22)	38	(12)
Cosmopolitans	21	(9)	24	(32)	32	(18)	36	(19)
High score on devotionalism								
Locals	42	(14)	52	(36)	63	(39)	67	(16)
Cosmopolitans	39	(12)	54	(24)	60	(31)	64	(14)

*Statistically significant at .05 level.

for the local-cosmopolitan hypothesis. It is clear that the effect of localism persists despite the control for age. Except for minor inversions the percentages of locals who are conventionally religious are consistently greater than cosmopolitans across all age categories. Also noticeable is the fact that local-cosmopolitan differences usually decline as age increases. Declines are most prominent with devotionalism and importance of faith. Why this should occur with these measures and not with the others is not readily apparent. Given the small cell sizes, one must necessarily be cautious in drawing firm conclusions.

One further point with regard to age: note in the case of orthodoxy the relatively stable pattern among cosmopolitans, up until age seventy and over when it drops off. This suggests that among cosmopolitans aging may not result in increases in belief. Contrary to conventional wisdom, aging may have very little influence in this direction among those who for one reason or another find traditional beliefs implausible. Further inquiry into this is of course required in order to be more definitive, in view of the small number of cases on which our observations are based.

SUMMARY

This chapter put the plausibility theory to its first empirical test. Significant differences between locals and cosmopolitans were shown to exist with respect to both religious belonging and meaning. Those individuals with strong local social ties, repeatedly, scored higher on the religious commitment measures. Controlling statistically for the effects of socioeconomic status, community size, and the respondent's age, added confidence in the results. In each instance the test factor analysis failed to disconfirm the theory, despite minor inversions here and there and despite overall reductions in most of the relationships. This, of course, does not prove the theory, but does lend support to its validity.

Two conclusions should be made. First is that the local-cosmopolitan distinction is a reasonably good predictor of traditional religiosity. Along with sex, age, social class, and education, this variable should be added to the list of social correlates commonly included in such studies. Empirically it compares favorably, if not better than, many of the correlates receiving attention in the past. Exactly how well it compares is examined in the next chapter, at which time we shall explore further its predictive power. This does not mean the measure will explain a huge variance in religiosity or that it is necessarily the best predictor available. Rather, the point is that most of the alleged social correlates explain very little. Gerhard Lenski, writing in 1962, observed that a combined set of the better predictors probably accounts for no more than one-third of the variance in religiosity measures.[19] There is little reason to expect this to be any greater today.

Second, the findings amply demonstrate that plausibility as a consideration adds to our understanding of both religious belonging and meaning. From a theoretical point of view, it would seem crucial to recognize traditionalist versus modernist approaches to religion and to understand that these differences arise out of the varying levels of plausibility in belief systems as a whole. Plausibility cannot be taken for granted in the modern world, as if all members in churches share equally in their normative commitments. In contemporary secular society, this consideration becomes increasingly serious, requiring that we treat commitment strength as a factor itself in developing theories of traditional religion.

It is worth noting in this regard what we have and have not established thus far in the analysis. The results give us reason to be fairly confident of the relation of local attachments to religion, and to rule out spuriousness as a serious possibility. As a first step this is crucial but it is only that—a first step—toward establishing the theory. In developing a general explanation for religious plausibility, we have to explore in greater depth the role that local-cosmopolitan orientations play in relation to other social correlates of religion. This raises another set of research questions about the broader social bases of traditional religion in contemporary society, to which we must turn in the next chapter.

⌈5⌉

Social Bases of Religious Plausibility

In the last chapter we saw that locals are more religious than cosmopolitans as measured by various indicators. Differences between the two hold even after taking into account the influences of other, presumably significant social factors. But this raises as many questions as it answers. Does it mean that the religious styles of the two character types are unrelated to such factors as social class, community size, and age of respondent? Or could it be that the local's orientation and outlook actually mediate these other social influences? This latter raises the interesting possibility that breadth of perspective may function as an intervening psychological mechanism helping to account for various of the influences on religion. If this is indeed true, local-cosmopolitan differences in religiosity are important not only in their own right, but because they fit into a larger explanatory framework of religion and its correlates in contemporary society.

It is well known, for example, that less educated church members adhere to more orthodox, literal beliefs. It is also known that older persons are more orthodox in their doctrinal beliefs, and rural and small-town residents are more conventional in beliefs and practices. In modern American society these three—the less educated, the aged, and rural, small-town folk—number among those coming from the most traditional sectors of contemporary life. They are all traditionalists, culturally speaking, by virtue of their peripheral location in the society. Does it follow then that they share a localistic world view? Are their definitions of social reality similar enough to account for their common religious styles?

In search of a more general interpretation of localism-cosmopolitanism and of its relation to these other social bases of religion, this chapter seeks answers to these questions. In the first part of the chapter, we take another look at social class, community size, and age, focusing this time on the way the community reference orientations function as social psychological mechanisms mediating other influences. Following that, we conclude the discussion on the social correlates by looking at a general model of religious plausibility linking the many types of influences into a single interpretation.

INTERPRETING SOCIAL CLASS EFFECTS

We can hardly avoid looking closely at social class influences, considering the amount of discussion and debate that it has evoked over the years. Despite the massive amount of research on social class and religion, however, relations between the two are not really well understood. Not only has previous research tended to exaggerate the strength of these relations, it is also true that theories of social class often leave much to be desired in the way of adequate interpretations.

Perhaps the most serious problem with social class theories of religiosity is the lack of a clear, unambiguous understanding of the link between an individual's social standing and religious commitment. Why this should be so is, partly at least, accounted for by the character of the data researchers typically rely upon. Those concerned usually rely upon "objective" social class indicators (e.g., years of education or occupational prestige scores) on which to draw inferences about religious styles, but they often do so without a clear understanding of the meanings that individuals attach to their social class standing. As a result not very much is known about the subjective consequences of social class standing for a person's basic value orientations. To be sure, researchers are inclined to make psychological assumptions about these cognitive and motivational consequences, but these often go unexamined or are simply taken for granted. So serious is this state of affairs in stratification research that Estus and Overington insist that the problem is not "the discovery of better indicators of church participation, but the development of better studies of the meanings of church membership in the life space of the individual member."[1]

No where is the lack of clarity better illustrated than in the case of education. Though education often gets cited as a correlate of religiosity, seldom do researchers clarify why, or exactly how, it affects people's commitments. The connection between education and literal religious beliefs is clearly obvious: high levels of learning are simply at odds with fundamentalist orthodoxy and a theology of a miraculous, soul-saving God who redeems people from hellfire and brimstone. But what about a person's *involvement* within religious institutions? Here the picture becomes blurred. For on the one hand, education is a status indicator reflecting the person's social standing, relative to others. The higher the social standing, the greater the chances of religious belonging and participation, including attendance at worship and involvement in congregational activities. Within American society, church participation is for many a symbolic means of representing one's middle-class position.

Yet education as status simply does not exhaust its import for religion. Education can just as easily undermine the plausibility of the beliefs on which traditional religion rests, and thus it may lead individuals to question orthodox doctrines in light of modern scientific principles. Through education people are exposed to new perspectives and values—"contact effect" as Stouffer described it.[2] And in a realm like religion where beliefs and values rest primarily on faith, such exposure can and does produce cognitive incompatibilities that can result in disbelief and disaffiliation. "Intellectual defection," as Mauss says, is a major source of religious disinvolvement, as evidenced by the low levels of religiosity among academicians.[3] If not disinvolvement, education is surely to result in a reorienting of religious commitment, as the example of liberal, activist clergy suggests—away from dogmatic assertion to this-worldly involvement and ethical concerns.

The relation of education to religion is thus complex and cannot be fully explained by either the *status* or *exposure* principles. Moreover, the two principles in reality can work against one another in giving shape to a person's religious beliefs and practices. Education may, for

109

example, generate status pressures leading in the direction of church participation, but at the same time reorient an individual toward more rational, this-worldly beliefs and values. For this reason it is necessary to keep these two aspects of the relationship separate and, if possible, to sort out their alternative effects. Some clarification of these two would seem essential in establishing a better understanding of the processes of secularization in modern life.

This is not easily accomplished, but the data at hand do permit an approximation. By conceptualizing localism-cosmopolitanism as an intervening perspective, we can view it as a social psychological mechanism transmitting a portion of the influence of education upon religious commitment. That is to say, formal schooling broadens people's outlook, or cosmopolitanism; and greater breadth of perspective should in turn mediate education's influence on style of religious commitment. In other words education is the source of influence, but the effects are indirect by means of the expanded mental horizons. Contrariwise, those effects of education *not* hinging on an expanded outlook, namely status, operate as direct rather than as intervening influences. By direct and intervening, of course, we have in mind only logical distinctions in types of influence, recognizing fully well that such constructs only approximate the psychodynamic processes involved.

That such a conceptualization may be helpful is shown by the data in table 5.1, which displays the correlation coefficients describing the association between education and level of religiosity. If breadth of perspective does transmit a portion of education's influence, controlling for this intervening variable should (a) increase the total correlation when the direct influence differs in sign from the intervening; or (b) reduce the zero-order relationship in instances where direct and indirect effects are of similar sign. We have to consider both possibilities because of education's differing relations with the several dimensions of religiosity. Education is positively associated with the belonging components, and negatively with the meaning.

These predictions hold in all six instances. With church attendance, church activities, and congregational friendships, the partials are somewhat larger; but with orthodoxy, importance of faith, and devotionalism they are weaker than the zero-order coefficients. The effects mediated via localism-cosmopolitanism, though not large, are dis-

TABLE 5.1

Education, Localism, and the Religiosity Measures

MEASURES OF RELIGIOSITY	ZERO-ORDER CORRELATION BETWEEN EDUCATION AND RELIGIOSITY	PARTIAL CORRELATION CONTROLLING FOR LOCALISM
Church Attendance	.09	.25*
Church Activities	−.09	.17
Congregational Friendships	.19*	.29*
Orthodoxy	−.30*	−.24*
Importance of Faith	−.24*	−.20
Devotionalism	−.27*	−.24*

*Statistically significant at .05 level.

cernable and offer support for the intervening-variable hypothesis. At the same time they amply demonstrate that education generates still other effects of a different sort. Especially interesting are the *conflicting* influences on religious belonging, as reflected by total correlations smaller than partials.[4] Education results in positive status effects plus indirect, negative exposure influences, and the two appear to oppose one another. Opposing effects as these are worth noting not only because of the empirical peculiarities they create but because of their theoretical significance. A systematic theory of education must take into consideration both types of effects, and to the extent possible provide some rationale for how the two operate in combination.

In sum, the results suggest that we do gain in understanding by conceptualizing breadth of perspective as an intervening mechanism. Education's consequences for religiosity are diverse, and by linking the variables in this way we shed some light on how these operate. More broadly, we see that in developing theories of social class, plausibility as a consideration should not be lost sight of. Both the exposure and status factors, or some other related set, require attention in describing the intimate linkages between social class and the individual's beliefs and practices. In the future, these complexities will no doubt become even more important assuming the plausibility of traditional religion continues to erode.

111

INTERPRETING COMMUNITY SIZE EFFECTS

Already the point has been made that in cities, as compared with rural areas, people are somewhat less likely to be religious. This is especially true with personal forms of religiosity, such as beliefs and private devotional activities. Not only with religion but with cultural patterns more broadly, rural-urban differences persist despite the "massification" of American society. Given this fact, the question that concerns us here is this: are these community size effects transmitted through local-cosmopolitan perspectives?

As previously mentioned, recent research suggests that the impact of urban residence on traditional values is best explained by the social characteristics of urban dwellers, not simply by demographic and ecological factors. One has only to recall Gans's urban villagers to be reminded that some people are in but not of the city. Insofar as people's values and outlook are concerned, urban dwellers are *not* uniformly less traditional than rural and small-town residents; instead they can be highly diverse in outlook, ranging from the highly cosmopolitan to the parochial. Quite clearly, even in the largest of cities people's perspectives vary immensely, so much so in fact that considerations other than community size and heterogeneity are necessary for explaining traditional versus nontraditional patterns of belief and behavior.

This observation calls attention to what is an important aspect of urbanism, namely, the individual's opportunity and/or willingness to expand social boundaries. Socialization into urban values and life-styles involves, minimally at least, the breaking down of narrow, particularistic ties with primary groups, and development of broader, rationally based social relationships. Put somewhat differently, we might say that urban life affects traditional values to the extent that urban dwellers discard narrow perspectives and adopt in their place broader social orientations. The cosmopolitan-oriented are in Fischer's words, the "modernizing agents" who foster innovative perspectives, establish unconventional life-styles, and build up deviant subcultures.[5] The larger the community, the greater the possibility of a critical mass of such modernizing agents who can transmit and diffuse such innovation.

112

In effect, urban influence on religion and traditional ways of thinking generally, implies new and alternative value systems that are implemented by social innovators.

Again an intervening variable model seems appropriate—a model in which urban influences are conceptualized as transmitted by means of cosmopolitan orientations. Should we control statistically for this intervening mechanism, assuming it accurately describes the actual causal processes involved, the zero-order relationships between community size and religiosity should attenuate. Unlike with education above, there is no reason here to expect both direct and indirect influences.

Table 5.2 reports the results, showing that community size is weakly related to the several dimensions of religiosity. Of greater interest here though are the partial correlations, all of which are smaller than the original coefficients. Unfortunately, weak relationships make it difficult to draw firm inferences from the reduction of the partials, but the results generally support the interpretation offered for urbanism. Whatever else may be involved, it would appear that urbanism entails an intervening social-psychological mechanism of the sort described by cosmopolitanism. As people's social attachments and orientations are broadened in urban life, they tend to break away from traditional forms of religious commitments.

Again, as with education, the patterns differ for religious belonging as compared with the meaning aspects. Correlations with the first set

TABLE 5.2

Community Size, Localism, and the Religiosity Measures

MEASURES OF RELIGIOSITY	ZERO-ORDER CORRELATION BETWEEN COMMUNITY SIZE AND RELIGIOSITY	PARTIAL CORRELATION CONTROLLING FOR LOCALISM
Church Attendance	−.11	.02
Church Activities	−.06	.01
Congregational Friendships	−.05	.02
Orthodoxy	−.15*	−.07
Importance of Faith	−.10	−.05
Devotionalism	−.12	−.08

*Statistically significant at .05 level.

of indicators reduce practically to zero. These were weaker from the outset and, in keeping with the findings of Nelsen et al. and Fischer,[6] such measures probably are less sensitive to community size than orthodoxy, importance of faith, or devotionalism. Controlling for the latter results in predictable decreases, but clearly the effects are less striking. About half of the community-size influence is not accounted for by the intervening orientations. Why this should be so is unclear.

But taken as a whole, the findings fall into place much as the recent subcultural explanations of urbanism would suggest. More is required for explaining changes in traditional religiosity than simply ecological-demographic factors. "A full understanding of life in cities," as Fischer says, "requires incorporation of ecological factors, subcultural development, and diffusion in a dynamic model."[7] Breadth of perspective offers one means of tapping the diffusion of urban values and as such provides a much needed psychological complement to the purely demographic approaches to rural-urban and community size differences in religion.

INTERPRETING EFFECTS OF AGE AND LENGTH OF RESIDENCE

Finally, we look at the respondent's age and length of residence in the community. These two refer to quite different phenomena, of course, one having to do with the life cycle and the other time spent living in a given locale. But both are temporal considerations important to the development of strong local social bonds, and both are known correlates of religious commitment. Accordingly, we examine the two together in this section.

Age as a factor in relation to religiosity is quite complex. In the last chapter we observed there are several interpretations for age, depending in part on the type of religiosity involved and also because age is itself a confusing correlate. Age taps at least three, perhaps more, aspects of experience: biological maturation, changes in roles and responsibilities as one proceeds through the life cycle, and intensification of social attachments by accretion. Each of these perhaps has a differing implication for religion. Biological maturation, for example, may facilitate the quest for religious meaning. Many individuals as they grow older tend to become more concerned about ultimate matters. In contrast, life-cycle stages are likely to produce erratic patterns of religiosity. Levels of religious participation often drop at the time of marriage and the birth of children, increase as children reach school age and then drop once children are no longer in the home.[8] As these two aspects of experience indicate, age is a surrogate index masking many meanings.

The third aspect of age mentioned above is what concerns us here: intensification of social attachments. With age people become more settled, develop friendships in their communities, and become involved in institutional activities as well as symbolically attached to their place of residence. Age is a crucial resource in this respect, for as people grow older both the range of their interpersonal contacts and the quality of their relations become, potentially at least, greater. Older people have the benefits not only of experience, but of long-standing relations with others in a community. This is especially true of course in instances where individuals have remained in the same community for a long time. While perhaps not any more important than the other aspects of age, nonetheless it is a consideration which should not be overlooked.

Following this line of reasoning, we can expect that localism once again mediates the effects of age on religion. At least it is likely to mediate a portion of these effects. Because age taps other aspects of experience as well, the community reference measure will no doubt account for only a part. A similar intervening should occur with the second variable of concern, i.e., length of residence. This latter is, as already observed in Chapter 3, strongly related to community attachment and orientation. Considering that length of residence refers directly to the respondent's stay in the local community, the orientational mechanism should mediate practically all of its effects on religiosity.

Correlations summarizing the data are shown in table 5.3, and as expected the patterns are consistent with the interpretation given to age. The partials controlling for localism are reduced in the case of age and religiosity, suggesting that a portion of the age effects may be mediated. Intervening influences appear to be greater with the belonging than with the meaning measures of religion. Localistic attachments associated with age carry a greater impact in the realm

TABLE 5.3
Age, Length of Residence, Localism, and the Religiosity Measures

MEASURES OF RELIGIOSITY	ZERO-ORDER CORRELATIONS		PARTIAL CORRELATIONS CONTROLLING FOR LOCALISM	
	With Respondent's Age	With Length of Residence	With Respondent's Age	With Length of Residence
Church Attendance	.21*	.17*	.11	.01
Church Activities	.18*	.12*	.08	.03
Congregational Friendship	.26*	.10	.15*	.00
Orthodoxy	.31*	.14*	.22*	.03
Importance of Faith	.32*	.10	.19*	.04
Devotionalism	.30*	.06	.26*	.01

*Statistically significant at .05 level.

of socioreligious group involvement. Proportionately less reduction in the partials with the religious meaning measures suggests that other aspects of age, not controlled for by means of the community reference measure, come into play in explaining these relationships. To account fully for age effects, controls tapping maturational, life cycle, and perhaps other types of intervening dynamics would be necessary.

The findings for length of residence are more straightforward. Here the partials attenuate to zero, or nearly so, across all six measures. Whatever influence length of residence has on religiosity, it is virtually all transmitted via localism-cosmopolitanism. Length of residence bears implications for church-type religious commitment, but apparently only because it predisposes residents to develop attachments to the local community.

Again we muster empirical support for breadth of perspective as an intervening social psychological dimension. In addition the data invite further inquiry into the sundry meanings of the aging process and its implications for religious commitment. Generally the findings prompt the conclusion that aging is important for many reasons, but especially because it entails an intensification of social attachments. Further attention to such effects should prove insightful in analyzing the correlates of traditional religion in contemporary society, considering the disproportionate number of older people who are members of churches. If nothing else, it offers an alternative interpretation to the aging process and one that promises to shed light on future religious trends.

THE BASIC MODEL[9]

Having examined the several correlates separately, it is now time we make a more general, multivariate assessment of the local-cosmopolitan hypothesis. The findings up to this point have generally confirmed our expectations, but because the approach has been that of focusing upon one variable at a time, a more rigorous inquiry is necessary. In this latter part of the chapter, our attention is given to the possibility of a more systematic interpretation linking the many variables in the analysis.

Our chief concern in this section is to offer a parsimonious interpretation for traditional religion, accounting for as many of its situational bases in modern society as possible. Already we have reviewed in some depth several of the major correlates, with an eye toward their social psychological meanings and implications. This led us to infer that plausibility is a critical consideration in explaining why these correlates—namely, social class, community size, and age—relate to church-oriented religion as they do. While other explanations may be given for how these factors operate, including the deprivation interpretation, none of these fully deals with the problems of plausibility in liberal Protestantism. They fail to consider that a crisis of faith and commitment has reached serious proportions, especially among the higher social classes, urban residents, and the young. Mainline denominations in the United States are losing members disproportionately among these sectors, and within churches as we have seen there are growing cultural cleavages along these lines. The lesser educated, small-town and rural residents, and the aged are all more traditional in outlook and values—characteristics that make for a close affinity with conventional church religion. For this basic reason then it makes sense to offer a general interpretation for these patterns of commitment.

In this and the previous chapter we have relied upon local-cosmopolitan reference orientations as an ordering principle. The usefulness of this approach lies mainly in the social psychological basis for linking the correlates to the problem of religious plausibility. The lesser educated, small-town, and older sectors of the society, by virtue of their more traditional cultural orientations, are prone to share a common social perspective—the limited, parochial social world of the local community. Ideologically they share a conservative stance, more committed to preserving traditional beliefs and behavior than to embracing new and untried ways. Their local world is in fact their defense, bound together as they are often by concerns about the larger society as a threat to their way of life. As the "massification" of modern society has increased, these several sectors have come to be remarkably similar in regard to cultural values and life-styles.

In analyzing their common values and outlook, it will be useful to treat localism-cosmopolitanism as an intervening variable. Specifically, the question we seek to answer is: does breadth of perspective mediate simultaneously the effects of these other correlates on religion? This assumes of course an individual's perspective is, to some extent, dependent upon structural variables like social class, community size, and length of residence. Schematically, this basic causal assumption is shown in figure 5.1.

This conceptualization is restrictive in the sense that it commits us to a simple "one-way" causal interpretation, thus disregarding other kinds of complexities among the variables.[10] On theoretical as well as empirical grounds, however, the assumption is reasonable. Social psychological orientations are often viewed as intervening variables in this manner, and even if empirically the relations among variables are more complex one would hardly argue that the primary influences operate in any other way. Finally, such assumption is necessary in order to utilize ordinary regression procedures in the data analysis.

Accordingly, a multivariate model was constructed making explicit

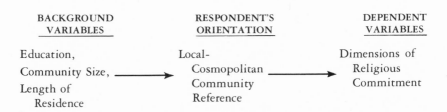

BACKGROUND VARIABLES	RESPONDENT'S ORIENTATION	DEPENDENT VARIABLES
Education, Community Size, Length of Residence	Local-Cosmopolitan Community Reference	Dimensions of Religious Commitment

FIGURE 5.1   Localism-Cosmopolitanism as Intervening Variable

the interrelations among the several types of variables. Theoretical formalization in this way serves several functions: one, it pulls the several variables into a single system of relationships, thereby permitting a simultaneous test of the theory; and two, it should help to show even more convincingly, in terms of direct and indirect relations, how local social attachments function in mediating the effects of social class, community size, and length of residence. Five variables are included in the model. These are:

X_1 Years of Education
X_2 Length of Residence
X_3 Community Size
X_4 Degree of Localism
X_{5a-f} Religiosity (six separate dimensions)

These have all been described in some detail, in this and the previous chapter. Note that respondent's age is left out of the model. Given our concerns about the alternative interpretations for age, plus the fact that length of residence has stronger relations with all the other variables, it seemed wise to rely upon the latter instead. Also, we rely upon years of education as our only measure of socioeconomic status. Education is more highly associated empirically with religiosity than either occupational prestige or income, and it is simply more promising in developing a theory of religious plausibility. Both empirical and theoretical considerations are of concern here, since our aim is to construct a general, but empirically testable, theory. Table 5.4 displays the matrix of correlations for these variables, their means and standard deviations.

Figure 5.2 is a graphic representation of the proposed system of relationships. Consistent with the previous analyses, it shows the influence of education upon religion as both direct and indirect through localism-cosmopolitanism, the influence of length of residence as indirect, and the influence of community size as indirect. Following the conventions of path analysis, double-headed arrows are used for describing the associations among the background, or exogenous, variables. The numbers entered on the diagram beside the bidirectional arrows are correlation coefficients. Influences upon the causally dependent, or endogenous, variables are depicted by means of causal

TABLE 5.4

Simple Correlations, Means, and Standard Deviations for Variables in the Model

VARIABLE		X_{5b}	X_{5c}	X_{5d}	X_{5e}	X_{5f}	X_1	X_2	X_3	X_4	MEAN	S.D.
X_{5a}	Church Attendance	.40	.30	.22	.11	.31	.09	.17	−.11	.42	2.91	.98
X_{5b}	Church Activities		.32	.07	.10	.20	.09	.12	−.06	.21	2.63	1.74
X_{5c}	Congregational Friendship			.14	.14	.24	.19	.10	−.05	.25	2.38	1.32
X_{5d}	Orthodoxy				.58	.19	−.30	.14	−.15	.29	3.11	1.63
X_{5e}	Importance of Faith					.39	−.24	.05	−.10	.16	7.56	3.61
X_{5f}	Devotionalism						−.27	.06	−.12	.13	3.87	1.28
X_1	Education							−.23	.18	−.31	13.07	3.52
X_2	Length of Residence								−.27	.38	13.41	4.74
X_3	Community Size									−.31	3.75	1.74
X_4	Local Community Reference										9.21	3.47

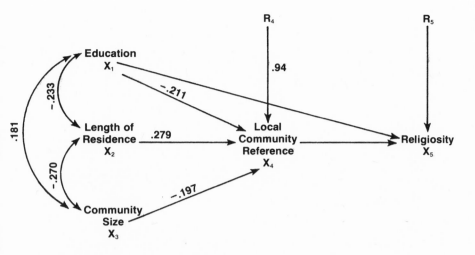

FIGURE 5.2 Basic Model of Localism-Cosmopolitanism and Religious Commitment

arrows, and the strength of these relationships is summarized by path coefficients. These latter are standardized partial regression coefficients (betas) and have the advantage, unlike correlations, of showing the strength of the relationships controlling simultaneously for all independent variables in the model. Shown also are the Rs, or residual variances, left unexplained by the explanatory variables.

Of interest in the model, first of all, are the relationships between the background variables and localism. Length of residence is positively associated whereas education and community size are negatively related. Of the three, length of residence is the strongest predictor of localism. This is not surprising considering that localism-cosmopolitanism as a cultural dimension cuts across, rather than coincides with, social class and rural-urban differences. Nevertheless, the overlap is sufficiently large enough to warrant the treatment of education and community size as contributing influences.

But our primary concern is with religious commitment. Because we have six measures of religiosity, direct influences on them cannot be shown in the diagram; instead, the separate effects of education and localism are displayed in table 5.5. As we would expect from the findings of Chapter 4, the relations of localism to religiosity are positive in all instances. The direct effects of education, however, are mixed:

TABLE 5.5
Partial Regression Coefficients in Standard Form and Residuals

| MEASURES OF RELIGIOSITY | INDEPENDENT VARIABLES | | RESIDUAL |
	EDUCATION	LOCALISM	
Church Attendance	.238*	.492*	.837
Church Activities	.168	.263*	.948
Congregational Friendships	.295*	.342*	.915
Orthodoxy	−.230*	.224*	.931
Importance of Faith	−.171	.155	.932
Devotionalism	−.211*	.196	.967

*Statistically significant at .01 level.

positive with religious belonging but negative with religious meaning. That is what we would expect, too, based upon the earlier inquiry. Interestingly the net effects of localism, relative to those of education, are stronger with church attendance, organizational participation, and congregational friendships but are slightly weaker with the subjective measures of religiosity. That is, a person's attachments to his or her local community, controlling for level of education, is more likely to influence socioreligious group involvement than personal faith and devotional practices. But with both the belonging and meaning aspects of religion the basic hypothesis is supported.

Overall, the results are unmistakably clear: *local community attachments, even when controlling for all other independent influences in the model, help to sustain traditional religious belief and behavior.*

Confident in this, we turn next to the intervening influences. By multiplying out the indirect paths and total correlations among the exogenous variables, we can obtain estimates for the indirect effects for several of the background factors plus the noncausal, or spurious and/or unanalyzed, influences that account for the observed associations in the correlation matrix. This procedure yields the decomposition of the correlations between education and the six religiosity measures shown in table 5.6.

Education's direct effect is obviously stronger, but its *indirect* effects via localism deserve attention. Especially with the belonging aspects of religion, the patterns of influences are of interest. Note that in these

TABLE 5.6
Decomposition of Correlations Between Religiosity and Education

MEASURES OF RELIGIOSITY	EFFECTS OF EDUCATION		SPURIOUS AND/OR JOINT ASSOCIATION
	DIRECT	INDIRECT	
Church Attendance	.238	−.103	−.050
Church Activities	.168	−.055	−.026
Congregational Friendships	.295	−.072	−.034
Orthodoxy	−.230	−.047	−.022
Importance of Faith	−.171	−.032	−.019
Devotionalism	−.211	−.041	−.020

three instances the indirect effects are negative, thus differing in sign from the direct, positive relations. These indirect influences, while certainly not large in any absolute sense, are about one-third the size of the direct. Coupled with the noncausal associations of similar sign, they help explain the generally low correlations between education and religiosity. More importantly, they provide insight into the complexities of education's influence. If we can regard the direct and indirect as status and exposure influences, respectively, then it is apparent the latter functions as a *counter* influence canceling out a portion of education's positive influence. The two paths of influence work against one another, thereby reducing what otherwise probably would be a stronger direct effect. Perhaps this explains the generally small relationships reported between education and religious belonging and involvement in several recent studies.[11] Beyond this, the data demonstrate that education, measured in terms of years of formal schooling, can generate multiple types of influences, each having differing consequences for religious commitment. Breadth of perspective is one such consequence; and without considering its implications for religious plausibility, one could be misled by looking at only the status significance of education. Assuming the plausibility of traditional religion continues to decline in contemporary society, the exposure effect will likely become even more important in the future.

Contrary to education, the impact of community size on religion is mediated almost entirely through people's local-cosmopolitan ori-

TABLE 5.7
Decomposition of Correlations Between Religiosity and Community Size

MEASURES OF RELIGIOSITY	EFFECTS OF COMMUNITY SIZE		SPURIOUS AND/OR JOINT ASSOCIATION
	DIRECT	INDIRECT	
Church Attendance	.005	−.096	−.021
Church Activities	−.003	−.052	−.004
Congregational Friendships	.005	−.067	.008
Orthodoxy	−.023	−.044	−.082
Importance of Faith	−.014	−.039	−.051
Devotionalism	−.001	−.049	−.073

entations. Similar decomposition of the correlations between community size and religiosity is shown in table 5.7.

The direct effects are negligible, as our theorizing and previous analyses led us to expect. Obviously community size exerts only a modest influence to begin with—yet what there is of it is transmitted by means of the community reference orientations. Why the noncausal, or joint association, component is so large with orthodoxy and devotionalism is not readily interpretable. This is puzzling in view of previous research indicating that community size effects are greater in the case of the personal, more subjective measures. Nevertheless, the path computations on these data make clear the indirect effects are greater than the direct.

These manipulations lend support to our theorizing about religious plausibility. Locals outnumber cosmopolitans in the smaller communities, but in communities small and large the locals are the traditionalists who hold to conventional Christian beliefs and practices. Whatever influence larger cities have upon traditional values, it appears to be transmitted primarily through cosmopolitan innovators who discard the older orthodoxies and institutional loyalties. Urbanism entails a broadening of social perspective that, in turn, results in some decline—however modest—in religiosity. As in the case of education, the absolute figures are of less interest than the goodness of fit generally for the intervening variable model.

SUMMARY AND CONCLUSIONS

This chapter put the local-cosmopolitan hypothesis to a more rigorous empirical test by showing that religious differences persist despite statistical controls simultaneously for education, community size, age, and length of residence. Not only do differences persist, but the analysis reveals indirect effects of education and community size transmitted via the orientational mechanism. Even though the relations are generally small, the model's fit with the data is good. In response to the questions posed at the beginning of the chapter, we can now say that people's local community attachments do indeed help account for the greater religious commitment on the part of the lesser educated, the residentially immobile, and small-town and rural residents.

On the basis of these results, we can be fairly confident that a general theory cast in terms of plausibility is possible. The local-cosmopolitan orientations offer an explanation for how the effects of the several correlates are mediated. Increasingly, in a secular society, we would expect religious and cultural differences between traditionalists and modernists to become pronounced, and as a result plausibility will become more and more of an issue in the analysis of religious patterns. Among those holding to traditional values and world views, church religion will continue to retain its meaning and significance; however, for those whose ultimate value systems are more modern, institutional religion as we know it today will lose its grip. Declining religious plausibility, for more so than deprivation, is the fundamental dilemma confronting the liberal Protestant churches today.

While we have concerned ourselves with social class, community size, and residential mobility patterns, there is no reason why a general theory of religious plausibility cannot be extended to include other variables as well. Quite clearly, more attention to studying the effects of age is needed. Other collectivities with traditional value orientations—for example, ethnic groups and some status groups—very likely function as plausibility structures for church religion today. Hence it may be possible to develop an even more encompassing theory of religious commitment using the local-cosmopolitan distinction.

Also, it should be noted that plausibility as a line of inquiry is especially promising in yielding insight into the process of secularization. The data examined show that education generates at least the two types of status and exposure effects—a composite set of counter influences deserving of further attention. Despite the model's simplicity, it helps in clarifying contradictory direct and indirect effects that can be explained in terms of the differing psychological dynamics at work. Intellectual defection leads to one consequence, social status influences to another. A better understanding of these, and related processes of social change in contemporary society, would obviously help in explaining more precisely secularization and its consequences. It would help enormously in coming to terms with the cultural crises confronting the liberal, mainline churches today.

Obviously data on other Protestant denominations are essential in generalizing our findings here. And yet, even the limited findings we have prompt us to explore further along the lines already begun. What are the mechanisms by which locally oriented traditionalists maintain a plausible faith in an increasingly secular world? And what consequences in the realm of social and political attitudes follow from such community attachments? These are questions we must take up in the chapters that follow.

[III]

MAINTAINING
RELIGIOUS
COMMITMENT

$\begin{bmatrix} 6 \end{bmatrix}$

Mechanisms of Institutional Belonging

Few observers of the current religious scene in America would challenge the fact that liberal Protestant churches are facing serious problems of institutional support. Since the peak years of social activism in the late sixties, many churches have suffered from declining attendance at worship services, lack of financial contributions, and membership losses. So serious are these institutional problems that some observers have even gone so far as to predict the demise of these churches and to suggest we are entering a "post-Christian" era. They see America's Protestant cultural heritage as rapidly vanishing, leading to a time when the mainline churches as we have known them will fade away.

But must we go this far in our prognosis? To be sure, many Protestant churches are experiencing deep strains as a result of membership losses, lack of participation, and sagging financial support, but this does not necessarily mean that as institutions they are dying. Rather what has happened is that these churches, as was noted in the Introduction, have established new institutional priorities emphasizing evangelism and personal faith and reduced commitments to social ethics and activist concerns. With this shift in priorities, there has also come as we have argued a more profound shift in the social basis of support for these churches: away from the cultural mainstream and more toward the conservative and traditional sectors of the society. Cultural traditionalists, in outlook as well as life-style, find themselves increasingly at home in the mainline churches now that they have backed off somewhat from activist concerns. And consequently, churches previously on the brink of collapse now find themselves regaining somewhat their equilibrium.

Already we have seen in Part II this shifting in the social basis of Protestant church life is important for understanding the changing styles of religious commitment in these institutions. But the implications are even more far-reaching than might appear. They bear not only on the *styles* but also on the *mechanisms* by which commitment is socially maintained. As in all normative organizations commitment to churches is a complex matter, influenced by many types of factors—religious and nonreligious, personal and social. Our concern here is with changing social infrastructure as the churches shift to a more traditional, conservative base and its subtle implications. What are the social ties that bind the committed members to the churches? In what ways might these ties help to nurture and to maintain their personal beliefs and convictions in a highly secular world? These are the questions that we seek to explore further. Our strategy is twofold: to look at religious belonging, or commitment to the church as an organization in this chapter, and at the more personal aspects of religious meaning in the one that follows.

ORTHODOXY AS AN EXPLANATION

Of all the issues confronting liberal Protestant churches today, few are as significant as the way in which beliefs help to shape commitment to the church as an institution. The crisis of institutional commitment, given its severity in recent years, has led some to argue it is directly related to the collapse of orthodox Christian belief. Declines in church attendance, parish activities, and financial support have occurred as have the rejections of beliefs in a personal, loving God and in Jesus Christ as a Divine Saviour—fundamental Christian beliefs that traditionally have served as the raison d'être for churches. As convictions about these historic, traditional doctrines have collapsed, so have many people's loyalties to the church as an institution.

There are good reasons for regarding beliefs as crucial to institutional commitment. For one thing, religious belief in Western tradition is at the heart of faith. "It is only within some set of beliefs about the ultimate nature of reality, of the nature and intentions of the supernatural," write Stark and Glock, "that other aspects of religion become coherent. Ritual and devotional activities such as communion or prayer are incomprehensible unless they occur within a framework of belief which postulates that there is some being or force to worship."[1] Even in the most theologically liberal churches, belief in God and the possibility of a personal relationship between man and God are the foundations around which the church's worship services, study groups, mission endeavors, and other functions are organized. Without a plausible belief system, much of what takes place in the institutional life of the church would not make sense.

More specifically, traditional orthodox beliefs are critical because of the authority historically they have possessed. Orthodox beliefs are explicit in supernatural imagery about a Deity who rewards those who believe and punishes those who do not; and about the individual believer's responsibility to accept salvation or risk eternal damnation. Such a belief system carries with it enormous power for motivating individuals to live out their faith according to prescribed norms. Loyal commitment to the church, traditionally, has been one of the most important of these, because of the theological interpretation of the church as the fellowship of the faithful as well as for social reasons. In living out the faith properly, believers have been encouraged to fulfill the public responsibilities of being an example to others of a firmly committed church member.

Previous research has shown that among laity doctrinal orthodoxy induces strong commitment to the institutional church, but that nonorthodoxy does not. Stark and Glock, who address themselves most directly to this matter, show that while orthodox believers are the most committed participants and supporters, those more heterodox in belief are more likely to stay home on Sundays, not to join in parish activities, and not to contribute financially to their churches.[2] Matters of social ethics, ever since the days of the Social Gospel movement early in this century, have been of greater concern to the liberal wing of Protestantism, and for this reason Stark and Glock are inclined to take a dismal view of the liberal church's future. Modernist, demythologized theology may be conducive to this-worldly ethical concerns, but appears not to generate the kind of commitment necessary to keep the church as an organization alive.

In an attempt to look further at the theological factors involved, the present study replicates as nearly as possible Stark and Glock's analysis in Chapter 11 of their *American Piety*. This analysis, as shown in Table 6.1, yields results very similar to theirs. Whereas only 28 percent of those holding modernist beliefs are regular church attenders, 55 percent of the orthodox believers report attending weekly or nearly so. The relationships are somewhat weaker with the remaining indicators, but clearly they too support the hypothesis. Compared with the nonorthodox, those who retain traditional orthodox views are more involved in religious activities, contribute more financially to the church, and regard their church membership as more important. Those involved in the institutional life of the churches are, as would be expected, the traditional believers.

Thus our North Carolina Episcopal data clearly confirm Stark and Glock's findings of an association between traditional belief and institutional involvment. The patterns are not as pronounced as theirs, but overall the results are unambiguous: *orthodox beliefs and church participation vary together in liberal Protestant denominations*. The active participants even in the mainline religious institutions are the orthodox believers, who increasingly as the nonorthodox stray away are left as the remnant of the faithful.

TABLE 6.1
Orthodox Belief and Institutional Support for the Church, in Percentages

	LITERAL	ORTHODOXY	INDEX
INSTITUTIONAL SUPPORT	Low	Medium	High
FOR CHURCH	(N=143)	(N=163)	(N=160)
Attending church weekly or nearly every week	28	37	55
Participating in two or more church activities	29	31	36
Contributing at least 1 percent of annual family income to church	18	35	46
Saying their church membership is "extremely important"	21	36	44

AN ALTERNATIVE EXPLANATION

Undoubtedly there is a relation between orthodoxy and church involvement, but the critical question is what *kind* of relationship. Does the erosion of orthodox belief lead to declining church participation? Or is it the case that nonreligious factors account for both the declining patterns of belief and of participation? Stark and Glock assume the former is correct and argue that the loss of orthodoxy is the crucial causal factor underlying the liberal church's plight currently. As members discard traditional beliefs in favor of modernist theology, they predict that the churches will suffer from a lack of practical commitment—especially financial support and personal participation—which they need to survive.

Such arguments have some intuitive appeal, for reasons already discussed concerning the role of beliefs in religious commitment. But they have their limitations, too, and it is these that concern us here. The major problem with theological explanations is that they often overlook the simple fact that belief systems convey meanings in a specific sociocultural context. That is to say, formal religious beliefs and symbols are always "filtered" through the believer's own experiences, and thus the interpretations given to belief bear the distinct imprint of cultural conditioning. Similar beliefs may be held by individuals in many divergent contexts but the realities that they conjure are not necessarily the same; rather, they become phenomenologically "real" as individuals find experiential referents in their own lives making the belief-elements meaningful. By anchoring formal religious precepts in experience, people are able to make sense out of the contingencies of their lives and to create symbolic religious worlds that lend order to and legitimate their own distinctive values and outlooks.

This approach to understanding religion, grounded in Durkheim's and Weber's works, stresses the basic value orientations of individuals and of groups and especially the manner in which shared values come to be expressed in religious ideology and participation. Society itself is one such context of shared values, often acknowledged as the basis for civil religious beliefs and rituals.[3] Social class is another context out of which values are generated and ritually affirmed in religious collectivities.[4] And likewise, in keeping with the interpretation proposed here, it would seem that for traditionalists generally in contemporary society their religiosity expresses far deeper, underlying value commitments to a highly esteemed way of life. To interpret fully their patterns of religious participation and belief, one must understand the shared values and outlook they bring to their affirmations of faith.

Accordingly, we would expect locals to live in symbolic worlds in which both traditional beliefs and church participation are intensely meaningful. Their beliefs and institutional involvement may be interpreted in terms of adherence to conventional social values, or more simply as ways of "acting out" commitments to a traditional social order. The twin aspects of religion—that is, meaning and belonging—may thus be viewed less as a result of theological than of reference orientations that predispose traditional, church-type styles of commitment. Such logic can be depicted more formally as in figure 6.1 where (a) localism is taken as a causally antecedent factor *both* for literal orthodoxy and institutional support, and (b) the relation between beliefs and institutional support is essentially, though perhaps not totally, spurious. This conceptualization extends but is logically consistent with the discussion in the previous chapters.

In a sense, of course, such argument is easily overextended. That some people participate in and support their churches out of conviction cannot be denied. But for the rank-and-file membership of the mainline

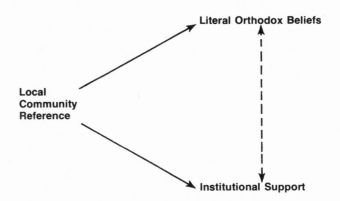

FIGURE 6.1 Local Community Reference, Orthodox Beliefs, and Institutional Support

churches it is highly questionable whether beliefs exert the *primary* influence. By comparison local community attachments are probably just as important if not more so. This latter was examined and the results are shown in table 6.2. Presented are the zero-order correlations between literal orthodoxy and institutional commitment plus the partial correlations once the respondents' localistic orientations are statistically controlled. Reduction in magnitude for these two coefficients offers a clue as to how well the antecedent factor explains variation in both types of religiosity, and hence the extent to which the belief— institutional support association is noncausal. Admittedly the correlations are weak to begin with, but even so the reductions are relatively strong. Church attendance is associated originally with literal orthodoxy at .22, but the coefficient drops by one-half to .11 with localism controlled. Similarly, the weak zero-order association between orthodoxy and church activity (.07) reduces to a negligible partial correlation of .01. Finally, the table shows that though financial support for the church is related to belief, this relationship reduces substantially from .38 to .10.

These data strongly suggest that local community attachments help explain the alleged relationship of orthodox belief with institutional support for the church. While the empirical associations are, as predicted, not totally spurious, the reductions in the partial correlations are of sufficient magnitude to indicate that localism can be legitimately conceptualized as a mutually antecedent factor and one that directly affects *both* the levels of belief and participation of church members.

TABLE 6.2

Zero-Order and Partial Correlations Among Literal Orthodoxy, Localism, and Institutional Support

INSTITUTIONAL SUPPORT	CORRELATION WITH LITERAL ORTHODOXY	CORRELATION WITH LITERAL ORTHODOXY CONTROLLING FOR LOCALISM
Church Attendance	.22*	.11
Church Activities	.07	.01
Financial Contributions	.38*	.10

*Statistically significant at .05 level.

135

As local community attachment declines, so does traditional orthodox belief as well as institutional loyalty and support. This would seem to be the case particularly for the liberal churches where for various reasons, there is greater tendency for members to sever local institutional affiliations and connections if they find them unfulfilling and/or incongruent with their own values. Given their greater geographical mobility, higher levels of education, and more cosmopolitan life-styles, members of the liberal denominations are more inclined to fashion a religious style—both personal beliefs and institutional commitments—in keeping with their choice of whether or not to become involved in local affairs. Thus it appears that *declining community attachment, more so than the erosion of traditional belief per se, is the critical factor in accounting for the declines in church support and participation*. Even if this overstates the case, it is unmistakably clear that nontheological factors in church commitment are important in their own right and deserve more attention than they often receive.

FURTHER EXPLORATIONS INTO CHURCH COMMITMENT

Having uncovered additional support for local community attachments as the social basis for church commitment, we inquire next into some of the more subtle forms of influence. Our strategy is that of looking at ways community attachments interact with other social influences in shaping people's commitment to the religious institution. In particular, we focus upon two social factors often cited in studies of church participation and support: social class and parental religiosity. In both instances it will be shown that relations with level of institutional commitment vary, depending on the respondents' local attachments and orientations. That is, localism "specifies" the relations between the two, thereby yielding additional insight into the dynamics of institutional commitment. Let us examine each of these patterns in some detail.

Social Class and Church Commitment

By now it should be clear that social class is frequently mentioned as a religious correlate. One aspect of social class that we have not commented on, however, concerns its implications for voluntary organizational activity. Higher-status people typically participate more in voluntary organizations of all kinds, and for this reason it might be argued that their involvement in the church is simply a reflection of this broader pattern of middle-class associational activity. Many writers hold to this interpretation of American church life, suggesting that the middle classes' church involvement is explained essentially in terms of associational, rather than purely religious, reasons.[5]

The logic underlying the argument is reasonable. Middle-class individuals do tend to participate more in voluntary organizations, and as Demerath, Lenski, and many others have shown, such individuals as compared to members of the working class are more likely to "do" their religion rather than "feel" or "believe" it. But even so, questions must be raised about whether middle-class associationalism fully accounts for their greater church participation. For one thing, empirical studies have shown that when organizational involvement is controlled, the relation between social class and church activity attenuates but does not totally disappear.[6] Middle-class propensities for joining and participating in voluntary organizations may help explain church commitment but do not fully account for such activity. The implication seems to be that extent of organizational involvement by itself is insufficient as an explanation. Additionally, the question of why individuals are associated with a given *kind* of activity, namely religious, must be dealt with as well. This is not to suggest that factors producing commitment in churches are unlike those operating in organizations generally, but rather to note that above and beyond these are considerations peculiar to religious commitment that also come into play.

Questions about middle-class associationalism as an explanation for church participation, arise also from recent reappraisal of social class differences in religious commitment. Close examination of earlier studies reveals that social class differences in religious participation are often modest at best. Moreover, were the small percentage spreads of these studies subjected to more rigorous multivariate analyses of con-

temporary social research, social class differences in religious involvement would probably be less than are commonly believed. In fact,
findings from a recent nationwide general population study indicate
(1) that socioeconomic status explains only about one percent of the
total variance in religious participation, and (2) that the SES-religious
participation relationship is stronger among some subgroups than
among others—for example, among those who are married and those
with school-age children.[7] Variations by subgroup indicate, as Rodney
Stark suggests, that social class differences are most likely for those
subpopulations of American society where religious perspectives are
regarded as "plausible options."[8] If religious inclinations are strong,
middle-class persons will participate appreciably more than will the
working class; but if traditional religious plausibilities are weak, the
two subgroups will differ very little. Stark's data bear out the point:
among "liberal Protestants" there is a five percentage point difference
in church attendance for lower and upper social classes, for "moderate
Protestants" seven points, and for "conservative Protestants" twenty-
three points. As plausibility increases, so do the social class differences.

If this logic is correct, we can hypothesize that social class effects
should be greater among the traditionally oriented locals than among
their cosmopolitan counterparts. Middle-class locals should be more
involved in churches not only because of their status level, but also
because such individuals tend to participate in those voluntary organizations where traditional and sacred values are deemed as important.
That is to say, religious belonging will be greater among those of the
middle class who find the underlying religious values meaningful to
begin with. Such reasoning prompts the expectation of interaction
effects: if middle-class *and* locally oriented, religious participation
should be greater than if only one or the other factors were operating
alone.

To test this hypothesis, we examine first the zero-order correlations
between the socioeconomic status indicators and church commitment
and then the relationships by level of localism. The zero-order associations as presented in table 6.3 are quite weak and very similar to
those reported elsewhere. Though modest, the relationships are positive
and of about equal strength. Education, occupational prestige, and
income are all relatively weak predictors of church commitment.

But our concern is whether there are any significant differences

138

TABLE 6.3

*Zero-Order Correlations Between Socioeconomic Status
Indicators and Church Commitment*

CHURCH COMMITMENT	EDUCATION	Socioeconomic Status OCCUPA-TIONAL PRESTIGE	INCOME
Church Attendance	.09	.10	.11
Church Activities	.09	.12	.08
Financial Contributions	.08	.12	.12

across local-cosmopolitan subgroups. Are middle-class locals more involved in churches? Do they attend worship services more, participate more in parish activities, and contribute more financially to their support? Is there an interaction between locally based organizations and middle-class associational activity, producing unusually high levels of church commitment?[9]

The regression coefficients in table 6.4 suggest an affirmative answer

TABLE 6.4

*Regressions of Church Commitment on Socioeconomic Status
Indicators Within Categories of Localism*

INDEPENDENT VARIABLE DEPENDENT VARIABLE	Low	Moderately Low	Moderately High	High	F–TEST*
Occupational Prestige					
Church Attendance	.04	.15	1.64	1.78	.01
Church Activities	−.05	.04	.23	.10	N.S.
Financial Contributions	.02	.02	.31	.58	.01
Income					
Church Attendance	.10	.09	.11	.33	N.S.
Church Activities	−.22	.19	.14	.17	N.S.
Financial Contributions	.09	.21	.23	.62	.01
Education					
Church Attendance	.03	.10	.23	.44	.05
Church Activities	.02	.02	.05	.19	N.S.
Financial Contributions	.04	.08	.36	.51	.05

*All F–tests have 3 and 464 df.

to these questions. All three socioeconomic status indicators are better predictors of church participation under conditions of strong local community ties. Even though only two of the tests are statistically significant, a pattern of increasing slopes across categories of localism is evident in all. The impact of social class varies directly with the individual's orientational stance—a pattern that is better crystallized around church attendance. Why church attendance should be more sensitive to the specification effect than church activity is unknown, although it is probably the case that church attendance is a more valid measure of associational involvement in a religious institution. People may "attend" church just as they occasionally participate in other voluntary organizations, but one cannot easily be so casual with respect to organizational memberships that often entail leadership responsibilities and group obligations. Observe that the pattern for financial contributions is among the most consistent and strongest of all: middle-class members who are locally oriented are the greatest contributors in these liberal Protestant congregations.

It is reasonable to conclude that social class effects on church commitment are conditional, depending upon some minimal degree of religous plausibility. In contemporary society, religious participation is less and less the uniformly middle-class and highly public phenomenon it is sometimes thought to be. The latter is increasingly an exaggerated view, more fitting perhaps as a description of church life of the fifties and sixties than of the seventies. This suggests not only that the impact of social class on religious participation may be declining in the more modernized sectors of the society, but also that further attention should be given in the future to developing better explanations of church commitment. Quite clearly social class as a single factor is not a major determinant of religious participation, but taken in conjunction with other related influences it is still a significant consideration.

Parental Religiosity and Church Commitment

A second topic for investigation is that of parental religiosity and its effects on the respondents' own commitment to the church. As is commonly known the religiousness of the home environment in which a child grows up is crucially important in instilling appreciation for religious values and adherence to religious norms. Members of a family are typically members of the same religious group, and consequently the family setting facilitates a child's interaction with others who share similar religious teachings. The more committed the family members, and especially parents, the greater the likelihood that their beliefs and norms will be reinforced for children.[10]

Even beyond childhood and the primary phases of socialization, parental religiosity may continue to exert an influence on an individual's commitments. Parents often serve as religious role models for young adults, reminding them of their earlier religious training and of the importance of faithfulness to their heritage. Normally it is assumed that such influence is positive, although there is some evidence showing parental religiosity may result in negative commitments.[11] Unfortunately very little is known about the conditions under which family religious background results in negative rather than positive influence. Nor for that matter is much known about the social psychological mechanisms generally that exert positive parental influence.

The zero-order associations between parental religiosity and the respondents' church commitment are presented in table 6.5. It is instructive at the outset to note that the correlations are all positive and about the same magnitude. Father's religiousness exerts a slightly stronger influence than mother's on most of the institutional commitment measures. Both appear to have greater effect on church attendance and church activities, and importance attached to church membership than on financial contributions. Though the differences here are not huge, the latter is consistent with the findings of

TABLE 6.5

Zero-Order Correlations Between Parental Religiosity
and the Respondent's Church Commitment

RESPONDENT'S COMMITMENT	MOTHER'S RELIGIOSITY	FATHER'S RELIGIOSITY
Church Attendance	.33	.31
Church Activities	.26	.27
Financial Contributions	.16	.23

other researchers that family religious background has a greater impact on religious participation than upon other aspects of the individual's commitment. The data here reaffirm what previous studies of Catholics, Protestants, and Jews have pointed out—namely, that parental religiosity is particularly important in influencing whether or not an individual will develop affiliational and associational ties with the church.[12]

However, the question we are most interested in is whether all individuals are equally dependent on parental role models and equally influenced by family religious traditions. This is often assumed to be the case in studies on parental influence, but there is reason to believe otherwise. If locals are more sensitive to primary-group demands, it seems reasonable to expect that they should more likely conform to parental religious styles. And conversely, persons with cosmopolitan outlook should be less inclined to base their personal life-styles on a model provided by parents and close kin. Essentially then the family's influence in religious socialization is likely not to be uniformly important for all individuals, but vary depending on the person's particular cognitive orientations.

To examine this, the respondent's religiosity measures were regressed on parental religiosity within categories of the local-cosmopolitan scale, in search of differences in the slopes. If differences exist, as with social class in the previous section, this would indicate important variations in the effects of parental religiosity. Data presented in table 6.6 suggest that the individuals' reference orientations do indeed specify parental influences. Just as expected we find stronger slopes generally among the extreme locally oriented subgroups. This expectation is met in six of the eight F—tests, thus indicating that respondents with local orientations are more influenced in their church commitments by their parents.

Note that in several instances negative relationships are uncovered for the highly cosmopolitan subgroup. Highly religious backgrounds can lead to a rejection of such commitments on the part of those not holding strong primary-group relations. But among those who do, the impact of parental religiosity not only reverses to positive but tends to increase in strength with the respondent's level of local social bonds. The patterns suggest that correlational studies may mask con-

142

TABLE 6.6
Regressions of Respondent's Religiosity on Parental Religiosity Within Categories of Localism

| MEASURES OF RELIGIOSITY | CATEGORY SLOPES FOR LOCALISM | | | | F–TEST* |
	Low	Moderately Low	Moderately High	High	
Father's Religiosity					
Church Attendance	−.16	.30	.31	.51	.05
Church Activities	.10	.18	.13	.19	N.S.
Financial Contributions	−.18	.30	.44	.52	.05
Mother's Religiosity					
Church Attendance	.18	.30	.34	.56	.05
Church Activities	.14	.14	.24	.26	N.S.
Financial Contributions	.19	.29	.37	.49	.05

*All F-tests have 3 and 464 df.

siderable variation in people's responsiveness to parental role models unless the effects of different cognitive styles are taken into consideration. Without examining the latter, parental religious influence will often appear to be weak when in fact there may be substantial positive effects among some subgroups.

Several other observations are worth noting. One is that specifications occur with both father's and mother's religiosity. If there is a sex differential in such influence, it does not show up here. Locals are consistently more influenced by both parents. And second, the interaction effects are not statistically significant in the case of church activities. Why this should be so is not clear although it will be recalled that similar results were obtained with social class. Perhaps because church activities is such a different type of associational indicator than church attendance and the others—involving as it does more demanding group obligations—it is simply less sensitive to orientational differences. Compared with the other commitment measures, its relations with the independent variables in this study have been generally weak.

CONCLUSION

This chapter has explored institutional commitment within the church, and specifically the extent to which nontheological factors explain church attendance, participation in church activities, and parish friendships. Further analyses of our data have shown (1) that orthodoxy's relation to such commitment is partially spurious, and (2) that among locals the influences of social class and parental religiousness on church participation are considerably stronger. The results underscore the critical role that local cognitive orientations play in predisposing church members to traditional beliefs and participation in the liberal Protestant denominations.

Institutional commitment within religion is a complex phenomenon, and certainly cannot be explained fully by any single-factor theory. As has been demonstrated time and time again, churches like other institutions draw into their fold people with many different and diverse reasons for participating. Especially the mainline churches, composed of large numbers of members with varied backgrounds and values, include many who have very limited, nominal types of commitment. For this reason two points deserve comment. First, theological beliefs as sources of institutional belonging are easily exaggerated. Not that beliefs are inconsequential or unimportant to the committed church member, but rather beliefs are often themselves reflections of more basic cultural patterns emphasizing churchgoing norms and ideologies. By means of socialization into traditional values, many people come to appreciate and uphold conventional beliefs and customs. More significant than whether or not beliefs are orthodox theologically is the way people's religious views lend meaning and legitimation to their values and life-styles. Second, cognitive factors affecting the way beliefs are held are critically important. Localistic orientation on a church member's part may be thought of as an example of cognitive simplicity, predisposing the individual toward very personalized and rigidly prescribed beliefs and behaviors. Like dogmatism, authoritarianism, intrinsic versus extrinsic motivations, and other such social psychological factors, local cognitive orientation exerts a significant influence upon styles of commitment. And no doubt in the future, if indeed churches

144

draw their members increasingly from the more traditional sectors of the society, it will become even more of a determining factor.

Be this as it may, our findings have provoked new speculations about the mechanisms underlying religious belonging. We now leave these behind and turn to a new, but related, topic for the next chapter—linkages between the twin aspects of belonging and meaning in religious commitment. Doubtlessly the same influences that shape institutional belonging will also manifest themselves in the more subjective realms of religiosity. If so, we should be able to uncover additional evidence in support of the plausibility explanation.

[7]

Belonging and Meaning

No matter how important institutional belonging may be, it tells us little about the more personal, subjective side of religiosity. This latter—having to do with an individual's system of meaning—is a much different sort of phenomenon, embracing a person's religious self-definition and personal identity. Because meanings are at the very heart of a belief system, any study concerned with religious plausibility must of course examine this aspect of religiosity as well. Moreover, in Western tradition an individual's private religious life, except possibly for mystics, is commonly linked to congregational and religious group participation. For most people the belonging and meaning aspects of commitment are bound together—a fact of religious life that poses a number of interesting questions. What is the nature of the relationship between belonging and meaning? Does belonging reinforce meaning, and if so equally for all church members?

This chapter explores these questions, with attention especially to the ways in which personal religious identity is maintained in contemporary society. Presumably in a traditional setting social influences play a big part is reinforcing religious beliefs and shared definitions of reality. But if these influences are weakening in a pluralistic, and increasingly secular, society, then the question of how an individual sustains such meanings is extremely important. Assuming that religious values and symbols are not widely shared in the society, it becomes necessary to specify those social contexts in which traditional religious belief systems persist and to sort out the mechanisms by which they are socially maintained.

Following the theoretical leads already established, we are concerned to see if locals are better able at maintaining strong belief systems. Earlier we have shown that they attend church more often, participate in more church activities, and have more friends in their congregations. But now we seek to find out if their socioreligious group involvement reinforces their meaning systems—in terms of beliefs, importance of faith, and devotional practices. To this we now turn.

SOCIORELIGIOUS GROUP INVOLVEMENT AND RELIGIOUS MEANING

To begin with, we look at the relations between religious participation and personal commitment. That these two aspects of religiosity are interrelated there is little question, but the extent to which the two covary is open to debate. Some argue that the several dimensions are not particularly well correlated, citing evidence that belonging and meaning, or behavior and belief, each vary to a considerable extent as independent components.[1] By and large, however, empirical studies concerned directly with the matter report moderate correlations between the two. For example, Stark and Glock report a correlation of .46 between ritual commitment and orthodoxy among Protestants; and King and Hunt in their nationwide sample of Presbyterians find a correlation of .34 between church attendance and creedal assent.[2] While these may not be strong, such associations are of moderate magnitude by social science standards. In multidimensional studies generally, in fact, the belonging-meaning correlations are only slightly weaker than those among the meaning scales themselves and among the several indexes of participation.

There is theoretical basis for expecting a relationship between the belonging and meaning aspects. From a sociology of knowledge perspective, we would reason that beliefs, values, and other facets of personal meaning are responsive to, if not deeply rooted in, people's networks of social interaction. This is not to advance a reductionist argument to the effect that ideas and beliefs are simply epiphenomena, but rather to suggest that the communities in which people share beliefs play a big part in shaping their content and in assuring their perpetuation. Essentially this is what Berger is proposing when he asserts that for a person's religious world to be plausible, one needs to be integrated into a "plausibility structure" wherein definitions of reality are reconstructed and maintained on a regular everyday basis.[3] Individuals who are well integrated into a believing community are reinforced in their own religious affirmations by others whose convictions and daily examples serve as reminders of the faith. Such a collectivity is indispensable for maintaining a strong and vital faith, especially in the modern setting where a secular rather than a religious ethos predominates. Speaking of American society in particular, Greeley makes a similar point when he says that religious groups play a "quasi-ethnic" role in providing people a sense of who they are and where they stand in a large, complex society.[4] Denominational affiliations make available opportunities for intimate fellowship, thereby facilitating primary-group identity for individuals who otherwise would perhaps not regard themselves as very religious.

To test the possibility of a belonging-meaning relationship, we shall examine the data on doctrinal beliefs and doubt, importance of faith in everyday life, and personal devotional practices. With each our attention is focused on the individual's social interaction within the socioreligious community, and the extent to which this undergirds personal religiosity.

Doctrinal Beliefs and Doubt

The central feature of a person's religious meaning system is belief—that is, the convictions one holds about the Deity, salvation, an afterlife, and so forth that are grounded on faith. It is these fundamental conceptions and beliefs, primarily supernatural in focus, that have provided faithful Christians down through the centuries with a framework of symbols and meaning in which to interpret their lives. Supernaturalism is by no means the only, or necessarily the most authentic, mode of Christian belief, but historically such tenets of faith have been professed by committed members of the Christian community.

Participation in the socioreligious group, as the data in table 7.1 indicate, appears to be related among church members to their levels of belief and extent of doubt. Those who are most involved by virtue of attendance at worship, participation in church activities, and congregational friendships, are also more orthodox in belief and tend less to doubt such basic doctrines of Christian faith as the existence of God, the divinity of Jesus, eternal life, Virgin Birth, Biblical miracles, and the Final Day of Judgment. These associations are best shown with church attendance and congregational friendships, and somewhat less so with church activities. Recall from the previous chapter that the church activities measure of institutional belonging was weakly related to orthodoxy. But still, the patterns for all three belonging measures are consistent across a range of doctrinal beliefs. Individuals enmeshed in the religious community by means of primary-group relations profess greater personal commitment, at least as indexed by traditional, supernatural beliefs.

Importance of Faith

Church people not only hold to supernatural beliefs about God, about Jesus Christ, and about salvation, they also attach considerable

TABLE 7.1

Respondents Who Are Highly Orthodox in Belief and Who "Never Doubt" Selected Doctrines by Socioreligious Group Involvement, in Percentages

RESPONDENTS	CHURCH ATTENDANCE		CHURCH ACTIVITIES		CONGREGA- TIONAL FRIENDSHIPS	
	Reg. (N=234)	Irreg. (N=251)	High N=190)	Low (N=290)	High (N=210)	Low (N=272)
High on Literal Orthodoxy	69	43	66	59	64	41
Saying They "Never Doubt":						
Existence of God	87	68	89	83	92	61
Divinity of Jesus	71	59	75	64	86	60
Eternal Life	76	60	73	61	73	48
Biblical Miracles	69	45	65	49	71	39
Virgin Birth	73	48	67	43	73	41
Final Day of Judgment	61	39	73	40	75	42

149

significance to how their convictions enhance personal experience and endow life with purpose and meaning. This is a more intrinsic and highly personal aspect of faith, having to do not with beliefs per se but with the extent to which people cultivate religious values and apply them to their everyday lives. Whereas doctrinal beliefs as handed down through the historic creeds demand a certain amount of acceptance on their own terms, the meanings derived from faith for any given believer are by comparison far more diverse and subjective.

Compared with orthodox beliefs, we see that importance of faith reveals weaker relations with socioreligious group involvement (see table 7.2). There are differences between the highly involved and marginal participants, but they are small and are not statistically significant. Interestingly, the meaning-salience of faith as measured by some of these very general items on the application of religion to life is about as high for those uninvolved in the church as for highly active, nuclear members. This is somewhat surprising, but not totally so considering that doctrinal beliefs and importance of faith tap quite different dimensions of personal commitment. Literalistic supernatural conceptions are probably less easily maintained by a believer in the absence of "confirming others"—perhaps because they rest upon a highly structured world view, and one shared regularly by those most active in the institutional life of the Christian community. But im-

TABLE 7.2

Respondents Who Are High on "Importance of Faith" by Socioreligious Group Involvement, in Percentages

RESPONDENTS	CHURCH ATTENDANCE		CHURCH ACTIVITIES		CONGREGA- TIONAL FRIENDSHIPS	
	Reg. (N=234)	Irreg. (N=251)	High (N=190)	Low (N=290)	High (N=211)	Low (N=272)
Saying religious faith is "of central importance"	49	42	42	33	40	38
Saying most of their decisions are made on the basis of faith	81	74	83	82	74	70
Agreeing that without faith life would not have much meaning to it	80	76	78	71	71	64

portance of faith taps a more personal, and deeply subjective religious response, highly dependent on the individual's own willingness to engage in introspection and self-searching. Church members are more likely to assign importance to faith than nonmembers, but ultimately such meanings are too subjective to be closely related to socioreligious group involvement.

Devotional Practices

Last we look at personal devotional practices that devout Christians engage in, such as Bible reading and prayer. Like doctrinal beliefs these practices have a long and rich heritage within the Christian community. Churches today as they have in the past exhort their members to cultivate the spiritual life through study, contemplation, and private prayer. Although individual acts of worship as these are highly personal in character, nonetheless the motivation for carrying them out often results from the encouragements received from within the church. Many church organizations—for example, Sunday school classes, Bible study groups, and mission study groups—promote devotional activities as part of the discipline expected of the more committed members.

Table 7.3 describes these practices, showing a definite relationship between socioreligious group involvement and personal devotional

TABLE 7.3

Respondents Engaging in Devotional Practices by Socio-Religious Group Involvement, in Percentages

RESPONDENTS	CHURCH ATTENDANCE		CHURCH ACTIVITIES		CONGREGA-TIONAL FRIENDSHIPS	
	High (N=234)	Low (N=251)	High (N=190)	Low (N=290)	High (N=211)	Low (N=272)
Praying Regularly*	78	53	84	51	71	48
Reading Bible Regularly	40	17	52	26	41	21
Reading Religious Literature Regularly	41	18	57	39	43	28
Having Family Devotions Regularly	34	11	31	10	27	12

*"Regularly" in each case refers to everyday, or more than once a week.

151

practices. Those members attending church regularly, participating actively in church organizations, and having friends within the congregation, engage more in prayer, Bible study, reading of inspirational literature, and family devotions. As with doctrinal beliefs earlier, the associations are all substantial, indicating a moderate degree of relationship between these several belonging and meaning dimensions. In fact, the relations are stronger than might be expected considering that devotionalism has become highly "privatized" and accessible to individuals both inside and outside of the church, and thus less and less linked to other forms of institutional religion. But despite these trends, it is clear that among church members socioreligious group involvement is a source of support and encouragement for traditional devotional activities.

PATTERNS FOR LOCALS

Next we turn to the question at issue: *are the effects of socioreligious group involvement on personal beliefs and practices greater for locals?* The reasons for expecting this should be clear by now. Because of their greater sensitivity to primary-group pressures, locals are more inclined to interpret the world in terms of its personal relevance, to link these interpretations to primary communities, and hence to limit the number of reference groups available to them. Particularistic orientations enable believers to obtain local group reinforcement for their religious self-conceptions, and likewise provide a significant frame of reference for filtering outside influences that threaten to weaken or negate religious consciousness. The net effect of such localistic ties should be a stronger, more plausible traditional religious identity.

Previously it was observed that Americans have a strong tendency to identify themselves religiously, especially along denominational lines. Strong belonging functions are served by religious groups in this society, but by the same token it can be said there is considerable variation in the depth of meaning Americans attach to religious affiliation. To join a church is for some little more than the affirmation of America's "religion of democracy," whereas for others it entails profound religious convictions embedded in the Judeo-Christian tradition. Probably for most Americans, however, religious identity is rooted in strong primary-group ties with kin and close friends, wherein the religious and ethnic components of their self-concepts are mutually reinforcing. This is often the case with sectarians and members of smaller religioethnic groups (e.g., Irish Catholics and Jews) who maintain close communal ties. Yet for others religious identification may be highly individualized and of little salience in their self-concept. For many in the mainline Protestant denominations, this is no doubt an apt description. The absence of rigid membership requirements, lack of strict doctrine, and tolerance of diversity in theological and social views, combined with strong American norms encouraging affiliation as a minimal gesture of religiosity, serve to inflate church rolls in the liberal denominations with many members having very weak commitments.

What all this suggests is that strength of religious commitment varies enormously among church members, depending upon their sociocommunal group involvements *plus* their orientations toward, and identifications with, such groups. The first is taken as a precondition for religious affiliation and identity in a pluralist society; the second, though less obvious, is also quite crucial as a psychological mechanism supportive of religious identity. An individual may be affiliated with a religious group as many nominal Protestants in liberal congregations are, but unless the membership is personally meaningful to the individual involved, it is unlikely to rank very high in terms of identity-salience. Dashefsky underscores the significance of the member's psychological frame of reference when he says religioethnic group identification entails "personal attachment to the group and a positive orientation toward being a member of the group."[5] Without both, religious membership is unlikely to result in a strong identity.

The subjective aspects of religious identification are especially critical for American Protestants. Compared with Catholics and Jews, there is greater *separation* of the ethnic community from the religious life for Protestants. This means that Protestant religious socialization depends very heavily on the individual's receptivity of childhood religious teachings, orientation toward parental role models, and quality of social interaction within the religious group itself. In the absence of a strong ethnic community, the individual's psychological bonds with significant religious others are instrumental in maintaining a religious identity. Strong bonds undergird religious teachings and values in the childhood years and even later in adult life may predispose people to appreciate their religious traditions. Without these dispositions Protestant group identity becomes quite vulnerable to secular influences. For not only do Protestants lack a strong ethnic community, the demise of traditional theology—especially among the mainline liberal denominations—confounds even more the difficulties involved in sustaining a plausible religious identity.

If socioreligious group involvement has its strongest impact on the beliefs and practices of those maintaining close primary-group ties, this should be evident when we examine the Episcopalians controlling for levels of localism. These results, presented in table 7.4, support

TABLE 7.4

Regressions of Personal Religiosity on Socioreligious Group Involvement Within Categories of Localism

INDEPENDENT VARIABLE DEPENDENT VARIABLE	CATEGORY SLOPES FOR LOCALISM				F–TEST
	Low	Moderately Low	Moderately High	High	
Church Attendance					
Orthodoxy	.04	.11	.19	.34	.05
Doubt	−.01	−.09	−.29	−.37	.05
Devotionalism	.21	.24	.26	.23	N.S.
Importance of faith	.14	.17	.11	.09	N.S.
Church Activities					
Orthodoxy	.04	.05	.11	.17	.05
Doubt	−.03	−.11	−.30	−.29	.05
Devotionalism	.23	.26	.19	.25	N.S.
Importance of faith	.11	.09	.14	.12	N.S.
Congregational Friendships					
Orthodoxy	.01	.00	.21	.37	.05
Doubt	−.03	−.15	−.16	−.31	.05
Devotionalism	.19	.09	.13	.07	N.S.
Importance of faith	.21	.16	.18	.13	N.S.

the prediction insofar as doctrinal beliefs and doubt are concerned, but do not with devotionalism and importance of faith. With the belief and doubt measures, there are consistent increases in the regression slopes across categories of the control variable. The stronger the local attachments, the stronger the effects of socioreligious group involvements on personal religious commitment. In effect, the data suggest that for locals the belonging and meaning dimensions of religion hang together very closely.

With devotionalism and importance of faith, there are no significant interaction effects. Both are less related to local community attachments as well as to socioreligious group participation than is the case with orthodoxy and doubt, and for this reason it is understandable why specifications are not uncovered. As we saw earlier in Part II, devotionalism and importance of faith differ considerably as forms of religion from traditional orthodoxy. They are highly privatized, less bound to the institutional church, and thus less dependent on a communal support structure. It is likely true, as Luckmann suggests, that the proliferation of inspirational literature in recent decades signifies an emergent form of "invisible" religion, directly accessible to individuals, and one that will flourish given the increasing personal autonomy and individualism that is characteristic of modern society.

These same trends hardly favor a close functional relationship between institutional belonging and personal meaning. Greater personal autonomy results in weaker commitments to the organized church, and consequently one would expect disaffected members to adhere less and less to institutionalized church values and meanings. The privatization of religion should lead to further separation of the meaning functions from intimate rootage in the institutional life of the church. At the same time, for loyal church members remaining in the fold this means that their close primary relations with fellow believers should become increasingly important to maintaining strong personal commitments. Especially in the realm of beliefs—that is, in adhering to traditional, supernatural interpretations of reality—the data suggest that group ties come into play. Those having local group loyalties are better able to integrate the belonging and meaning components of religious commitment, and to maintain a plausible belief system in the midst of a secular, nonbelieving environment.

ANOTHER TEST: UPHOLDING BELIEF IN THE FACE OF CHAOS

Before concluding this chapter, we look briefly at another, quite different type of situation in which the group context functions to sustain religious meanings. If as we have found locals have stronger belief systems resulting from their firmer plausibility structures, then their faiths should better withstand the jarring effects of personal crisis. People's religious worlds, humanly constructed as they are, are forever threatened by chaotic and disruptive events. Bafflement, pain, injustice, unexpected and paradoxical events, all threaten the taken-for-granted world in which people live, and unless such crises can be interpreted satisfactorily they may undermine a person's meaning system. At the very least, it is essential to personal well-being for a person to adjust to personal crisis by restructuring one's own views about the nature of ultimate reality.

Of all the chaotic and disruptive events of life, death is the most baffling to try to explain.[6] Sudden, unexpected deaths of a loved one or friend can push a person's analytic capacities to their limits, in search for some ultimate rationale and meaning. For many church members traditional beliefs about God, salvation, and eternal life offer a cognitive frame for resolving, if not explaining, death. Yet still others within the church find little comfort from the resources of faith, because they are unable to reconcile death with their own personal beliefs.

Fortunately a question in the Episcopal Survey asked for respondents experiencing the death of a relative or close friend to indicate if this had affected in any way their faith, and if so how. Cross-tabulating these responses with religious group participation and orientations, we can see what influences these latter have in mediating the disconcerting and shattering effects brought on by such events. If group ties are a serious factor in reducing the threat-potential to belief, this should be most evident among locals actively participating in congregational life; and conversely, less so among cosmopolitans similarly involved.

TABLE 7.5

Effect of Death of Relative or Friend in Weakening Belief by Socioreligious Group Involvement and Local-Cosmopolitan Orientations, in Percentages

RELIGIOUS GROUP INVOLVEMENT OF RESPONDENTS	PERCENTAGE SAYING DEATH HAD WEAKENED BELIEF	
	Locals	Cosmopolitans
Regular church attenders	9	27
Irregular church attenders	22	41
High on church activities	5	35
Low on church activities	19	31
High on congregational friendships	12	30
Low on congregational friendships	21	42

In table 7.5 this prediction is examined, and the results are consistent with the our expectation. In every instance the proportions saying that death had weakened belief are lower among locals, suggesting that psychological attachments to the group exert a potent influence in warding off threats to personal faith. Note also that in every instance but one, active participants in the socioreligious group are better able than inactives to hold on to a plausible and satisfying belief system. This is congruent with our theoretical perspective throughout the chapter, pointing to the fact that group involvement and local orientations interact to produce a supportive effect on maintaining the church member's beliefs and religious identity. Given that such effects are observed in the case of death, it is reasonable to expect the same with other, less traumatic crises in life.

CONCLUSIONS

This chapter has emphasized the importance of religious belonging as a basis for individual religiosity. Essentially the hypothesis pursued was that church members who are highly involved in the socioreligious group *and* locally oriented should evidence stronger subjective commitments to religion. Data pertaining to orthodox beliefs, doubt, and the impact of death on personal faith support the hypothesis. However, with respect to devotionalism and the importance of faith, the predictions were not supported.

By and large, the evidence underscores the fact that a strong relationship between the belonging and meaning functions helps to sustain personal commitment. In a pluralistic society, as Greeley proposes, the meaning function of religion is salient largely because of the strong belonging function that religion fulfills. Social forces propelling individuals to identify with a socioreligious group, likewise serve to reinforce religious consciousness by helping create a homogeneous and supportive context of meaning. It would seem that group support of this kind is particularly important for maintaining traditional, orthodox belief. Supernatural conceptions and world views are less and less shared in the populace at large. Locals, strongly integrated into a community of belief, are thus better able to maintain a world of traditional meanings and to enjoy the benefits of faith in times of personal crisis.

We can speculate about the exceptions to the hypothesis—devotionalism and importance of faith. Earlier in Chapter 4 we observed weaker relations between local community attachments and these two dimensions, and similarly here we find little, if any, evidence of interactive influence. Very likely these aspects of religion are more privatized and less dependent upon a socially supportive context. Largely as a result of privatization, devotional practices have lost much of their traditional meaning as individual acts of worship, and have become instead rituals *in search of* a plausible belief system and religious identity. The importance of faith measure, too, taps deeply subjective and intrinsic meanings, cultivated more perhaps by the individual through serious introspection and contemplation than by religious group belonging.

Thus while we find support for the belonging-meaning hypothesis, quite clearly it is necessary to distinguish among the several components of meaning. And as we shall see in the next section, these distinctions become even more serious when we turn to the matter of faith and its consequences.

[IV]

FAITH AND ITS CONSEQUENCES

⌐8⌐

Social Ideology and Its Cultural Context

In this final section we take up the general topic of religious belief and its consequences. Few topics in liberal Protestant circles have prompted as much attention, or for that matter as much controversy, as has this one. Are those who profess Christian belief more anti-Semitic than those who do not? Are orthodox believers more prejudiced toward racial and ethnic groups of all kinds? Do orthodox beliefs cause conservative social and political views? Are they in opposition to an activist stance toward the church's role in society? Despite considerable research on these matters, we still lack satisfactory answers.

As we saw in Chapter 1, theories pertaining to the "consequential" dimension typically emphasize the importance of theological beliefs. The greater the doctrinal orthodoxy, presumably the greater the conservatism in social and political views. But throughout this study we have taken this explanation to task, pointing out its shortcomings both conceptually and empirically. Again in this section we do the same, but now we have to confront the issues more directly. Recall that the chief concern underlying our approach is the changing social and cultural context for church religion in contemporary society. The basic assumption is that as religion has shifted contexts, Protestant ideologies have come to reflect more and more the cultural attitudes of traditionalists. Not that theological beliefs have become unimpor-

161

tant, but rather as they become "captive" to a more conservative outlook, contextual factors such as the believer's cultural orientations easily come into greater play, interacting with beliefs to form defensive, and at times reactionary social ideologies. The result is a belief system combining religious and nonreligious elements, but one which lacks the qualities of constraint and integration that are often assumed to exist among liberal Protestants.

Two considerations are involved here: (1) the nature of the cultural belief system that characterizes the highly involved church members, and its implications for the orthodoxy-consequences issue; and (2) the precise manner in which religious meaning elements function, either in reinforcing or shattering cultural beliefs. Both considerations point to complexities in belief systems that are seldom fully examined, but nonetheless call for careful analysis. Especially in the liberal Protestant churches, attention to these issues promises to yield some new insight into the struggles and strains over social action that have gripped these institutions over the past decade. Chapter 8 makes a start in this direction by examining the cultural correlates of orthodox beliefs and their relation to local-cosmopolitan orientations. The following chapter addresses the related matter of how the intrinsic religious elements operate in creating a pattern of consequences far more complex than is often thought to be the case.

ORTHODOX BELIEFS AND SOCIAL IDEOLOGY

First we look at doctrinal orthodoxy in relation to three sets of consequential attitudes: church activism, political views, and prejudice. Past research on all three has led to mixed conclusions. Doctrinal orthodoxy has sometimes been found to correlate with conservative attitudes towards the church's involvement in public affairs, with conservative, and often reactionary, political sentiments, and with prejudice toward racial, ethnic, and religious minorities. Although the explanatory significance of orthodox belief is much debated, recently a number of researchers have called into question its *causal* role suggesting that it is probably less important than often thought. No other issue in the recent study of religion better illustrates how methodological advances of the last decade have helped to challenge and reassess views that were widely accepted only a few years ago.

Church Activism

By *church activism* is meant the effort, on the part of Protestants, to have the church involved in public affairs and, more generally, to make the ethical teachings of faith relevant to the society. In the sixties this was a source of considerable friction among the liberal Protestant churches. Prodded by the civil rights movement, the new youth culture, and a growing awareness of the church's lack of influence, prominent church leaders called for new emphasis on Christian social action, and for the church to reorganize itself as a more effective institution within society. In opposition to the activists, many others—both clergy and laity—insisted that churches should move to abandon concern with social problems and stick to personal evangelism, Biblical morality, and attention to the needs of the individual.

Remarkably little is known about the factors that help shape the ethical commitments of Protestant laity. Previous studies show that though church members often approve of the church's involvement in public issues in the abstract, they are less likely to support specific actions on the part of their church or clergy.[1] In Campbell and Fukuyama's study of the United Church of Christ, for example, 69 percent of the laity agreed that "ministers have a right to preach on controversial subjects from the pulpit" whereas only 38 percent thought that "denominations have a right to issue policy statements on social and economic issues."[2] While a good deal of support for church activism is voiced in principle by the laity in the liberal denominations, quite clearly this support diminishes when specific courses of action are taken or proposed as binding on all members of the religious group.

The issue of most concern here is the source of ethical attitudes on the part of Protestant laity—specifically, whether nonorthodox, modernist beliefs are causally related to church activism. Unlike doctrinal orthodoxy with its stress on the individual and personal responsibilities, modernist theology places greater emphasis on the church's social obligations. Stress upon this latter and its close relationship with demythologized faith is a theme found in many studies. For example,

163

in their San Francisco Bay area study, Stark and Glock found that 73 percent of the lay respondents scoring low on ethicalism were highly orthodox while 50 percent of the most ethical were highly orthodox. In addition, they found that those who scored highest on the "ethicalism" scale were members of the liberal denominations, thus tending toward less orthodoxy generally.[3] However, these differences are not very large, less perhaps than one might expect; and the researchers in their analysis do not introduce any statistical controls for social class, education, age, or any other characteristic that might account for the relationship.

Quinley's more extensive analysis of Stark and Glock's data reveals even less difference in lay views between the orthodox and the nonorthodox than appears. Support for church activism is greatest among those with higher incomes, who attend church most frequently, and who hold nonorthodox beliefs.[4] Quinley's results are consistent with others who report that the greater church activism among nonorthodox laity is a more complex phenomenon, and one *not* very strong at that. Certainly the patterns are weaker than those existing among Protestant clergy. Among clergy there is a definite tendency for those with modernist beliefs to place strong emphasis on social ethics, but among the laity such inclinations are far more diffuse, erratic, and highly sensitive to the social context in which they are found.

In the present study, the relations among these variables are shown in table 8.1. Three agree-disagree statements were included in the Episcopal survey, two tapping very general views on the church's social involvement and a third support for a minister's participation in the civil rights movement. Broken down by type of belief, we find as expected the orthodox more conservative, and the nonorthodox giving greater approval for social action. The differences are stronger than those reported by Stark and Glock: 76 percent of the orthodox favor the church's sticking to religious matters and not getting involved in social and economic issues as compared with 49 percent of the nonorthodox; 31 percent among the orthodox agree that an ideal religion should include social and political involvement whereas almost twice that many, or 60 percent, of the nonorthodox express proactivist views.

Shown as well are the respondents' attitudes toward ecumenism. Strictly speaking *ecumenism* refers to the reunification of the church, and specifically to interdenominational efforts toward cooperation, and

TABLE 8.1
Orthodox Beliefs and Religious Activist Attitudes, in Percentages

RELIGIOUS ACTIVIST ATTITUDES	ORTHODOX (N=251)	NONORTHODOX (N=211)
Church Activism		
"The church should stick with religious matters and not get involved in social and economic issues."	76	49
"A minister who participates in social controversies such as the civil rights movement should generally be supported by his parish."	29	41
"An ideal religion . . . includes involvement in social and political issues of the day."	31	60
Ecumenism		
"The Episcopal Church should resist mergers with other Protestant denominations in the United States."	62	38
"It would be wonderful if the Catholic Church and the Protestant denominations could eventually combine to form one large Christian church."	27	46

hopefully merger in the future. But for many church people the spectacle of a supradenominational church carries with it the fear of a larger and more controversial organization involved in social issues above and beyond their local control. Because ecumenical efforts were defined in this way in the late sixties and early seventies the respondents' views are included here along with church activism. Again we find orthodox believers adhering to the conservative position, opposed to ecumenical mergers among Protestant groups as well as with the Catholic Church. The nonorthodox, less concerned with of the particularistic claims of their own tradition and more inclined toward an activist church, express their views in the form of support for ecumenism. As with church activism, the differences reveal alternative theological and ethical commitments on the part of the orthodox and the nonorthodox regarding the individual, society, and the church's role in controversial issues.

But note these are all zero-order relationships—as with Stark and Glock's data—without benefit of multivariate statistical controls.

Whether the associations will diminish as a result of bringing other variables into the analysis is a matter for later consideration, once we have reviewed similar patterns with political attitudes and prejudice.

Political Attitudes

Despite the numerous studies reporting on the political attitudes of church members, the conclusions they yield are mixed. Unquestionably orthodox believers hold stronger anticommunist views than do the nonorthodox. When confronted with ideological differences of this kind, the most committed believers take an unambiguous position. Differences between the orthodox and nonorthodox become ambiguous, however, on matters of less ideological significance. For example, there is conflicting evidence over whether the orthodox tend to vote Republican in American society, and whether they adhere to a more pronounced Protestant work ethic. Not that studies have not reported empirical relations between religious and political beliefs, but they are typically weak, and as Wuthnow says, "elusive."[5]

Weak relations are well demonstrated in the data cited in Hadden's *Gathering Storm in the Churches*, obtained from the Faith Lutheran study. Using an index of Biblical literalism similar to ours in this study, he shows there is virtually no relationship between religious belief and political ideology among Lutheran laity. Fifty-two percent of the literalists adopt a strong free-enterprise ideology but so does 51 percent of those scoring low on the literalism index. Forty-nine percent of the literalists agreed that "most people who live in poverty could do something about their situation if they really wanted to," as compared with 48 percent of the liberal believers. Theological outlook would seem to have little if any influence on what the laity believe concerning political ideology. "Those who are biblical literalists," as Hadden says," are no more or no less likely to express liberal views on these issues."[6]

In other studies stronger relations are sometimes reported. Most research shows some association between literal orthodoxy and political conservatism.[7] Upon closer scrutiny it is evident also that the orthodoxy and conservatism patterns reflect, in part at least, other types of influences. For example, southern studies typically reveal stronger positive relations between the two; and socioeconomic status is often

166

a confounding influence, resulting in some spuriousness in the observed patterns.[8] In general, the conclusion would be that some associations exist between the laity's religious and political views, but these vary from one political issue to another and are often influenced by social and cultural factors operating to magnify these out of proportion.

Table 8.2 displays the results from the present study. In keeping with most research, our data suggest the orthodox believers are more conservative politically—a pattern manifest with every item. The first two items tap responses to civil disobedience, the third provision of foreign aid, the fourth labor union support, and the last political ideology in a very general sense. Remarkably little variation in the pattern occurs, with orthodox literalists in every instance adopting the more conservative position. Less difference between the orthodox and nonorthodox is observed in the case of labor union support. This is probably an indication, however, not so much of a lack of economic and political ideology as of the strong antiunion sentiment characterizing our southern sample.

Thus there appears to be some association between the laity's religious beliefs and social ideology. Literal orthodoxy accompanies economic as well as political conservatism. But whether these simple

TABLE 8.2

Orthodox Beliefs and Political Attitudes, in Percentages

POLITICAL ATTITUDES	ORTHODOX (N=251)	NONORTHODOX (N=211)
"The best way to stop rioting in the streets is to give the police more power."	47	31
"Government should have the right to prohibit certain groups of persons who disagree with our form of government from holding public meetings"	54	33
"The U.S. should give assistance to the poorer countries of the world even if those countries remain politically neutral."	28	49
"Labor unions generally do more harm than good."	62	51
"The government that rules the least is best."	65	43

bivariate associations persist once other variables are controlled is an open question, and one we must turn to later in this chapter in order to get a more definitive answer.

Racial and Ethnic Attitudes

Next we look at the relation of religious beliefs to racial and ethnic prejudice. As a topic of study for social scientists interested in religion, prejudice has received more attention than church activism or political ideology. This is explained partly of course by the nature of intergroup prejudice—the fact that it engenders intolerance and animosity among people in a pluralist society and can become a serious threat to social order. In addition, there are some curious paradoxes associated with religious belief. On the one hand, religious principles motivate people to espouse noble and humanitarian ideals, to love those who are different, and to seek justice and equality for all human beings. Yet on the other hand, people often believe that theirs is the one true faith; that only certain people are God's chosen people; and that they should, if called upon, defend the faith vigorously against infidels and heretics. Gordon Allport makes the point quite succinctly:

> Brotherhood and bigotry are intertwined in all religion. Plenty of pious people are saturated with racial, ethnic, and class prejudice. But at the same time many of the most ardent advocates of racial justice are religiously motivated.[9]

That these two contradictory forces coexist within religion is obvious enough, but the sources from which they spring and the dynamics by which they operate are not very well understood. It is not surprising then that many studies show an association between orthodox beliefs and ethnocentrism among Protestant church members. These associations vary in intensity depending upon the out-group involved, but similar Protestant attitudes hold toward Jews, Catholics, and blacks. Glock and Stark's *Christian Beliefs and Anti-Semitism* is the best known work advancing the argument that Christian beliefs are supportive of prejudice against Jews.[10] Anti-Catholic attitudes are less frequently identified as such, but Protestant orthodoxy is often found to be correlated with generalized prejudice and ethnocentrism toward minorities. By all odds, most of the research has focused on blacks as the target of prejudice, and here too empirical studies show that orthodox believers are more intolerant. The greater the commitment to doctrinal orthodoxy, the greater the prejudice toward racial and ethnic minorities generally.

This pattern is especially pronounced among fundamentalist believers. People adhering to literalist conceptions and interpretations of the supernatural score higher on prejudice measures.[11] Beliefs in the Virgin Birth, the infallibility of the Scriptures, and the literal meaning of miracles—that is, fundamentalist beliefs—are more associated with ethnocentric attitudes than are other aspects of the Christian faith. Evidence in support of this is found not only among the more conservative denominations where lay members are more prejudiced generally, but also within the liberal churches where individual members vary considerably in belief and outlook.

Our data are no different in this respect as is shown in table 8.3. We see that orthodox literalists are less supportive of the government intervening to help blacks obtain access to schools, jobs, and housing. Similar patterns exist on items pertaining to all-white residential neigh-

TABLE 8.3

Orthodox Beliefs and Prejudicial Attitudes, in Percentages

ATTITUDES	ORTHODOX (N=251)	NONORTHODOX (N=211)
"The Federal Government should stay out of the question of whether white and Negro children go to the same school."	78	51
"If Negroes are not getting fair treatment in jobs and housing, the government should see to it they do."	42	66
"White people have a right to live in all-white neighborhoods if they want to."	86	63
"Although some Jews are honest, in general Jews are dishonest in their business dealings."	33	21
Willingness to "welcome as fellow member of social club":		
Negroes	9	37
Jews	19	39
Catholics	28	42

169

borhoods and Jewish stereotypes. Literalists are more inclined than nonliteralists to agree that "white people have a right to live in all-white neighborhoods" and to regard Jews as "dishonest in their business dealings." The latter is somewhat less related to religious beliefs, but the overall pattern is the same for all the agree-disagree items. We also see that literal orthodoxy is related to willingness to welcome minority individuals as fellow members of a social club. With all three groups—blacks, Jews, and Catholics—the literalists hold to greater social distance than do the nonliteralists. As was expected the views of orthodox Protestants differ very little toward the several minorities. Greater differences exist between the two types of believers in the case of antiblack prejudice, but similar relationships are found with Jews and Catholics.

Very clearly the results imply a general relationship between religious orthodoxy and ethnocentrism. As such, they are in keeping with most of the research that has examined this issue. Whether or not the patterns will hold up under closer multivariate scrutiny remains to be seen, and it is to this that we now turn.

IN SEARCH OF AN EXPLANATION

The relationships between orthodoxy and the several "consequences" described in the previous section are summarized in table 8.4. Indexes for each of the dependent variables are constructed from the composite items—for church activism, ecumenism, political intolerance, racism, anti-Semitism, anti-black prejudice, and anti-Catholic prejudice.[12] Shown are the zero-order correlations with orthodoxy, all of which are relatively weak but most of which are statistically significant. Thus we are dealing with relations that are small but significant, on statistical as well as substantive grounds. The crucial question, of course, is whether the associations survive once controls are applied for other variables.

Two differing kinds of influences may operate. First, there are general orientations stemming from the respondent's background, such as localism, which might predispose those who are orthodox believers also to narrow-mindedness and prejudicial attitudes. These are basically factors that are causally antecedent, or independent of, both orthodox beliefs and the consequences. Second, there may be intervening factors

TABLE 8.4

Correlations Between Consequential Attitudes and Both Literal Orthodoxy and Localism*

CONSEQUENCE	WITH LITERAL ORTHODOXY	WITH LOCALISM
Church Activism	−.10	−.30
Ecumenism	−.12	−.32
Political Intolerance	.24	.37
Racism	.18	.32
Anti-Semitic Prejudice	.13	.21
Anti-Black Prejudice	.20	.26
Anti-Catholic Prejudice	.10	.17

*Correlations coefficients greater than .12 are statistically significant at .05 level.

that are essentially religious that help to explain the syndrome of beliefs and attitudes. For example, particularistic and/or extrinsic religious orientations might come into play, affecting the way in which orthodox beliefs bear upon the consequences. Both types of factors are of concern to us in this study, the former in this chapter and the latter in the next.

At present we are concerned with the first of these—that is, whether the orthodoxy-consequence association is spurious, owing to the causally antecedent influence of the respondent's breadth of perspective. Already we have seen that localism is related to orthodoxy, but we have yet to examine local-cosmopolitan differences in the consequential attitudes. Table 8.4 displays these correlations as well and makes amply clear that locals are not only more orthodox, but are also less activist in theological outlook, less interested in ecumenism, more conservative politically, and more prejudiced toward Jews, blacks, and Catholics. Several observations here are worthy of attention. One is the consistency: locals are traditionalists, and in one attitudinal realm after another they respond in a predictable manner. Whether pertaining to church-related or to more general consequences, their attitudes reflect that of a narrow world view. A second is the size of the relationships: though by no means large, these correlations are larger than those found with orthodoxy. Localism is more strongly associated with each of the consequential variables than is literal, orthodox belief.

Taken as a whole, the results suggest that a broad set of conservative, traditionalist responses are associated with localism. *People with a limited social outlook tend to conform to the traditional norms of the culture, including in the American case strong elements of white Anglo-Saxon Protestant ethnocentrism, racism, and political conservatism.* This broad syndrome of attitudes reflects a cultural style characteristic of many mainline church members, and one originating essentially out of orientations and predispositions extraneous to theological dogma.

Viewed from this perspective we have a clearer basis for explaining orthodoxy's relation to the consequential attitudes. Religious beliefs need not "cause" so much as "legitimate" people's attitudes. As Geertz says, "in religious belief and practice a people's style of life . . . is rendered intellectually reasonable; it is shown to represent a way of life ideally adapted to the world as it 'really' . . . is."[13] Especially among those whose social outlook is limited, literal orthodox beliefs offer a simplistic interpretation of life and rationalization for traditional values, norms, and life-styles. Literal beliefs serve to sacralize their world view—to infuse their perspectives with transcendent meaning and authority, and to shield them against anomie.[14] Why this should be so is accounted for by Converse's principle of attitudinal constraint. As will be recalled from Chapter 2, Converse was concerned with differences in political belief systems between political leaders and their mass constituents. Moving down the information scale from leaders to followers, he saw two changes occurring in the belief system: first, the degree of constraint among the idea-elements in the total belief system should decline; second, objects central to the belief system are likely to shift from the "remote, generic, and abstract to the increasingly simple, concrete, or close to home."[15] Following this reasoning, we would expect that for locals, as compared with broader-minded persons, their religious ideologies are less oriented to abstract theological principles, structured more around their cultural characteristics, and hence less constrained as a system of beliefs and attitudes. Accordingly, the local's conservatism in matters of social ethics is explained largely by factors other than religious belief.

This possibility raises several interesting issues. Are the relationships between orthodoxy and the consequential attitudes spurious? Totally or only partially spurious? Exactly how is the religious belief system structured for a person whose social outlook is limited? Lacking much in the way of attitudinal constraint, we would expect among locals their breadth of perspective plays a greater part than theological beliefs per se in explaining social ideology.

To gain insight on these issues, it should be helpful to postulate three very simple analytic models (see figure 8.1). All three assume that breadth of perspective is the critical causal factor, but they differ in the way in which theological beliefs are conceptualized as functioning in the total belief system. One possibility is that doctrinal orthodoxy "interprets" the relationship between narrow perspectives and its consequences; that is, religious belief serves as an intervening influence in linking the other two components. Such a conception is not inconsistent with theories of prejudice and conservatism that underscore the importance of theological beliefs.[16] A second possibility is that both orthodox beliefs and the the consequential measures are directly dependent on breadth of perspective but are themselves not causally related to each other. In this instance the association between beliefs and consequences is totally spurious, resulting from the fact that both variables have a common antecedent factor. Finally, a third model predicts a direct effect of religious belief on the consequences as well as direct and indirect effects of breadth of perspective. This is a more complex model suggesting that the orthodoxy-consequences relationship is partially, but not entirely, spurious. By implication it suggests that both sets of factors—social orientations and theological beliefs—should be considered in an analysis of church members' ideologies.

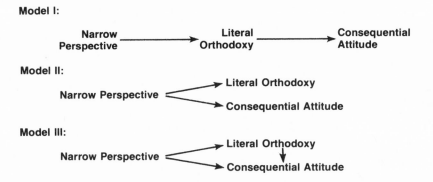

Model I:

Narrow Perspective ⟶ Literal Orthodoxy ⟶ Consequential Attitude

Model II:

Narrow Perspective ⟨ Literal Orthodoxy / Consequential Attitude

Model III:

Narrow Perspective ⟨ Literal Orthodoxy ↓ Consequential Attitude

FIGURE 8.1 Alternative Models of Breadth of Perspective, Literal Orthodoxy, and Consequential Attitudes

Some clues about the appropriateness of these models are offered in table 8.5. Shown are partial correlations that provide a set of results against which to evaluate the three alternative possibilities. If Model I were correct, the partial correlations between localism and consequences, with orthodoxy as the test factor, should drop to zero. The data in the first part of table 8.5 show emphatically this does not occur. In none of the seven tests does this prediction hold. In fact, the greatest reduction in the partials occurs with political intolerance but it diminishes only from .37 to .32. Thus very little evidence is mustered for the intervening beliefs model.

Somewhat more support is found for the second, although it too is limited. When localism is controlled, as in the second part of table 8.5, the associations are all reduced. These partials are substantially smaller than their counterparts in Model I, suggesting that local community reference does account for much of the variation in both orthodoxy and the consequential measures. But the partials generally

TABLE 8.5

Partial Correlation Coefficients for Consequential Measures and Localism with Orthodoxy Controlled, and for Consequential Measures and Orthodoxy with Localism Controlled

CONTROL VARIABLE INDEPENDENT VARIABLE	CONSEQUENTIAL MEASURES	PARTIAL CORRELATION
Controlling for Orthodoxy	Church Activism	−.285
Localism	Ecumenism	−.263
	Political Intolerance	.323
	Racism	.289
	Anti-Semitic	.183
	Anti-Black	.218
	Anti-Catholic	.149
Controlling for Localism	Church Activism	.014
Orthodoxy	Ecumenism	.035
	Political Intolerance	.150
	Racism	.096
	Anti-Semitic	.078
	Anti-Black	.140
	Anti-Catholic	.057

do not drop to zero as would be expected if the orthodoxy-consequential relationship were totally spurious. Clearly the orthodoxy relationship persists in most instances even if in a somewhat attenuated form.

By process of elimination, we turn to Model III. Both localism and doctrinal orthodoxy are proposed here as having direct influence. Doctrinal orthodoxy is also assumed to be directly affected by localistic orientations. Instead of either the "interpretation" or the "spuriousness" explanations above, the data suggest a more complex pattern of relationships in which the influence of narrow perspectives is expressed both directly and indirectly through literal orthodoxy. More than anything else, the consistency of the partials across a range of church-related and secular consequences lends support to Model III.

From this we conclude generally that there is support for the localistic world view explanation. Not that theological beliefs have no independent effects, *but rather the overwhelming influence stems from breadth of perspective, either directly or indirectly upon the consequences*. The more limited the social perspective, the less church members are constrained to develop integrated, theologically based belief systems. To the contrary, their social ideologies tend to reflect the fact that parochial interests and loyalties have replaced religious principles as the central, organizing objects in their belief systems. Considering the crucial part that a person's breadth of perspective plays, a fundamental observation about belief systems should be noted: historic theological doctrines are always filtered through the believer's cultural experience. Formal beliefs and creeds, no matter what their teachings about social ethics, are always apprehended by people in a given cultural context having distinctive values, assumptions, and perceptions about the nature of life. This being the case, it is not surprising to find locals committed to a social ideology bearing the imprint primarily of their more conservative world view.

RETURNING TO THE BASIC MODEL[17]

Having uncovered evidence in support of the world view argument, we turn next to a retest of the basic model introduced in Chapter 5. If the world view explanation holds, it must do so in a more systematic analysis of religious orthodoxy and its social correlates. For this we turn to the basic path model, augmented in this instance by the addition only of the consequential'attitudes. Shown in figure 8.2, the consequences are treated as dependent upon three direct influences: literal orthodoxy, education, and local community reference. Education is brought into the explanatory scheme directly here, given its importance in attitudinal research generally plus our earlier finding of direct and indirect effects in the sense of status versus exposure influences. As with the previous model the path coefficients summarizing direct effects are not shown in the diagram, but are presented instead in table 8.6.

Consistent with the previous findings, the results of this more systematic test underscore the effects of localism on *both* literal orthodoxy and the consequential measures. Orthodoxy has an influence on the latter, but it is clear its impact is secondary to that of education and localism. This is true for all seven dependent variables, which suggests that the relationships among breadth of perspective, orthodoxy, and the consequential dimension hold generally for church-related as well as secular measures. The evidence is quite clear: the orthodoxy-consequential relationships are partially spurious. By con-

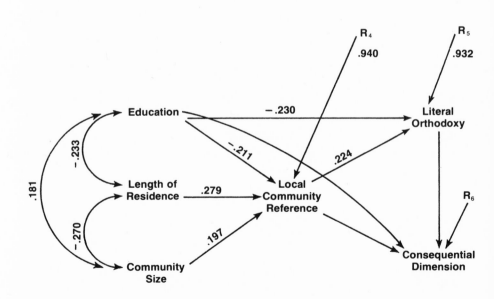

FIGURE 8.2   Basic Path Model, Plus Consequences

TABLE 8.6

*Path Coefficients Between Consequential Measures and
Independent Variables, and Residuals*

CONSEQUENTIAL MEASURE	INDEPENDENT VARIABLES			
	EDUCATION	LOCALISM	ORTHODOXY	RESIDUAL
Church Activism	.141	−.264	−.192	.909
Ecumenism	.134	−.310	−.167	.911
Political Intolerance	−.127	.301	.154	.902
Racism	−.133	.284	.226	.924
Anti-Semitic	−.082*	.179	.072*	.934
Anti-Black	−.183	.261	.122*	.927
Anti-Catholic	−.122*	.177	.050*	.946

*Not significant at .05 level.

trolling for education and breadth of perspective, orthodoxy's impact is considerably reduced.

Localism is the strongest of the three predictors in every instance. This shows that with all the model variables simultaneously controlled, breadth of perspective persists as a significant factor in explaining church members' attitudes toward racial, ethnic, and religious minorities, political views, and activist orientations. Its greater influence over education is especially noteworthy. As was discovered with the religiosity measures earlier, local community attachment accounts for attitudinal responses on the part of many individuals above and beyond that of education. Such attachment is likely to carry with it an orientation to the dominant cultural norms, no matter what the individual's level of education or social class standing.

In this respect the manner in which localism functions in the model as an intervening mechanism is revealing. Note that a portion of education's influence is mediated by means of localism-cosmopolitanism. To the extent that education increases a person's social horizons, it should result in greater cosmopolitanism; and by implication, individuals with broadened perspectives should be better able to transcend cultural traditions and thus to bring their attitudes into greater consistency with religious beliefs. Such effects are depicted in the model at hand from education via localism to consequence, and from education via localism via orthodoxy to consequence. Calculations of this indirect influence show that it is about one-third of the total relationship. That is, about one-third of education's influence on the attitudes can be interpreted in terms of what Stouffer describes as "contact effect," or as Becker labels it, "mental mobility."

The indirect effects are sufficiently large enough to make breadth of perspective an interesting and important consideration, and at the same time small enough to indicate that education's influence on the consequences is theoretically complex.[18] Some indirect effects for length of residence and community size are also found in the model, but by comparison with education these influences are small. Overall, the results invite further attention in research to developing theories elaborating in more detail the interrelations among these several variables.

SUMMARY AND DISCUSSION

This chapter has reviewed orthodoxy's relation to three sets of consequential attitudes: church activism, minority prejudice, and political ideology. Though a relationship is demonstrated, for most of the consequences the influence of orthodoxy is minimal in a context that considers seriously education and local community orientation. Localism is the strongest predictor, across all seven of the consequences examined. The consistency of the empirical pattern is itself striking.

Beyond this, however, the results are provocative along substantive lines. Let us sketch a few of the implications for liberal Protestantism today.

First of all, the data suggest that analysts should proceed with caution in advancing theological, or religious belief, explanations for conservative attitudes in the realms of race, ethnicity, and political ideology. Orthodoxy's relation to these variables is often weak to begin with, and if proper nontheological factors are controlled for, researchers are likely to uncover influences of a different sort that are stronger than beliefs. Breadth of perspective is one such influence, but there are many others—psychological, cultural, and social. In this respect the findings and interpretations offered here are in keeping with those of others who recently have challenged theologically based explanations, on either theoretical or methodological grounds.

Methodological weaknesses in the research on religious beliefs often abound and are easy to document in study after study. Theoretically speaking, however, the conceptual difficulties with theological arguments are more serious. Studies on religious beliefs are often narrowly focused upon creedal content, as if prejudice or some other conservative consequence were a direct and rational implication of the beliefs themselves. This reasoning, common to much Protestant ethic research, overlooks the simple fact that theological doctrines are always filtered through people's social and cultural experiences. People's beliefs interact with their everyday lives, to create a phenomenal world of meanings especially suited to their range of experiences. What emerges in a given situation as "operant religion" will differ considerably from the "formal religion" of the historic creeds, and more concern with the former is essential to understanding how belief systems function in people's daily lives.[19]

Second, and at a somewhat lesser level of reflection, questions are raised about how to explain changing patterns of institutional commitments within the liberal Protestant churches. It would appear from the evidence herein reported that theories that try to account for ethicalism, or a social activist religious orientation, in terms of a decline in orthodoxy require some reexamination. The inverse association between orthodoxy and church activism is not very strong among the Episcopalians in this study. Moreover, if the constellation of localistic orientations, beliefs, and sentiments is taken into consideration, quite clearly the case for the declining belief argument becomes tenuous indeed. Thus it would seem that an important causal factor in explaining the social activist orientation of many members in the liberal churches is not so much the *decline* of traditional belief as the social experiences that lead a person to commit himself or herself to a nonconventional ideological position. Breaking out of conformity to traditional norms and narrow cultural orientations is the crucial consideration, resulting in changes in religious ideology—away from literalistic conceptions toward greater ethical values. A nonlocal, or cosmopolitan, social orientation is in this respect an important psychological mechanism facilitating value systems for persons who are less dependent on the norms in their immediate social environment.

Finally, the implications pertaining to education and its effects upon the consequential attitudes are important. Research on ethnocentrism over the past two decades has repeatedly shown that education is positively associated with tolerance toward minorities; yet these studies often fail to explain fully *why* education has such effects. The findings here strongly support the view proposed by Gabennesch that a crucial function of education is breadth of perspective; and that by conceptualizing education in this way, it is possible to explain authoritarian attitudes in social psychological rather than purely personality terms. Specifically, the issue has to do with the intervening linkage between education and tolerance. Unfortunately the effects of education on attitudes are often measured by years of formal schooling—a measure useful for some purposes, but which fails to tap education's orientational and/or developmental influences. The latter is most directly concerned with the tolerance-producing potential of education and should not be neglected when studying liberal Protestants. For unless education results in broadened perspectives on the part of individuals, the chances are that their attitudes will not be significantly altered.

These are all important directions for further research that we cannot pursue here. Important to note in all of this, however, is that discussion has focused on the nonreligious world-view factors that help to shape people's belief systems. Our concern throughout has been to underscore the significance of these extrinsic factors. But what about *intrinsic* religious meanings? Are there not dimensions of religious meaning aside from doctrinal belief that exert influence on people's attitudes, say, in a liberal rather than a consevative direction? Answers to these questions, dealt with in the next chapter, promise to provide still more insight into the complexities of the belief systems held by many liberal Protestants.

[9]

Broadened Perspectives and Subtle Effects

In the last chapter we saw that breadth of perspective was a significant factor in explaining church members' attitudes, but in arriving at this conclusion several issues emerged that deserve further attention. We observed, for example, that literal orthodoxy exerts some impact on social and political conservatism independent of people's localistic perspectives. Although not a strong impact, yet it does prompt speculation about religion as a source of influence. Why do religious beliefs have such influence? Is it because religion predisposes people generally to conservative ideologies and attitudes? Or is there something peculiar with literal orthodox beliefs themselves that result in these influences?

Further, there is the issue of what kind of influence religion generates in the life of a religious person. It is commonplace in emperical research to find that orthodox beliefs are associated with conservative social and political views, and indeed this study confirms such a pattern. But is religious belief and conviction not also a *liberalizing* influence— generating attitudes of favor rather than disfavor toward others, and positive instead of negative views toward responsible social ethics? This side of the argument is rarely put forth and demonstrated empirically even more rarely. Nonetheless the possibility exists and invites careful study, to see what sorts of liberal sentiments are expressed, and if perhaps the two opposing strands of influence are discernable in religious belief systems.

We know a fair amount about the psychological dynamics of belief systems, plus such characteristics as dogmatism, authoritarianism, and intrinsic versus extrinsic qualities in religious commitment. Studies of these phenomena have resulted in greater understanding of religiosity, its nature and consequences; but by and large these insights have not been fully incorporated into sociological, or even social psychological, theories of commitment. Often, what happens is that researchers in a given theoretical tradition carry on without much exchange with other traditions, with the result that there exists very little in the way of systematic theory about beliefs and their consequences. This is indeed unfortunate in studying liberal Protestants, for of all established religious groups, we would anticipate finding among them conflicting sentiments—positive as well as negative views—about the implications of religion for social ethics. Serious conflicts among lay members over social matters and religious responsibility over the past decade amply demonstrate the deep-seated ambiguities of commitment among liberal Protestants.

The belonging and meaning paradigm offers a framework for pulling together some of these ambiguities. Already we have observed that locals generally are belongers in religious groups, concerned with maintaining commitment to the institutional church and its beliefs and practices. Because of their strong social attachments, their ideologies are shaped largely by particularistic, "close-to-home" values. On the other hand, cosmopolitans in the religious institution are social activists, known more for their strong ethical concerns than for congregational involvement. Their commitment is based primarily upon liberal theological principles of social justice and ethics; concerns about social morality, and not the institutional norms of the church, structure their ideologies. Given the higher levels of constraint in their belief systems, it follows that *ethical principles occupy a more central position in their overall system of meaning*. For this reason we can expect that cosmopolitans are less committed to religion as a cultural system, and more to religion as a set of abstract ethical and theological teachings.

The cosmopolitan's greater breadth of perspective is important here, analytically speaking, because of its implications for *dereification*. A reified belief system is one in which extrinsic elements in religion become highly fused with the religious and ethical teachings. Conversely, dereification implies reduced significance for the extrinsic aspects, and greater constraint among the idea-elements within the belief system. Broadened cognitive orientations allow individuals to *transcend* cultural particularisms and to critically evaluate their views according to a consistent value standard. In effect, greater breadth of perspective should lead to the discarding of the cultural trappings of faith, and to a more highly integrated, ethically oriented belief system. This being the case, we have a basis for understanding better the ideological conflicts among liberal Protestants; but to account more fully for why this is so, we must explore in greater depth the many facets of liberal Protestant belief systems.

To do this, the chapter examines (a) further variations in local-cosmopolitan ideology; (b) major themes of the cosmopolitan's belief system; and (c) how breadth of perspective results in liberalizing influence. These will help to round out the analysis begun in the previous chapter and provide a more balanced perspective on religion and its consequences.

LOCALISM, LITERAL ORTHODOXY, AND REIFIED BELIEFS

First we look at literal orthodoxy's relation to four indexes of cultural attitudes: Americanism, conventionalism, anomie, and achievement orientation[1]. These represent a diverse range of attitudes in contemporary American society, some more pertinent perhaps to religion than others. But all are highly normative matters, evoking strong positive or negative sentiments, and easily become fused with religious values and symbols. For this reason it makes sense to examine them in the context of reification. That is, we would expect literal orthodox beliefs to be closely associated with such views and to play a significant part in aiding individuals to interpret their life experiences. As shown by table 9.1, there is evidence to suggest this is the case. With each of the cultural attitudes, there is a direct positive relation: the more intense the response, the greater the literalistic interpretation.

But the major question here concerns breadth of perspective, and how the religious and nonreligious elements in the belief system vary

TABLE 9.1

Levels of Literal Orthodoxy and Cultural Attitudes,
in Percentages

| | LITERAL ORTHODOXY INDEX | | |
CULTURAL ATTITUDE	Low (N=142)	Medium (N=165)	High (N=155)
High on Americanism	26	47	64
High on Conventional Values	33	48	59
High on Anomie	43	52	61
High on Achievement Orientation	23	42	66

for locals and cosmopolitans. Among locals—and hence belongers in religious institutions—the belonging and meaning functions of religion should be closely associated. Because they are strongly attached to the groups in which they belong, their systems of meaning will reflect particularistic, cultural elements linked with traditional lifestyles and values. This should result in a highly conservative and diffuse set of beliefs associated with literalistic orthodoxy among locals, but less so among the cosmopolitans.

Table 9.2 presents the correlation coefficients describing the patterns for the two subgroups separately. This shows that in all instances the relationships are substantially stronger among the locals. Not only is this true for literal orthodoxy, but for several other measures of religiosity as well. Although the orthodoxy correlations are somewhat stronger, the local-cosmopolitan differences hold generally for all four of the institutional commitment indicators. The dynamics of reification appear to embrace a broad spectrum of attitudes in the case of locals, resulting in the general fusion of religious and particularistic idea-elements.

This is best demonstrated with the Americanism index, which is intended as a measure of commitment to the country's way of life. Democracy and free enterprise are its celebrated values—the "operative faith" of the American people, in Herberg's terms.[2] Substantial associations between religiosity and Americanism indicate that among locals, there is considerable symbolic unity of church religion and national identity and purpose. To be religious is to affirm the American

TABLE 9.2

Correlations Between Religiosity and Cultural Attitudes, Among Locals and Cosmopolitans

MEASURES OF RELIGIOSITY	AMERICAN-ISM	CONVEN-TIONAL VALUES	ANOMIE	ACHIEVE-MENT
	Locals (N=235)			
Literal Orthodoxy	.53*	.36*	.27*	.51*
Church Attendance	.34*	.28*	.15*	.23*
Church Activities	.24*	.22*	.18	.23*
Importance of Church Membership	.49*	.41*	.23*	.46*
	Cosmopolitans (N=224)			
Literal Orthodoxy	.14	.17*	.03	.13
Church Attendance	.12	.07	−.03	.16*
Church Activities	.09	.09	−.06	.11
Importance of Church Membership	.16	.12	−.08	.19*

*Statistically significant at .05 level.

way of life. Similar, though less striking, patterns are obtained with the conventional values index and achievement orientation. Among those who are belongers in the religious institution, religiosity is associated with tried-and-true values plus an individualist, inner-directed ethic that stresses material success, self-reliance, and middle-class conformity. The fact that we find specifications with both the institutional participation and belief measures of church religion, suggests the religious and cultural elements coalesce to form a highly charged belief system.

Particularly interesting are the correlations between religiosity and anomie. They all reduce substantially among the cosmopolitans, leading to the speculation that the alleged relationship between anomie and strict, "sectlike" commitment may be partially explained by the respondent's breadth of perspective. Alienation and normlessness are correlates of literal belief, but apparently much more so among those with a reified world view. At the very least, the data show that religious responses to anomie are far more prevalent among those with limited outlooks.[3]

In sum, the findings support the reified world-view interpretation. Among locals, religious belonging and meaning are closely interrelated, with the implication being that church religion functions to sacralize such widely held values in American society as individualism, inner-directedness, conventional morality, and patriotism. Considering the constellation of elements involved, such a belief system is characteristic of those individuals or groups who find in religion legitimation for a comforting and reassuring faith, if not a defense for traditional values and life-styles. Certainly such beliefs are unlikely to foster a social activist or challenge ideology.

THE SEARCH FOR MEANING

Next we turn to the fundamental question underlying this and the previous chapter: how to explain the sources of social activism and ethicalism in religious commitment? Data presented in Part III indicate that the decline-of-orthodoxy explanation fails to account satisfactorily for liberal concerns over social ethics. Cosmopolitans as we have seen evidence ethical concerns independent of their doctrinal conceptions. Quite clearly, their social activist leanings and liberal attitudes are better explained by their broader world views than by demythologized theology. And yet, the intervening links in the world view explanation are unclear. What exactly are the *religious* implications of a broadened social perspective? As literal religious beliefs and conceptions lose their reified character, what types of religious motivation surface in the process?

The lack of strong institutional ties with the church among cosmopolitans implies, among other things, a style of commitment that is highly individualized and privatized. This fact leads us to expect that the search for personal meaning and truth is an integral part of their religious style; and that self-definition and self-understanding in terms of religious and ethical principles play heavily in their case. Ethical concerns are paramount for cosmopolitan members, so we have argued, essentially because their social orientations emancipate them from particularistic, narrow-minded views and encourage the exploration of in-depth meanings of faith in their lives. Evidence in support of this can be mustered in two ways in the present study: directly by looking at the reasons respondents give about being religious, and what they say about how doubt affects their faith; and indirectly by examining the patterns of denominational switching among locals and cosmopolitans. Let us look at each of these in turn.

Reasons Given for Being Religious

Fortunately the Episcopal survey included a question designed to tap respondents' views on why they are religious. The items were carefully selected so as to allow respondents to choose between traditional, church-related reasons and more personal explanations. Results from this cross-tabulation are shown in table 9.3, indicating that the modal response for cosmopolitans is the search for meaning in life. Forty-three percent selected this response as their first reason, to be followed by worship through prayer and meditation as the second choice. Both responses refer to personal, individualistic reasons that differ conspicuously from those given by the locals. Aside from prayer and meditation, participation in church activities and serving as an example for others are the major responses endorsed by the traditionalists.

By far the most striking observation is the significance which the

TABLE 9.3

Reasons Given for Being Religious by Locals and Cosmopolitans, in Percentages

TO BE RELIGIOUS MEANS:	LOCAL (N=238)	COSMOPOLITAN (N=226)
1. to participate regularly in the activities of one's church.	26	5
2. to continually search for the ultimate meaning of life.	9	43
3. to be a person who is thoughtful of others.	9	5
4. to worship God through prayer and meditation.	37	38
5. to make one's life a good example for other people.	17	6
6. to actively work to promote social justice for all men.	2	3
Total	100	100

cosmopolitans attach to the search for ultimate meaning. Whereas the traditionalists are content with conventional explanations for being religious, such as divine worship and making one's life an example for others, the cosmopolitans seek instead to relate religious values and meanings to secular life. Noteworthy in this respect are the responses cosmopolitans give when faced with a choice between personal meaning, prayer and meditation, and social justice. Even though they are strongly committed to an activist position, basic theological convictions and quandaries appear more important than simply ethical or humanistic principles. In addition to their concern for current social issues, modernists share a heritage of Christian faith that encourages the honest search for truth, pursuit of the meaning of life, and the application of religious values in the personal and social domains of life.

Doubt and Its Functions

The honest search for truth and pursuit of meaning can, and often does, lead to doubt about religious truth. Religious doubt is itself a multifaceted phenomenon, depending on what aspects of belief are in question and how doubt is used by the believer. We can go even further and claim as some psychologists have, that religious doubt is a sign of a healthy faith. At the very least, doubt as mature reflection upon, and reformulation of, theological conceptions is an integral and necessary part of personal religious growth.

That cosmopolitans doubt more than locals is intuitively obvious, but less obvious is the possibility that doubt may function *differently* for the two. Cosmopolitan preferences for demythologized beliefs may reflect not only greater cognitive flexibility, but also their efforts at reconstructing traditional beliefs to make them more acceptable. This involves reinterpreting beliefs, symbolically rather than literally, and casting off mythological elements in favor of more existential meanings. As a result of such endeavors, it is quite possible that cosmopolitans will come to appreciate the importance of doubt as an integral part of the religious life. Doubt need not necessarily destroy the vitality of faith, but instead may offer an individual a means of creating a more authentic, and perhaps even stronger, personal belief system.

While the evidence is not particularly strong, there is some support for this in table 9.4. In a follow-up question to the items on doubt, respondents were given a chance to describe more fully their doubt about God in the past, and how it may have affected their faith. Cosmopolitans more readily admit to occasionally questioning God's existence even if they have never seriously doubted. But even more important, cosmopolitan respondents acknowledge more than locals, either having gone through an intensive period of doubt which is now resolved or regard doubt as part of a mature faith. In either case, doubt results not in any serious loss of personal faith but rather in its strengthening. Among those who feel that doubt has actually weakened faith, the differences between the two groups are quite minimal.

Generally speaking, it appears that doubt is a more pervasive quality of the cosmopolitan's religious commitment. By scrutinizing traditional doctrines and teachings, they are able to create for themselves a more satisfying belief system emphasizing existential meanings and truths. Persons with cosmopolitan orientations are better able to do this because of their broader, and less reified, social perspectives. Compared with locals, they have a more critical capacity for sorting

TABLE 9.4

Respondents' Views on Doubt and Its Effects, by Degree of Localism (N=462), in Percentages*

ASPECTS OF DOUBT	LOCAL	MODERATELY LOCAL	MODERATELY COSMOPOL- ITAN	COSMOPOL- ITAN
Occasionally question but never really doubt God's existence	17	28	29	38
Have gone through a period of very real doubt about God's existence but no longer hold such doubts	4	6	6	15
Often doubt but feel doubt is part of a mature faith	1	5	7	14
Often doubt and feel doubt has weakened faith	2	3	4	4
Have never doubted that God exists**	75	58	52	27

*Ns do not necessarily add to 100 percent. Another questionnaire item—nonbelief in God—is not included above.
**Statistically significant at .05 level.

189

out the various strands of religious meaning and reality, and are able to discard outdated literalisms in favor of more plausible conceptions. Greater flexibility in cognitive style facilitates the search for ultimate truth and makes it easier to reject particularistic and culture-bound elements without necessarily weakening personal faith. Consequently, they are better able to transcend traditional beliefs and imageries and at the same time retain convictions about religion's ethical and moral values.

Denominational Switching

Finally, we look at patterns of denominational switching and reasons given for joining the Episcopal Church. In American society, especially among Protestants, denominational switching is quite common. Stark and Glock report that more than 40 percent of American Protestants are not in the same denomination as were their parents.[4] Further, they show an intragenerational pattern of movement for the sixties—away from the conservative churches toward more liberal denominations. This trend is perhaps less today, but nevertheless many who reject orthodox religious beliefs, for whatever reasons, do turn to churches with liberal, modernized theologies in search of an alternative belief system. Given what we already know about cosmopolitans, we would expect them to number among those who are attracted to liberal denominations.

Fortunately for this study the sample consists of Episcopalians. Of all Protestant denominations, according to Stark and Glock, the Episcopal Church shows the largest increase in their net membership as a result of upward denominational shifting.[5] Thus, if cosmopolitans are indeed shifters, we should find them here. Having rejected traditional, literalistic beliefs, they should turn to this denomination in search of a demythologized faith. Forty-four percent of all our respondents, in fact, were previously members of other denominations. Of these, as table 9.5 indicates, 72 percent are cosmopolitans—thus confirming the prediction of differential orientations among the shifters. Further inspection of the data shows that cosmopolitan shifters come primarily from Methodist, Southern Baptist, and sectarian backgrounds. The latter are all more conservative theologically, in keeping with our expectation that breadth of perspective may play a

TABLE 9.5

TABLE 9.5

Switching of Denominations Among Locals and Cosmopolitans, in Percentages

	PERCENTAGE SWITCHING*
Locals	28
Cosmopolitans	72

*Statistically significant at .01 level.

part in motivating individuals to shift into more liberal denominations. A broadened social outlook facilitates upward denominational switching, usually because it is accompanied by fewer sociocommunal attachments and because greater openness in outlook encourages acceptance of liberal, modernized beliefs.

This interpretation of cosmopolitan switching into the Episcopal Church is supported more directly by the reasons given for changing church affiliation. Switchers were asked to rank-order their reasons, and were given six statements to choose among. Table 9.6 lists these along with the first preferences of locals and cosmopolitans. Looking at the modal responses, we see that cosmopolitans typically cite the item concerning how the denomination's doctrines match personal

TABLE 9.6

Reasons for Affiliating with Episcopal Church for Locals and Cosmopolitans, in Percentages

REASONS	LOCALS (N=238)	COSMOPOLITANS (N=223)
1. My children were attending this church	3	9
2. My spouse was a member of this denomination.	24	16
3. It was the church nearest my home.	12	5
4. Many of my friends belong to this denomination.	24	—
5. This denomination fits in better with my present work and manner of life.	4	21
6. The doctrines of this denomination best matched my own religious beliefs.	22	45

*Does not total 100 percent since other reasons were also given.

beliefs. The next most frequently cited reason is how the denomination "fits in better with my present work and manner of life." On the other hand, locals give as reasons, aside from doctrines, the influence of spouses and friends. These latter of course we would expect in view of the primary group ties that shape the organizational affiliations of locals. Interestingly, though, locals are less likely to cite the influence of children. If children are leading their parents to church, apparently they disproportionately lead cosmopolitans—perhaps because they give greater attention to children's preferences to begin with.

Considering the theological background of the cosmopolitan shifters, it is not surprising they should emphasize *religious* reasons for joining the Episcopal Church. By shifting denominations they acknowledge their rejection of orthodoxy while at the same time affirm their loyalty to the Christian heritage and its values. They have adopted demythologized beliefs but this need not necessarily mean the abandonment of theology as a critical dimension of personal faith and the search for meaning. Instead it probably indicates that for those who adhere to a demythologized religious position, Christianity is professed as a faith and a heritage that instructs people, as Hadden writes, in "the meaning of life rather than a dogmatic tradition proclaiming to possess ultimate reality."[6] Religion is more than the institutionalized beliefs and practices of a given church, and the cosmopolitans who have found their way to the Episcopal Church are in search of these other aspects.

A GENERAL HYPOTHESIS

Up to this point our discussion has focused on the differences in religious motivation for locals and cosmopolitans. The explanation has been cast directly in terms of reification and more indirectly along the lines of breadth of perspective. Stated formally, the basic argument was that breadth of perspective leads to dereification, which in turn opens up greater possibilities that believers will search for religious meaning and truth. Cosmopolitans tend less to "belong" to religious institutions and to reify their belief systems; and consequently general ethical principles replace particularistic elements as the central objects of their religious orientation.

Having found support for this line of reasoning, we are now prepared to entertain a more general interpretation. *Because of their broader social perspectives, cosmopolitans attach more significance to religious "meaning" than to "belonging," which predisposes them to stronger liberal religious sentiments.* Essentially the causal argument is as illustrated by figure 9.1.

Breadth of Perspective ⟶ Meaning-Salience in Religion ⟶ Liberal Religious Sentiments

FIGURE 9.1 Proposed Causal Argument for Liberal Religious Sentiments

By *liberal religious sentiments* is meant personal concerns about social ethics and the ethical implications of religious doctrines and teachings. *Meaning-salience* refers to the importance an individual believer attaches to religious ideas and principles—that is, religion's cognitive role. This aspect of personal commitment is to be contrasted with *belonging-salience*, which pertains to involvement and participation in congregational activities.[7]

For several reasons this promises to be a fruitful line of inquiry. First is that meaning-salience as an orientation to religion is probably related to a larger constellation of *intrinsic* religious concerns. King and Hunt find, for example, a good deal of overlap among measures tapping personal religious growth and striving, salience of religion in thought and feelings, devotionalism, and application of religious and ethical principles in life. All these appear as they say to be "different components of Allport's 'intrinsic'."[8] Second is that these components of intrinsic commitment have been shown generally to nurture more humanitarian, ethically oriented concerns. Especially with prejudice, intrinsic religious commitment tends to generate liberal sentiments.[9] Devotional practices and habits, also, are known to foster a sensitivity to human concerns.[10] Intrinsic religious sentiments simply differ qualitatively.

To test more fully this hypothesis, we look again at the belonging and meaning issue, and then the interrelations among religious meaning, literal orthodoxy, and breadth of perspective. By so doing we should better be able to understand how theological and nontheological factors interact in religious belief systems.

BELONGING VERSUS MEANING

On the basis of the previous discussion, locals are expected to score higher on belonging, and cosmopolitans higher on meaning. The percentages reported in table 9.7 show, however, the differences are not so clear-cut. To be sure, locals do score higher on the belonging-salience index. Sixty-one percent attach extreme significance to this component of religious identity, as compared with only 30 percent of the cosmopolitans. But on the meaning dimension we find results, on the surface at least, which seem to contradict our expectations. Both groups score high on meaning-salience, and interestingly a greater percent of the locals fall into this category than do the cosmopolitans. Surprising as this may appear, however, it may indicate simply the tendency for locals to be "indiscriminately proreligious." Unsophisticated, traditionally oriented persons are inclined to agree more readily to religious items in a questionnaire without serious and differentiated responses.

With this potential bias in mind, an index was created that would better indicate the significance of meaning for the individual respondent. Such an index was possible for each respondent by subtracting the belonging-salience score from the meaning-salience score, thereby producing a measure of *difference* between the two indexes, or *relative importance of religious meaning*. Persons attaching about equal significance to belonging and meaning were scored quite low on the relative index. But persons originally scoring higher on meaning than on belonging received considerably higher relative scores, and in the case of the

TABLE 9.7

High Scores on Meaning-Salience and Belonging-Salience Among Locals and Cosmopolitans, in Percentages

TYPE OF RELIGIOUS ORIENTATION	LOCALS (N=238)	COSMOPOLITANS (N=223)
Percent Scoring High on Meaning-Salience	72	66
Percent Scoring High on Belonging-Salience*	61	30

*Statistically significant at .05 level.

TABLE 9.8

Relative Importance of Religious Meaning among Locals and
Cosmopolitans, in Percentages*

RELATIVE IMPORTANCE OF RELIGIOUS MEANING INDEX	LOCALS (N=238)	COSMOPOLITANS (N=223)
High	11	48
Medium	36	21
Low	53	31

*Statistically significant at .05 level.

opposite where the belonging scores are higher, negative differences were treated as falling in the low index category.

Table 9.8 displays these results, showing as expected that cosmopolitans do indeed attach greater relative significance to meaning-salience. Wide percentage spreads here make clear that for many cosmopolitan members in liberal Protestant churches, concerns about theology, religion's role in personal decision making, and the implications of faith for life take precedence over purely institutional concerns. For them the salient religious questions have to do with theology as a source of meaning and personal growth, and as a source of religious and ethical principles. Because these are more individual, private kinds of religious concerns, they are indicative of an "invisible" religion characteristic of many who are no longer actively involved in church activities.

THE DYNAMICS OF DEREIFICATION

Without question, cosmopolitan-oriented Protestants attach more significance to religious meaning than to belonging and are more liberal in their social attitudes. But is the causal sequence of influences as proposed above? Our findings strongly suggest this is the case, although we have yet to look at the ethical attitudes. And to this we now turn.

In testing the hypothesis, it seems advisable to include in our considerations the role that religious beliefs play in social ideology. Already in the last chapter we have seen that beliefs exert influence on people's ethical attitudes and behaviors. The influence was not overly large, but we can hardly dismiss it altogether. Moreover, there is an interesting, and indeed paradoxical, fact that we must confront: *orthodox beliefs are related to consequential attitudes and ideologies just the opposite of intrinsic religious meanings*. Orthodox beliefs are typically associated with conservative social views. But intrinsic religious commitment, as we have discussed already, is a much different type of religiosity tending to nurture a liberal outlook and humanitarian concerns.

Why should this inconsistency occur? It would appear that beliefs and meanings are integrally related and that such differences would be unlikely. Nevertheless, the two do differ functionally. Beliefs have strong cognitive components, making it possible for people to structure their conceptions of reality. Religious beliefs convey imageries of ultimate reality and of the way in which the supernatural world impinges upon present-day life. Intrinsic meanings, however, pertain less to conceptual matters than to basic orientations toward, or motivations for, religious commitment. What matters in this respect is not the cognitive frame for interpreting reality, but rather whether religion as a meaning system is ultimate, or simply instrumental, to the person's motivation. Ultimate versus instrumental motivation is not a trivial distinction, since in the believer's motivation system fundamental orientations of this kind predispose how religion will be used, how it is applied to personal and social life, and even the limits of its influence on personal values and sentiments.

These differences help explain the basis for such inconsistency. Literal fundamentalist beliefs are most common among those with narrow, reified conceptions of reality; and hence for these people the cognitive functions of religion play a crucially important role in providing them with interpretations and legitimations. These cognitive functions are probably most pronounced among the indiscriminately proreligious— those who in Allport's terms tend to accept culturally based, often extrinsically oriented, beliefs and ideologies. By comparison, among those with broadened social horizons traditional religious imageries are less plausible, their belief systems generally are more flexible, and theological and ethical teachings are more salient as organizing principles. Intrinsic religious meanings are more central to their belief systems, and as a result the belonging and consensual elements have diminished significance and lose much of their motivational power.

From this vantage point we can better understand the ideological conflicts within the liberal Protestant churches. Traditionalists rely very heavily upon a literal cognitive framework in interpreting reality, and this in turn encourages a compartmentalized view of life wherein the religious and the nonreligious spheres are maintained as separate. Consequently, doctrinal orthodoxy gets cast into the role often of the defender, and not the challenger, of the status quo in society. With modernists the situation is quite different. Concerned more about ethical principles and their application to modern life, they find intrinsic religious meanings far more acceptable and relevant than the older orthodoxies. Their search for religious meaning results in the reconstruction not only of belief, but also of religion's relevance to all of life.

Not only conflicts between individuals and groups but also internal psychological conflicts *within* a person can be accounted for in this way. With broadened social perspectives, individuals experience important changes in their beliefs as a result of the dereification process. Dereification entails as a minimum two psychological dynamics bearing directly upon the religious belief system: (1) the declining plausibility of literal cognitive frameworks, and (2) the increasing importance of meaning-salience as a constraining force. In effect, the latter replaces the former among cosmopolitan-minded modernists as the basic motif underlying their belief system. Breadth of perspective creates the condition whereby the liberalizing effects of intrinsic religious meanings come into play.[11]

This interpretation is supported by the data in table 9.9. Presented here are the standardized regression coefficients describing the relative predictive power of both literal orthodoxy and meaning-salience for locals and cosmopolitans. Among locals literal orthodoxy is consistently stronger than religious meanings, thus indicating that for these respondents there is a close affinity between cognitive structures and social ethical attitudes. Among cosmopolitans to the contrary, we see that their attitudes are more sensitive to the influence of religious meanings. Given their flexibility of outlook, and more constrained belief systems, they rely less on traditional, supernatural imageries in formulating a religiously based social ideology. Instead, they are more concerned with the pursuit of religious truth, and its relevance to contemporary American life.

TABLE 9.9

Standardized Regression Coefficients Showing the Dependence of Consequential Variables on Literal Orthodoxy and Religious Meaning, for Locals and Cosmopolitans

CONSEQUENTIAL MEASURES	LITERAL ORTHODOXY	RELIGIOUS MEANING**
Locals (N=235)		
Church Activism	−.31*	.12
Ecumenism	−.27*	.14
Political Intolerance	.29*	−.10
Racism	.36*	−.11
Anti-Semitic	.14	.03
Anti-Black	.25*	−.08
Anti-Catholic	.09	.04
Cosmopolitans (N=227)		
Church Activism	−.11	.30*
Ecumenism	−.10	.32*
Political Intolerance	.14	−.31*
Racism	.15	−.27*
Anti-Semitic	.02	−.09
Anti-Black	.12	−.17
Anti-Catholic	.01	−.12

*Statistically significant at .05 level.
**Relative Importance of Religious Meaning Index

Observe also that these two sources of influence not only vary in magnitude for locals and cosmopolitans, but generally *oppose* one another as well. There are a couple of exceptions, but on the whole meaning-salience in religion relates to the consequences with a sign opposite to literal orthodoxy. This suggests that religious commitment can be a source of psychologically conflicting, and even contradictory, moral forces which must be taken into consideration when assessing religion's influence in social and political affairs. Conflicting forces are apparent in both church-related and secular consequences, pointing to a general pattern that seems to hold across a broad spectrum of cultural attitudes and ideologies.[12] Even among locals where the rigidities of reification are quite strong, meaning-salience exerts a counter effect. Though weak by comparison, nonetheless it functions as a moderating influence in the belief system. The influence increases with breadth of perspective, to the point that intrinsic religious considerations outweigh the more conservative forces.

CONCLUSIONS

Whatever else we may have discovered in this chapter, our major conclusion is that religious belief systems are highly complex and sensitive to the interactive influences of theological and nontheological factors. The findings demonstrate the importance of breadth of perspective, and especially the way in which community-based orientations condition how literal orthodox beliefs and religious meanings affect the social ideologies of liberal Protestant church members.

Theoretically speaking, the empirical results prompt several conclusions. The first centers upon reification as a belief system characteristic. In describing how beliefs function in the formulation and support of social ideologies, it is essential to know something about the belief system as a whole—its degree of constraint, centrality of religious and ethical principles, and constellation of cultural values. A reified belief system is one in which parochial and particularistic norms come to be infused with religious significance, to the point where the functional role of beliefs proper is not easily distinguished from nontheological, or extrinsic, aspects of commitment. As we have seen, these internal belief system patterns vary substantially across the local-to-cosmopolitan spectrum. The broader the social outlook, the greater the possibility the social ideologies of church members will reflect basic religious and ethical motifs.

Other implications follow from this fundamental fact about belief systems. One is that we should be careful not to mistake the cultural trappings of religion for the total phenomenon itself. Religion always bears the imprint of its cultural setting, but apparently more so for some people than for others. Among those believers able to transcend cultural traditions, the fruits of faith often bear little resemblance to their original setting; indeed, religion is a source of immensely varied, and at times contradictory, forces in people's lives. On the basis of our findings, it would appear that religion is most likely to lose its strong ethical qualities among those believers who rely upon traditional cognitive frameworks in interpreting reality. Perhaps it is for this same reason that Wuthnow reaches the conclusion that "only when orthodoxy is combined with 'particularistic' or radically 'fundamentalistic' views does it show frequent correlations with conservative secular attitudes."[13]

Another, and perhaps the most important, consideration concerns the intrinsic religious motiviation that characterizes those with broadened social perspectives. Breadth of perspective encourages the believer to discard the cultural trappings of faith, and to stress instead the importance of basic religious values and ethical teachings. This means that among our cosmopolitan oriented modernists, religion's influence is often liberalizing in character, propelling them to very strong ethical and humanitarian sentiments. It is not surprising at all, then, that the liberal Protestant denominations are riddled with internal strains and conflicts. Because of the established social position that these churches occupy, they house within their membership both highly committed traditionalists and equally concerned modernists whose faiths differ in many respects. The mainline churches may be becoming increasingly conservative, yet they remain culturally diverse and include in their membership many liberal modernists whose faith leads them to ethical concerns and an activist stance. Tension between these two is unavoidable, simply because the value conflicts and cultural cleavages that surface here are in a larger sense the conflicts and cleavages of the society as a whole.

[V]
CONCLUSIONS

[10]

Conclusions and
Implications

Having now reached the end of the study after working our way through dozens of tables and several path models, we need to take stock of our findings in terms of their general significance. Our concern has been the liberal Protestant churches—their institutional problems currently, the cultural crises they face, and the dynamics of change within these institutions. What have we learned about these churches? What distinctive insights, if any, has our approach shed on the institutional dilemmas they confront in the contemporary world? What does it all mean for the future of liberal Protestantism in America?

ANSWERS TO THE BASIC QUESTIONS

It would be helpful to summarize very generally the answers to the three basic questions that have concerned us in this study. Recall that the questions were the following:

1. What are the basic sources of religious commitment in the liberal Protestant churches?
2. How is religious faith maintained in a changing, secular social milieu?

203

3. Are the ethical concerns of these church members a consequence of faith, or are they a reflection mainly of traditional values and outlook?

In seeking answers to these, we made the assumption that mainline Protestant denominations are undergoing today severe problems of plausibility. These problems are by no means new considering the history of conflicts in liberal Protestantism throughout the twentieth century, but it would appear that internal institutional strains have reached peak proportions in recent times for several reasons. Protestantism's declining hegemony among American religious traditions is one factor; the seriousness and intensity of feelings over the social problems—especially civil rights and the Vietnam War—which the mainline churches faced in the late sixties is another. But more basic than either of these is the growing polarization within American culture between traditionalists and modernists, and the fact that these churches are becoming increasingly captive to the values and outlook of the more conservative, traditionally minded sectors of the society. While these cultural cleavages are by no means limited to churches, the liberal Protestant denominations are especially vulnerable because of their established position in American society.

Our first main set of findings pertained to the social sources of religious commitment. Traditionally oriented locals in the study were found to be consistently more religious on all the conventional indexes, in terms of both institutional belonging and beliefs and meaning. Even with other social correlates statistically controlled, the patterns of religious difference persisted. Not only were local community references a good predictor, they were also shown to operate as intervening social psychological orientations, mediating the influence of such factors as education, community size, and length of residence. Taken as a whole, these are important insights. They point to the fact that differences in cultural style between traditionalists and modernists constitute a major axis of cleavage in contemporary Protestantism. And furthermore, they underscore the close relation between local community attachments and traditional styles of religious commitment in these institutions. As the social basis for religion in modern society has shifted, the local community has become for many a meaningful symbolic world in which to adhere to traditional ways of believing.

We did not compare empirically the explanatory power of the local community reference with other better-known correlates of religion, but it probably stands up as good as, if not better than, most others. On the basis of an earlier study, there is evidence suggesting that it alone predicts religious styles as well as social class, education, and age combined.[1] Without exaggerating its importance, we can with a good deal of confidence say that *local-cosmopolitan cultural differences are as important as, and perhaps more important than, social class in explaining contemporary religious styles in the liberal Protestant churches.* Considering how much attention has been given to social class in previous research, quite clearly the time has come to take more seriously the cultural differences.

With this in mind, we went on to explore related aspects of commitment in liberal Protestantism. The second set of findings focused on how religious commitments are socially maintained in a communal context. Here we were concerned with two important matters: how to explain institutional belonging, and how to explain the persistance of traditional beliefs and meanings in a secular milieu. Regarding the first, our evidence suggests that local community ties better explain institutional belonging than does literal orthodox belief. The results call into question interpretations of church commitment emphasizing beliefs as the most critical factor in determining if people affiliate with churches, attend religious services, or contribute financially to their support. Doctrinal belief may be partly an explanation but hardly the whole. People's networks of social interaction within their local communities plus their interest in and willingness to participate in local voluntary activities are equally important. Locals are belongers in all sorts of community organizations and activities—a fact that helps to account for their greater involvement in religious organizations as well.

Not only institutional commitments but also people's fundamental conceptions of religious reality are influenced by their local community attachments. Our evidence indicates that because locals are belongers in the religious institution, they are better able to maintain a traditional, supernatural world view than are cosmopolitans. In general, social interaction within a socioreligious community, combined with strong local reference orientation, serves to reinforce the belief systems shared by members of the group. We found this to be especially true with orthodox beliefs, though less so for intrinsic religious meanings and devotional practices.

This is not to say the communal context of religion fully determines an individual's religious belief or cognitive meaning system. Obviously it does not and could not in the liberal Protestant churches where individuals enjoy considerable freedom in devising their own personal meaning systems. Nevertheless, it is within such social enclaves as these that the historic and literal beliefs of Christianity are affirmed today, the strict doctrines of faith adhered to, and transcendent religious worlds shared and maintained. The stronger the individual's ties with the believing community, the easier it is to keep the traditional meanings plausible. Group life reinforces the world view, thus serving as a support structure within the religious institution.

Admittedly this describes the situation sectarians face in trying to keep alive a "deviant" conception of reality. Yet it seems increasingly the case today that the social dynamics of reality maintenance are becoming similar for the mainline, established churches. To be sure, their membership is more heterogeneous, and their religious styles are more diverse. But the fact is that traditional religious views are plausible for a dwindling number of loyal and highly committed members who maintain relatively close ties with one another and who find the conventional beliefs and doctrines congruent with their more conservative outlook. And consequently, for the increasing numbers of those who do not maintain such ties and who are more likely to experience cognitive strains in adhering to traditional beliefs, it is not surprising that their commitments to the religious institution weaken and their religious worlds suffer from a lack of plausibility.

Finally, there is a set of findings relating to the social ideologies of the church members. These are of particular interest in demonstrating how theological and nontheological influences coalesce in forming belief systems. By and large, our evidence leads to the conclusion that the role of orthodox beliefs in influencing so-called consequential variables, such as prejudice toward minorities and conservative attitudes toward the church's social responsibilities, is easily exaggerated. Controlling for local community orientations, we found that the correlations reduced substantially between literal, orthodox beliefs and conservative, cultural attitudes. Not that the influence of beliefs was unimportant, but rather localism emerged as a stronger determinant of provincial and authoritarian views than doctrinal orthodoxy. Moreover, both beliefs and attitudes appear to covary with breadth of perspective, lending support to the possibility of a nontheological interpretation.

But subjective religious commitments involve more than literal, supernatural conceptions, as we discovered in looking at intrinsic religious meanings. We found that among cosmopolitans the meaning components of commitment were more important than the belonging. Their ability to transcend local custom and outlook facilitates a concern for pursuing the religious and ethical implications of faith. Given their more constrained belief systems, many extrinsic religious elements are discarded in favor of searching for religious truth and applying religious teachings to life.

Viewed as a whole, this last set of findings bears serious implications for liberal Protestantism. Among other things it suggests that broadened perspectives are a source of *both* religious and attitudinal change. Cosmopolitanism fosters a concern for intrinsic religious meanings and ethically constrained belief systems that in turn, nurture liberal social views and activist concerns about the church's social and political involvements. Given the composition of the liberal churches, especially their middle and upper-middle social class and highly educated clientele, it is understandable why these churches are riddled with institutional conflicts over social issues. The social orientations of many of these members generate strong ethical sentiments, which places them directly in opposition to conservative traditionalists. The disputes and disagreements that surface reflect not simply a lack of consensus over church priorities, but deep-seated and divergent value conflicts. So deep and pervasive are these value differences, in fact, that at bottom the liberal church's most serious institutional dilemma is its inability to unite members around a common goal and purpose.

GENERALIZABILITY OF THE FINDINGS

How confident are we of the results? Obviously the data base is limited. We have a sample of slightly less than five hundred Episcopalians all residing in North Carolina. This is hardly a sufficient sample from which to generalize about liberal Protestants, or for that matter about even Episcopalians in this country. Not only a more representative sample but also one including members of other Protestant denominations is needed for further inquiry.

From the very outset, however, our concern was not so much to generalize as to explore the divergent cultural styles of locals and cosmopolitans. Whatever the limitations of our data, we have sought to compensate for these by means of careful and systematic inquiry into a wide range of topics important to the study of religion. Our intent was to examine empirically issues arising out of a cultural perspective of liberal Protestantism's dilemma. In this respect it is in keeping with Martin E. Marty's interpretation of value conflicts between cultural traditionalists and cultural modernists as one of the major themes for mainline Protestantism throughout this century.[2] Similarly, it is akin to Dean R. Hoge's Presbyterian study wherein he suggests that the liberal churches are undergoing problems currently because they are "positioned between two world views"—pointing to the fact that they are caught in the middle trying to accommodate traditional religious as well as secular cultures.[3] Implied is a twin-culture interpretation of the religious problems, emphasizing the seriousness of the cultural gap confronting these institutions today.

The present study takes seriously this twin-culture interpretation and has sought to develop it further by means of the local-cosmopolitan framework. This latter provides a paradigm for gaining clarity on the cultural differences that beset contemporary Protestantism and for understanding the social dynamics that occur in religious institutions. Viewed in this way, ability to generalize the findings is not as important a concern as is the provocativeness of our in-depth analysis for further study of these cultural strains. Similar studies are needed in other denominations, in order to see if our description of local-cosmopolitan social differences in the Episcopal Church applies elsewhere. With additional studies of this kind, we should at some point be able to assess better the generalizability of our paradigm for liberal Protestantism.

IMPLICATIONS FOR LIBERAL
PROTESTANTISM

Even with our limited data, we gain perspective on several issues of interest concerning the liberal Protestant churches and their future in contemporary American society. On this score our line of analysis seems especially promising—if not for questions answered, at least for questions raised. There are two broad issues especially important, both of which deserve far more attention in future investigations into religious commitment. One is the role of plausibility structures, and the other the importance of residential locality.

Protestantism and Plausibility Structures

Throughout the study we have been concerned with the importance of plausibility structures for church religion today. We need not review here the definition of such structures, or their fundamental functions for religion; however, we may find it helpful to quote from Dean M. Kelley the following:

> . . . . the meanings which religion provides gain their validity from a continuing group experience: they do not stand alone, in the abstract, nor above human prehension. Religious meaning doesn't "take" unless it is transmitted from one person to another, vouchsafed by the commitment of the bearer. From this point of view, there is no such thing as individual or instant or disembodied religion.[4]

Kelley's point is that despite the proclivities of individuals, essentially religion is a shared experience. By this he means not simply that religious services and activities are organized as group phenomena; but instead that *systems of meaning, religious or otherwise, fulfill their functions of ordering experience and of world building in a social context in which people share their perceptions, and interact with one another on the basis of these shared definitions of reality*. This context of shared experience—no matter whether found in a religious congregation, a suburban neighborhood, an ethnic group, or wherever—is what constitutes a plausibility structure.

Probably less is known about how such structures function in the liberal Protestant churches than in any religious groups. The boundaries of social interaction and shared experience are firmly established in sects and cults, and also in more subtle ways in conservative Protestant churches. American Catholicism continues to benefit somewhat from its immigrant heritage and ethnic communalism, although this is rapidly undergoing change.[5] Likewise, American Judaism encompasses strong ethnic loyalties, more ethnic in fact than religious in the traditional Jewish sense.[6] But the mainline Protestant churches, compared with these other institutions, are far less encapsulated as religious groups. Their theology does not justify building walls between the believer and the larger society; nor do they enjoy as great a benefit from self-contained natural communities, such as ethnic or minority groups. To be sure, many of these church members enjoy the communalities of upper-middle-class life as evidenced by similar life-styles, affluence, and individual as well as family status symbols. Yet social class has not proven to be as strong a religious support structure for this wing of Protestantism as it has among conservatives. Liberal Protestants seek out others of similar class standing as friends and confidants, but they simply develop fewer such ties in their own congregations than do conservative, lower-status Protestants.[7]

In the past there was also little reason to study Protestantism's social infrastructures. American Protestantism historically has been a majority group, with the result that Protestant identity was regarded as almost synonymous with American identity. Obviously this is no longer the case, and increasingly we confront the fact of a pluralist society where white Protestants are becoming more and more conscious of themselves as one among several religious identities. "Protestantism in America today," wrote Will Herberg almost twenty years ago, "presents the anomaly of a strong majority group with a growing minority consciousness."[8] In the years since Protestant consciousness as a minority has increased, especially among those with strong religious group ties and who maintain commitment to their churches.

In his *White Protestant Americans*, Charles H. Anderson observes that by far the largest differences in Protestant communal orientation are between churchgoing and nonchurchgoing Protestants.[9] Strong differences also exist between church conservatives and liberals. Protestant intellectuals and academics are known to have weak ties to the religious

210

community, more so probably than those with Catholic backgrounds.[10] All these observations indicate that in the liberal Protestant church context, *white Protestant group consciousness is strongest for a declining number of highly committed, tradition-oriented members*. These are the Protestants most likely to think of themselves as becoming a religious minority in American society and who are most concerned to preserve the Protestant heritage.

As this happens the issue of plausibility structures becomes more and more important. Already there appears to be a direct connection between Protestant communalism and religiosity. If the trends now set in motion continue into the future, we can anticipate that these relations will become even stronger. Protestant associational and communal ties—including friendships, organizational participation, and intermarriage—should all become more important in creating a supportive social climate for religious beliefs and sentiments. Future research will need to explore these and determine more exactly the role they play in aiding Protestant church members in maintaining a religious faith. If it is also true, as we have argued, that reference orientations are highly significant for liberal Protestants, then more attention should be given to these social psychological considerations. Because liberal Protestants lack institutional mechanisms regulating social interaction, their own subjective predispositions and choices of reference groups become extremely important. Further explorations of these psychological mechanisms and especially of their relation to Protestant group participation should enhance our understanding of how traditional religion will persist in the future.

Residential Locality and Religion

In this study we have examined one such plausibility structure—the local residential community as a reference group for religious commitment. Our attention was focused primarily upon the dynamics of belief system maintenance and the changing modes of belief and participation in contemporary society. Underlying the social psychological dynamics, however, was a basic assumption that residential communities increasingly serve as significant social bases for traditional religion.

For despite the fact that the world is becoming increasingly cos-

211

mopolitan, it is also true that most people carry out their lives primarily within local communities. Here it is the vast majority of Americans grow up, choose their mates, find work, establish friendships, and develop and maintain institutional ties. In their daily routines, their comings and goings ordinarily do not take them far from their residences. Improvements in transportation have increased the distances traveled but not as much, perhaps, as one might think. As Peter H. Rossi points out, the daily lives of most Americans are still lived within a fifty-mile radius of their homes.[11] The persistence of strong local community orientations in the much-heralded mass society is itself evidence of the importance of these social bonds. They indicate two things: one, the fact that people's daily lives are acted out largely within the confines of community-based networks of interaction; and two, that residential localities serve as significant reference groups for their behaviors and attitudes. Both are important in understanding how vast numbers of Americans think, the standards against which they evaluate themselves, and the extent to which close-to-home loyalties command their respect and commitment.

And in both of these respects, there is reason to expect that religion benefits enormously. Organized religion has always depended on a relatively stable interactive network as a means of implementing religious values in everyday life. Its reliance upon preexisting communal structures is well illustrated by the parish system—the Christian ecclesiastical structure so common in the West, organized on a territorial basis. Parishes in the strict sense do not exist today as they once did, but the communal dynamics function much the same. Religious congregations, organized on the basis of voluntary choice and support, rely directly upon a local community clientele. In places where residential locality bonds are strong, these solidarities find expression in the religious community in the form of vitality and growth; but where they are weak or virtually nonexistent congregations decline and sometimes die, as has been the fate of many American inner-city churches over the past couple decades.

Aside from these more general considerations, residential localities are especially important to Protestantism in contemporary American life. Factors both of theological heritage and of contemporary social change account for this. Compared to Catholicism and Judaism, historically Protestantism in this country has more fully institutionalized principles of voluntarism and congregational autonomy. Its lack of a stronger sacramental and liturgical heritage, combined with the peculiarly American emphases of voluntarism and separation of church and state, led in the early days of the American experience to a view of congregations as "gathered" churches, or as religious fellowships endowed with local autonomy and lay control set apart from the society. But by the early decades of this century, mainline Protestant denominations had brushed aside much of this interpretation and embraced instead a more inclusive vision of the church and society coexisting together. This shift marked a transition in theological interpretation from "gathered" churches to "community" churches—that is, friendly fellowships open to all, organized to meet the needs of all those living nearby, and intended to give visible expression to the unity of the community.[12]

Not surprisingly, liberal Protestant identity in this country is inextricably bound up with the dominant cultural values. Achievement, career, family, small-town values, the American Way of Life—all these are fused with distinctively religious meanings. This has obviously been a mixed blessing. On the one hand, it has given Protestantism the character of an "established" church in American society, thereby making it possible to command a hearing and mount influence across broad sectors of the population. But on the other hand, it has meant that Protestantism has been most vulnerable to becoming a cultural religion and of losing its meaning as a transcendent faith. The liberal churches especially face this problem, as is evidenced by conflicts over church priorities and the wide variety of possible relations between the meaning and belonging functions of religion.

Recent social change has served to intensify and exacerbate these underlying Protestant tensions. Weakened ties to the residential community for many people and the resulting cultural cleavages between traditionalists and modernists make it extremely difficult for these churches to arrive at a synthesis of cultural meanings acceptable to all quarters. Traditionalists hold out for conventional values and world views, and modernists finding these implausible seek instead for new religious conceptions and identities. In all of this, it is clear that the locus of conflict is not simply theological but encompasses at a broader level tensions in the larger culture between traditional Christian and secular, scientific world views.

As the gulf between these two widens, it is conceivable that religious institutions will take on some new functions as well. Many individuals in modern society consciously choose to identify with their residentially based friends, organizations, and institutions. Compared with relations in the larger anonymous society, here they find the securities and supports necessary to their well-being and psychic balance. This being the case, it is not unreasonable to suppose that local communal bonds in Protestentism may serve important stabilizing functions. As religiously committed Protestants come to think of themselves more as a minority and as espousing values at odds with the larger secular order, belief systems extolling the virtues of traditional American culture may be helpful in adjusting to a rapidly changing society. The Protestant churches would seem to be well-suited for serving as a bridging institution, by providing for their members a familiar world of meaning and by helping them to deal with the complexities of a rapidly changing world.

PROSPECTS FOR THE CHURCHES

If our diagnosis of the current situation is correct, we can make some general predictions about the churches themselves—their future, their institutional styles, and their changing social and cultural characteristics. This is a risky matter, however, since the track record of social scientists in social forecasting is not very good. As often as not, social scientists miss the mark in their predictions.

But by venturing some predictions, we have opportunity to make very clear what is, and is not, expected on the basis of our theoretical perspective. Certainly there is no implication anywhere that liberal Protestant churches are about to fade from the scene. Many churches have of course suffered from membership loss and declining contributions, and many more will in the future. But rather than paint a gloomy picture of institutional decline, it is more helpful to describe the changing social conditions for the mainline churches and to draw

214

from this as many implications as possible. For after all, predictions of the church's demise, like those of the millennium to come, have to do with some far removed, future state of affairs, but do little in the way of bringing about a better understanding of the realities the churches face at present.

With this in mind, we offer four predictions concerning liberal Protestantism:

1. *These churches may experience even further declines in the years ahead, but they should persist indefinitely as cognitive-minority institutions.* Despite whatever new surges of life may come from the recent evangelical revival in some quarters, this will not likely alter trends in liberal church decline. At some point in the foreseeable future, however, the declines should stabilize as the churches adapt themselves to new social realities and concern themselves with preserving their theological heritage. Though they are likely to function increasingly as cognitive-minority institutions, this need not imply a sectarian conception of the church necessarily. Given their theological heritage and middle-class clientele it is doubtful these institutions would become anything like sects in the classical meaning of the term. More likely is the possibility that groups of highly committed traditionalists within the churches will come to resemble *ecclesiolae*—that is, small bands of strict and faithful believers amidst a larger congregation of casual, lukewarm members. The imagery of *ecclesiolae in ecclesia* (little churches within the church)[13] is suggestive. It points to a situation not only of high levels of traditional commitment on the part of some, but to the institutionalization of alternative levels of commitment within the church.

2. *Among committed members, communal ties should strengthen.* A growing Protestant minority consciousness will encourage within-group relations such as closer friendship patterns, organizational participation, and shared activities. Many members will begin to appreciate more deeply their relations with fellow believers and to discover common bonds with one another. As this happens, local community ties should increasingly overlap with the religious, thus serving to mutually reinforce one another and to provide a firm plausibility structure for traditional believers.

3. *As the active members of these churches become more traditional in*

outlook, they will likely espouse more conservative and provincial cultural attitudes. Increasing proportions of traditional, locally oriented members will encourage a culturally conservative and defensive posture. As a result there could be growing signs among rank-and-file members of intergroup prejudice, intolerance, and other forms of closed-mindedness. If this happens it will follow, of course, not from theology or even from the churches as such, but from the intensification of commitment to traditional values and ideology. Accordingly, the stance toward the church's role in public affairs will likely lean on the side of retreat and withdrawal rather than active involvement.

4. *Even though religious and cultural homogeneity may increase, liberal churches will continue as conflict-ridden institutions.* There are several reasons for thinking that conflict is endemic to these institutions. Because of their theological heritage and established social position, they draw into their ranks many who are disillusioned with other denominations and who seek a more relevant faith. This should continue as an attraction, though perhaps less so in the future as the churches become more conservative in character. Nonetheless, the cosmopolitan outlook on the part of many will continue to encourage the search for meaning as well as a liberal social ethic. Modern, secular influences will also continue to prompt reformulations of belief and to undermine traditional ways of believing. Ironically, these modernizing influences result in stronger instrinsic commitments to religious values but at the same time undercut commitment to the church as an institution. The churches are left with conservatives as their most active participants, but even so the potential for conflict is always present—as, for example, with controversies currently over abortion, homosexuality, and women's ordination. Both the clergy and progressive-minded laity are committed to liberal concerns, and hence conflicts are likely to surface whenever passions run high in the society and polarizations develop over issues of great importance.

These, then, are our predictions. Whether they prove to be correct or not, the fact is that liberal Protestantism's future will continue in the years ahead as a topic of considerable importance, and one that is closely linked to the American future. To a considerable extent, the future of this religious tradition depends on how successfully the churches can retain, and capitalize upon, a distinctive theological heritage in a time when the winds of change are blowing in a more conservative direction. If they can do this, there is the possibility of forging a new cultural synthesis attractive to larger segments of contemporary society, which might perhaps disprove our predictions. But if they cannot, the future as we have described it may be upon us sooner than we realize.

APPENDIX A
The Data

This appendix further discusses the data, focusing on sampling design, sample representativeness, response rate, and data collection procedures. In order not to complicate the general discussion in the Introduction, it seemed advisable to reserve these for discussion here:

Sampling Design   As a study of lay Episcopalians, 890 adult members from within the North Carolina Diocese were randomly selected to receive mail questionnaires. Members were systematically selected from the diocesan newsletter list. Since newsletters were mailed to all adult members without subscription from diocesan headquarters, this sampling procedure yielded a representative sample of church members from large and small churches and from rural and urban areas. The clergy were informed of the study but were not included in the sample.

Response Rate   Usable questionnaires were returned by 518 respondents. Discounting 28 errors in listing due to deaths and unknown addresses, this resulted in a response rate of 60 percent. For the present study, nonwhites were eliminated. Race was ruled out as a confounding factor since the research involved, in addition to religious beliefs and practices, racially salient items such as prejudice toward minorities and political ideology. With the non-whites eliminated, we have a final sample size of 486 white Episcopal lay members.

Representativeness   As pointed out in the Introduction, the sample was judged to be representative of the North Carolina Diocese. Our confidence in this follows from data gathered on nonrespondents some weeks after the general questionnaires were returned. In order to check on representativeness, a short follow-up questionnaire was sent to all members of the sample who failed to return the study questionnaire. This contained mainly social background questions providing us with some basis for comparing respondents and non-respondents. The follow-up questionnaire resulted in an additional 91 returns.

These data revealed only negligible differences between respondents and nonrespondents. On the variables of age, sex, level of education, and occupational type, differences between the two were statistically insignificant. With respect to rural-urban background, the respondents were slightly more inclined to come from larger cities. This difference, however, is hardly large enough to cause much alarm. Generally it would appear that any response bias resulting from lack of representativeness of the diocesan population would be quite minimal.

But how representative are these data of Episcopalians nationally? We really don't know. On several indicators, however, the sample statistics are roughly comparable to results obtained in other, nonsouthern surveys. For example, the proportion of Episcopalians who were previously affiliated with other denominations in this study is almost identical with that of a 1965 National Opinion Research Center survey. Whereas 45 percent of the NORC national sample were previously members of other churches, 44 percent had been so affiliated in the North Carolina sample. It should be noted, also, that many of the substantive findings reported in this research are very similar to, say, those of Glock and Stark in their many publications. Generally speaking, Episcopalians in the South are somewhat more inclined toward orthodox beliefs than are Episcopalians in Glock and Stark's northern California sample; but other differences between the two, such as church attendance, devotional practices, and parish friendships, are quite small.

To be sure, there is a regional religious culture which is distinctive in the South; and I would not try to argue that some regional biases probably surface in the present study. But it is easy to exaggerate such differences, especially when dealing with an established, upper-middle-class group like the Episcopalians. Even should biases exist these are far less serious, as was noted in the Introduction, in a study that is theoretical and analytic rather than primarily descriptive in focus. My intention is not to provide a descriptive profile of Episcopalians, but to examine a set of interrelationships among variables inferred from a theoretical framework which should hold across mainline Protestant groups.

Data Collection Procedures Opportunity for the present study developed in 1968 when sociologists at the University of North Carolina were sought by the research offices of the Episcopal Church to design and carry out a study evaluating a diocesan exchange program. The North Carolina Diocese had been involved in an exchange relationship with another diocese, and thus the study was aimed at collecting a large body of data pertaining to the attitudes and behaviors of church members.

The questionnaire instrument was designed, pretested, and mailed to respondents by the sociologists, but authorization for the study was from the Church. Members throughout the diocese were informed of the study (though not of its specific details), and a letter from the presiding bishop of the diocese was mailed along with the questionnaire to all respondents. Whether such authorization and request for cooperation had any biasing effects, and if so how, are unknown.

The cover letter on the questionnaire was written by the sociologists (see Appendix C). The questionnaire was lengthy, and perhaps for this reason the response rate was not higher. Nevertheless many respondents indicated that filling out the questionnaire was a learning experience, helping them learn much about their own beliefs and views. Questionnaires were mailed out in the spring of 1968, and after a month respondents not having returned theirs were sent a second plus a letter requesting their cooperation. Beyond that, only the short follow-up questionnaire was sent to nonrespondents.

APPENDIX B
Scale Construction

Described below are the measures and indexes used in the study. In addition to the scale items, shown as well are the coefficients describing the interrelations among them. Agree-disagree items were reflected where necessary in the scale construction.

Literal Orthodoxy   (starred responses indicate literal, orthodox beliefs)— Cronbach's *alpha* = .78.

God is:
*   *a. a powerful and sometimes wrathful judge of man's behavior
*   *b. a personal Being who watches over and cares for our lives
*   *c. the creator and ruler of the universe
*   d. the beauty and majesty of nature
*   e. that part of each person which is basically good
*   f. a kind of higher power or force in the world
*   g. ultimate or unconditional love

Jesus:
*   *a. Jesus was divine in the sense that he was in fact God living among men
*   *b. Jesus was divine in the sense that while he was only a man, he was uniquely called by God to reveal God's purpose to the world
*   c. Jesus was divine in the sense that he embodied the best that is in all men

d. Jesus was a great man and teacher, but I would not call him divine

e. Frankly, I'm not entirely sure there really was such a person

Bible:

    *a. The Bible was written by men inspired by God, but it contains factual errors

    *b. The Bible is God's Word and all that it says is factually true

    c. The Bible is valuable because it was written by wise and good men, but God has no more to do with it than he did with other great literature

Heaven and Hell:

    *a. physical places where all men live after judgment by God

    b. simply words that are used to express final rewards or punishments

    c. ways of speaking about man's acceptance of, or separation from, God

Devotionalism Pearson correlation = .52

Two items pertaining to frequency of personal prayer and frequency of Bible reading (every day, more than once a week, more than once a month, several times a year, seldom or never)

Importance of Faith, or Meaning-Salience (weighted responses indicated by numbers in parentheses)—Cronbach's alpha = .70

My religious faith is:

    (1) Only of minor importance for my life, compared to certain other aspects of my life

    (2) Important for my life, but no more important than certain other aspects of my life

    (3) Of central importance for my life, and would, if necessary come before all other aspects of my life

Everyone must make many important decisions during his life, such as which occupation to pursue, that goals to strive for, whom to vote for, what to teach one's children, etc. When you have made, or do make decisions such as these, to what extent do you make the decisions on the basis of your religious faith?

    (1) I seldom if ever base such decision on religious faith

    (2) I sometimes base such decisions on my religious faith but definitely not most of the time

    (3) I feel that most of my important decisions are based on my religious faith, but usually in a general, unconscious way

    (4) I feel that most of my important decisions are based on my religious faith, and I usually consciously attempt to make them so

Without my religious faith, the rest of my life would not have much meaning to it (agree-disagree)

Belonging-Salience (single item)

All in all, how important would you say your church membership is to you?

Fairly unimportant
Not too important
Fairly important
Quite important
Extremely important

Doubt   Average Pearson intercorrelation = .61

Six items tapping frequency of doubt (never, sometimes, often, don't believe in) with respect to: Existence of God, Divinity of Jesus, Eternal Life, Biblical Miracles, Virgin Birth, and Final Day of Judgment

Church Activism   Average Pearson intercorrelation = .53

A minister who participates in social controversies such as the civil rights movement should generally be supported by his church (agree-disagree)

The church should stick with religious matters and not get involved in social and economic issues (agree-disagree)

An ideal religion . . . includes involvement in social and political issues of the day (agree-disagree)

Ecumenism   Pearson correction = .67

The Episcopal Church should resist mergers with other Protestant denominations in the United States (agree-disagree)

It would be wonderful if the Catholic Church and the Protestant denominations could eventually combine to form one large Christian church (agree-disagree)

Political Intolerance   Average Pearson intercorrelation = .54

The best way to stop rioting in the streets is to give the police more power (agree-disagree)

Government should have the right to prohibit certain groups of persons who disagree with our form of government from holding orderly public meetings (agree-disagree)

The U.S. should give assistance to the poorer countries of the world even if those countries remain politically neutral (agree-disagree)

Racism Average Pearson intercorrelation = .60
  The Federal Government should stay out of the question of whether white and Negro children go to the same school (agree-disagree)
  White people have a right to live in all-white neighborhoods if they want to (agree-disagree)
  If Negroes are not getting fair treatment in jobs and housing, the government should see to it they do (agree-disagree)

Social Distance Items (Negroes, Jews, Catholics)
  "marry into the group"
  "welcome as a member of a social club"
  "have as next door neighbors"
  "work in same office"
  "have as speaking acquaintance only"
  "avoid all contact"

Americanism Average Pearson intercorrelation = .68
  To be a really good American, a person must believe in God (agree-disagree)
  A healthy democracy does not necessarily require that its citizens believe in God (agree-disagree)
  It doesn't matter which church one belongs to, but whether he believes in God or not (agree-disagree)

Conventional Values Average Pearson intercorrelation = .45
  Premarital sexual intercourse is always wrong (agree-disagree)
  The older a person grow the more respect he should be given (agree-disagree)
  A person should generally consider the needs of his parental family as a whole more important than his own needs (agree-disagree)

Anomie Average Pearson intercorrelation = .42
  It often seems as if there's not much point in life (agree-disagree)
  In spite of what people say, the lot of the average man is getting worse, not better (agree-disagree)
  These days a person doesn't really know whom he can count on (agree-disagree)
  There's little use writing to public officials because often they aren't interested in the problems of the average man (agree-disagree)

Achievement Motivation (single item)
  The extent of a man's ambition to better himself is a pretty good indication of his character (agree-disagree)

APPENDIX C
The Episcopal Church Study Questionnaire

Dear Episcopalian:

The Episcopal Church recently asked us, as sociologists particularly interested in the study of religion, to conduct a research project designed to develop a better understanding of the beliefs, feelings, and activities of contemporary Episcopalians. This questionnaire is one of the major parts of this research effort.

To be certain that our findings from this questionnaire represent all of the different kinds of persons in the church today, we have drawn a random sample of Episcopalians from diocesan mailing lists. Your name was one of those drawn. As a result, we are asking you to assist us by completing this questionnaire and returning it to us in the enclosed, pre-paid envelope. The value of our results depends upon the cooperation of each and every person receiving a questionnaire.

Let us say a few words about the questionnaire.

First, you will be assured complete anonymity. No place in the questionnaire are you asked to indicate your name, nor is there any identifying code. We are only asking that you print your name on the enclosed post card and return it *separately* when you mail back your questionnaire.

Secondly, in preparing this questionnaire, we had to make a choice between a very limited number of questions, which would take only a few minutes to answer but which would provide only superficial information, or a longer, more thorough format. We decided that if the study is to be of real value, both to the church and to the development of social scientific knowledge about religion, the second alternative was necessary. We hope you will appreciate our decision, and we think you will find that the half-hour to an hour which will be required to complete the questionnaire will be time well-spent. The persons who have completed an earlier draft of the questionnaire told us that they found the experience not only interesting but personally rewarding.

Thirdly, it is very important that the person to whom this questionnaire was addressed be the one who fills it out. Only if that person is no longer living in the home or is not an Episcopalian should someone else in the family complete the questionnaire. (If this latter is the case, would you please so indicate at the end of the questionnaire.)

Finally, please ignore the small number in parentheses throughout the questionnaire. These are simply to help in tabulating the responses.

We hope you enjoy filling out the questionnaire and we thank you deeply for your cooperation.

ROBERT E. STAUFFER
W. CLARK ROOF
Department of Sociology
The University of North Carolina

PART I

To begin with we would like to ask you about your present religious participation and about your religious activities generally.

(A27)   1.   How long have you been a member of your present parish?
        (   ) Less than a year
        (   ) 1 to 2 years
        (   ) 3 to 5 years
        (   ) 6 to 10 years
        (   ) More than 10 years
        (   ) I have always been a member

2. Have you ever been a member of a denomination other than the Episcopal Church?

( ) Yes ( ) No

If "Yes", please answer Questions 2a and 2b; if "No", skip to Question 3.

2a. What denomination were you a member of? (If more than one, indicate the most recent in (a), the second most recent in (b), etc.

(a) _____

(b) _____

(c) _____

2b. I affiliated with the Episcopal Church because: (If more than one, rank in order of importance with numbers 1, 2, 3, etc.)

( ) My children were attending this church.

( ) My spouse was a member of this denomination.

( ) It was the church nearest my home.

( ) Many of my friends belong to this denomination.

( ) This denomination fits in better with my present work and manner of life.

( ) The doctrines of this denomination best matched my own religious beliefs.

( ) Other reasons (Please specify) _____

_____

3. All in all, how important would you say your church membership is to you (Check one).

( ) Fairly unimportant

( ) Not too important

( ) Fairly important

( ) Quite important

( ) Extremely important

4. How often do you attend Sunday worship services? (Check one)

( ) Every week

( ) Nearly every week

( ) About three time a month

( ) About two times a month

(   ) About once a month
(   ) About every two or three months
(   ) Once or twice a year
(   ) Never

(36)   5.   Compared with five years ago, would you say you attend worship services today more, less, or about the same? (Check one)
(   ) Attend more now than five years ago.
(   ) Attend less now.
(   ) Attend the same.

(37)   6.   How well do you think you fit in with the group of people who make up your church congregation? (Check one)
(   ) I really don't fit in too well with this group.
(   ) I fit in, but not too well.
(   ) I fit in fairly well.
(   ) I fit in very well.

(38-41)   7.   In column A below, please list all church organizations, groups, or activities in which you participate, such as choir, woman's clubs, boards, etc. (If none, check here (   ) and skip to Question 8)

In column B, please indicate how many out of the last five meetings of each of these you have attended.

In column C, please indicate whether or not you have ever held an office in these organizations.

A (Name) (List)	B (Meetings Attended) (Circle Number)	C (Ever an Officer) (Circle)
(1)_____	1 2 3 4 5	Yes No
(2)_____	1 2 3 4 5	Yes No
(3)_____	1 2 3 4 5	Yes No
(4)_____	1 2 3 4 5	Yes No
(5)_____	1 2 3 4 5	Yes No

(42)   8.   Would you say you are more active, less active, or about the same in church activities now compared with five years ago? (Check one)
(   ) More active now than five years ago.

228

(   ) Less active now.

(   ) About the same.

9.   Think of your four closest friends. (Do *not* count relatives, persons living in other parts of the country, or the spouses of your friends). How many are members of your parish out of the four?

(   ) None

(   ) One

(   ) Two

(   ) Three

(   ) Four

(44-48)   10.   Approximately how often do you engage in each of the following activities? (Check one for each activity)

	Every Day	More Than Once a Week	More Than Once a Month	Several Times a Year	Seldom or Never
A. Have personal prayer	( )	( )	( )	( )	( )
B. Read the Bible	( )	( )	( )	( )	( )
C. Read religious literature	( )	( )	( )	( )	( )
D. Have family devotions	( )	( )	( )	( )	( )
E. Discuss religious matters with friends	( )	( )	( )	( )	(')

(49)   11.   Approximately what percentage of your total (gross) family income do you give to support your church generally? (Check one)

(   ) Less than 1 percent.

(   ) About 1 to 2 per cent.

(   ) About 3 to 5 per cent.

(   ) About 6 to 8 per cent.

(   ) About 9 to 10 per cent.

(   ) More than 10 per cent.

12. Has the percentage of your financial support, relative to your income, changed in the last five years for either (1) General parish budget, or (2) Additional Contributions?

(1) General Parish budget   (2) Additional contributions

(   ) Increased   (   ) Increased considerably
      'considerably   (   ) Increased somewhat
(   ) Increased   (   ) Decreased somewhat
      slightly   (   ) Decreased considerably
(   ) Decreased   (   ) About the same
      considerably
(   ) About the same

(52) 13. Thinking back to when you were a child, approximately how often did you attend Sunday Services and/or Church School? (Check one)

(   ) Every week.
(   ) Nearly every week.
(   ) About three times a month.
(   ) About two times a month.
(   ) About once a month.
(   ) About every two or three months.
(   ) About once or twice a year.
(   ) Seldom or never.

(53) 14. My religious faith is: (Check one)

(   ) Important for my life, but no more important than certain other aspects of my life.
(   ) Only of minor importance for my life, compared to certain other aspects of my life.
(   ) Of central importance for my life, and would, if necessary come before all other aspects of my life.

(54-59) 15. Many religious people today have doubts about some of their religious beliefs; others, of course, do not. Please indicate whether you never, sometimes, or often doubt each of the following beliefs, or whether you don't hold the belief at all.

	Never Doubt	Some-times Doubt	Often Doubt	Don't Believe In
The existence of God	( )	( )	( )	( )
The Divinity of Jesus	( )	( )	( )	( )
Eternal Life	( )	( )	( )	( )
The Miracles described in the Bible	( )	( )	( )	( )
The Virgin Birth	( )	( )	( )	( )
The Final Day of Judgment	( )	( )	( )	( )

(60) 16. Thinking back over your life with regard to your belief or doubt about God's existence, indicate which of the following best applies to your experience. (Check one)

(　) I have never doubted that God exists.

(　) I have occasionally questioned but never really doubted God's existence.

(　) I have gone through a period of very real doubt about God's existence but no longer hold such doubts.

(　) I often doubt that God exists, but feel such doubt is part of a mature religious faith.

(　) I often doubt that God exists and feel this doubt has weakened my religious faith.

(　) As noted above, I don't believe that God exists.

(61-63) 17. There are, of course, many ideas concerning the *nature of God*. Please indicate which of the following comes closest to expressing *your* idea of God's nature. Select as many alternatives as you wish, but *if you choose more than one please place a "1" next to the alternative which is most central to your conception of God, a "2" next to the alternative which is second most central, and so on.* God is:

(　) A powerful and sometimes wrathful judge of man's behavior.

(　) A personal Being who watches over and cares for our lives.

(　) The creator and ruler of the universe.

(　) The beauty and majesty of nature.

(　) That part of each person which is basically good

231

( ) A kind of higher power or force in the world.
( ) Ultimate or unconditional love.
( ) I do not believe God exists.

(64) 18. Various persons having differing conceptions of Jesus. Some say he was divine, but they may differ with regard to what this means. Others do not believe that Jesus was divine, although they may still attribute great importance to him. Please indicate which *one* of the following statements is closest to *your* conception of Jesus. (Check one)

( ) Jesus was divine in the sense that he was in fact God living among men.

( ) Jesus was divine in the sense that while he was only a man, he was uniquely called by God to reveal God's purpose to the world.

( ) Jesus was divine in the sense that he embodied the best that is in all men.

( ) Jesus was a great man and teacher, but I would not call him divine.

( ) Frankly, I'm not entirely sure there really was such a person.

(65) 19. Again, there are several different ideas which various persons hold regarding eternal life. Please indicate which one of the following comes closest to *your* conception of eternal life. (Check one)

( ) Eternal life refers to life with God in heaven after death.

( ) Eternal life refers to some kind of non-earthly existence after death but probably not in a heaven.

( ) Eternal life refers to one's soul returning to earth to live in another body.

( ) Eternal life refers not to life after physical death, but rather to a "rebirth" in this life through faith in God.

( ) Eternal life refers to the on-going influence one exerts after death through his children, friends, and deeds.

( ) I don't believe in eternal life.

(66) 20. The word *soul* is also given various meanings by persons. Which of the following best fits your definition of the soul? (Check one)

232

(   ) A part of man that lives after death.

(   ) Another word for conscience.

(   ) A way of speaking about a man as a religious creature standing before God.

(   ) I feel that the word "soul" is a meaningless concept.

(67)   21.   Similarly, which of the following descriptions best matches your understanding of the word *Devil*? (Check one)

(   ) A symbol of the world's separation from God.

(   ) The moving force of evil in the world.

(   ) A physical being which the Bible tells us about.

(   ) I feel the word "Devil" is a meaningless concept.

(68)   22.   The words *heaven* and *hell* are also a part of traditional religious language. Which of the following best fits your understanding of the meaning of these words? (Check one)

(   ) Physical places where all men live after judgment by God.

(   ) Simply words that are used to express final reward or punishment.

(   ) Ways of speaking about man's acceptance of, or separation from, God.

(   ) These words have no meaning for me.

(69)   23.   Here are statements which have been made about the Bible. Please indicate which *one* is closest to your own view.

(   ) The Bible was written by men inspired by God, but it contains factual errors.

(   ) The Bible is God's word and all that it says is factually true.

(   ) The Bible is valuable because it was written by wise and good men, but God had no more to do with it than he did with other great literature.

(70)   24.   Church mission work can take many directions. Please indicate from the following what you feel the chief aim of church mission work should be. (Check one)

(   ) To save those throughout the world who will be lost unless Christ is made known through the work of missionaries.

233

(   ) To give financial support to those less fortunate than us.

(   ) To enter into a mutual relationship with people elsewhere in the world so as to build understanding and cooperatively engage in God's work.

(   ) To improve the well-being of people by giving them new and improved methods of agriculture, industry, education, and health.

(   ) I don't feel the church should be involved in foreign mission work of any type.

PART II

Below are a series of statements on current affairs and other matters with which some people agree and some disagree. We are interested in how you feel. Even if you have not thought about some of these statements before, please indicate the response which is most consistent with your general outlook.

(B27)   1.   The Church should stick with religious matters and not get involved in social and economic issues.
     (   ) Agree Strongly   (   ) Agree Somewhat
     (   ) Disagree Somewhat   (   ) Disagree Strongly

(28)   2.   There's little use writing to public officials because often they aren't interested in the problems of the average man.
     (   ) Agree Strongly   (   ) Agree Somewhat
     (   ) Disagree Somewhat   (   ) Disagree Strongly

(29)   3.   Big cities may have their place but the local community is the backbone of America.
     (   ) Agree Strongly   (   ) Agree Somewhat
     (   ) Disagree Somewhat   (   ) Disagree Strongly

(30)   4.   The Federal Government should stay out of the question of whether white and Negro children go to the same school.

( ) Agree Strongly ( ) Agree Somewhat
( ) Disagree Somewhat ( ) Disagree Strongly

(31) 5. Although some Jews are honest, in general Jews are dishonest in their business dealings.
( ) Agree Strongly ( ) Agree Somewhat
( ) Disagree Somewhat ( ) Disagree Strongly

(32) 6. To be a really good American, a person must believe in God.
( ) Agree Strongly ( ) Agree Somewhat
( ) Disagree Somewhat ( ) Disagree Strongly

(33) 7. Despite all the newspaper and TV coverage, national and international happenings rarely seem as interesting as events that occur right in the local community in which one lives.
( ) Agree Strongly ( ) Agree Somewhat
( ) Disagree Somewhat ( ) Disagree Strongly

(34) 8. In spite of what people say, the lot of the average man is getting worse, not better.
( ) Agree Strongly ( ) Agree Somewhat
( ) Disagree Somewhat ( ) Disagree Strongly

(35) 9. The U.S. should give assistance to the poorer countries of the world even if those countries remain politically neutral.
( ) Agree Strongly ( ) Agree Somewhat
( ) Disagree Somewhat ( ) Disagree Strongly

(36) 10. A healthy democracy does not necessarily require that its citizens believe in God.
( ) Agree Strongly ( ) Agree Somewhat
( ) Disagree Somewhat ( ) Disagree Strongly

(37) 11. When it comes to choosing someone for a responsible public office in my community, I prefer a person whose family is known and well-established.
( ) Agree Strongly ( ) Agree Somewhat
( ) Disagree Somewhat ( ) Disagree Strongly

(38) 12. The best way to stop rioting in the streets is to give the police more power.
(   ) Agree Strongly   (   ) Agree Somewhat
(   ) Disagree Somewhat   (   ) Disagree Strongly

(39) 13. A person who does not believe in God should not be permitted to teach in our public schools.
(   ) Agree Strongly   (   ) Agree Somewhat
(   ) Disagree Somewhat   (   ) Disagree Strongly

(40) 14. These days a person doesn't really know whom he can count on.
(   ) Agree Strongly   (   ) Agree Somewhat
(   ) Disagree Somewhat   (   ) Disagree Strongly

(41) 15. White people have a right to live in all-white neighborhoods if they want to.
(   ) Agree Strongly   (   ) Agree Somewhat
(   ) Disagree Somewhat   (   ) Disagree Strongly

(42) 16. The most rewarding organizations a person can belong to are the large, state and nation-wide associations rather than local community clubs and activities.
(   ) Agree Strongly   (   ) Agree Somewhat
(   ) Disagree Somewhat   (   ) Disagree Strongly

(43) 17. A minister who participates in social controversies such as the civil rights movement should generally be supported by his parish.
(   ) Agree Strongly   (   ) Agree Somewhat
(   ) Disagree Somewhat   (   ) Disagree Strongly

(44) 18. If Negroes are not getting fair treatment in jobs and housing, the government should see to it that they do.
(   ) Agree Strongly   (   ) Agree Somewhat
(   ) Disagree Somewhat   (   ) Disagree Strongly

(45) 19. The extent of a man's ambition to better himself is a pretty good indication of his character.
(   ) Agree Strongly   (   ) Agree Somewhat
(   ) Disagree Somewhat   (   ) Disagree Strongly

20. It would be wonderful if the Catholic Church and the Protestant denominations could eventually combine to form one large Christian church.
( ) Agree Strongly ( ) Agree Somewhat
( ) Disagree Somewhat ( ) Disagree Strongly

21. Without my religious faith, the rest of my life would not have much meaning to it.
( ) Agree Strongly ( ) Agree Somewhat
( ) Disagree Somewhat ( ) Disagree Strongly

22. Most people are inclined to look out more for themselves than for others.
( ) Agree Strongly ( ) Agree Somewhat
( ) Disagree Somewhat ( ) Disagree Strongly

23. Government should have the right to prohibit certain group of persons who disagree with our form of government from holding orderly public meetings.
( ) Agree Strongly ( ) Agree Somewhat
( ) Disagree Somewhat ( ) Disagree Strongly

PART III

"Being religious" no doubt means different things to different people. We are interested in what you think it means to be religious. Please place a "1" next to the alternative which *comes closest* to what you think and a "2" by the alternative which is second closest to what you think.

1. To be religious means:
( ) To participate regularly in the activities of one's church.
( ) To continually search for the ultimate meaning of life.
( ) To be a person who is thoughtful of others.
( ) To worship God through prayer and meditation.
( ) To make one's life a good example for other people.
( ) To actively work to promote social justice for all men.

2. Please indicate how important each of the following characteristics would be to you in an ideal religion. For each characteristic, check whether it would be very important, somewhat important, of low importance, or irrelevant.

| | How Important | | | |
	Very	Some-what	Low	Irrel-evant
a. Provides salvation or redemption of the soul	( )	( )	( )	( )
b. Provides intellectual clarity about the fundamental problems of living.	( )	( )	( )	( )
c. Provides a solid basis for family life	( )	( )	( )	( )
d. Includes involvement in social and political issues of the day	( )	( )	( )	( )
e. Includes belief in God	( )	( )	( )	( )
f. Provides a strong community feeling or closeness with your fellow men	( )	( )	( )	( )
g. Provides a focus for personal adjustment and development	( )	( )	( )	( )
h. Includes a church and clergy	( )	( )	( )	( )
i. Not in conflict with rational scientific premises and laws	( )	( )	( )	( )
j. Provides welfare services and material aid for people who need them	( )	( )	( )	( )
k. Includes prayer and worship	( )	( )	( )	( )
l. Provides explicit rules for moral conduct	( )	( )	( )	( )

3. Everyone must make many important decisions during his life, such as which occupation to pursue, what goals to strive for,

whom to vote for, what to teach one's children, etc. When you have made or do make decisions such as these, to what extent do you make the decisions on the basis of your religious faith? (Check one)

(   ) I seldom if ever base such decisions on religious faith.

(   ) I sometimes base such decisions on my religious faith but definitely not most of the time.

(   ) I feel that most of my important decisions are based on my religious faith, but usually in a general, unconscious way.

(   ) I feel that most of my important decisions are based on my religious faith, and I usually consciously attempt to make them so.

(65) 4. Since you became an adult, has anyone who was very close to you (either a relative or a close friend) died or been killed?
(   ) Yes   (   ) No

If "Yes", please continue with Questions 4a and 4b; if "No", skip to Question 5.

(66) 4a. What was the effect of this death on your religious beliefs? (Check one)

(   ) My religious beliefs were strengthened because of the comfort they gave me during this tragedy.

(   ) This death had little or no effect on my religious beliefs.

(   ) My religious beliefs were weakened because I couldn't imagine a loving God allowing this death to happen.

(67) 4b. Was the death: (Check one)

(   ) A "natural" death resulting from old age?

(   ) An unexpected death of someone who would have had many years yet to live?

(68-70) 5. Listed below are the names of various kinds of groups of people. Also listed (across the top) are various kinds of social contacts people can have with one another. Thinking of the typical members of each group, please check as many of the types of contact you would be willing to have with each group.

239

		Would Marry Into Group	Would Welcome As Fellow Member of Social Club	Would Have as Next Door Neighbors	Would Work in Same Office	Have as Speaking Acquaintances Only	Would Avoid All Contact
a.	Jews	( )	( )	( )	( )	( )	( )
b.	Methodists	( )	( )	( )	( )	( )	( )
c.	Africans	( )	( )	( )	( )	( )	( )
d.	Atheists	( )	( )	( )	( )	( )	( )
e.	Mexicans	( )	( )	( )	( )	( )	( )
f.	Englishmen	( )	( )	( )	( )	( )	( )
g.	Panamanians	( )	( )	( )	( )	( )	( )
h.	Liberals	( )	( )	( )	( )	( )	( )
i.	Negroes	( )	( )	( )	( )	( )	( )
j.	Communists	( )	( )	( )	( )	( )	( )
k.	Conservatives	( )	( )	( )	( )	( )	( )
l.	Catholics	( )	( )	( )	( )	( )	( )
m.	Orientals	( )	( )	( )	( )	( )	( )

PART IV

Here are some more statements about life, religion, and society with which some persons agree and others disagree. Again, please indicate how you feel about each of them by checking the appropriate response.

(71) 1. Members of the same family should hold similar religious beliefs.

( ) Agree Strongly ( ) Agree Somewhat
( ) Disagree Somewhat ( ) Disagree Strongly

(72) 2. Rural and small town life is basically man's best from of living, especially for rearing children.

( ) Agree Strongly ( ) Agree Somewhat
( ) Disagree Somewhat ( ) Disagree Strongly

3. Most businessmen can no longer feel pride in having made the product which their company sells.
( ) Agree Strongly   ( ) Agree Somewhat
( ) Disagree Somewhat   ( ) Disagree Strongly

4. Premarital sexual intercourse is always wrong.
( ) Agree Strongly   ( ) Agree Somewhat
( ) Disagree Somewhat   ( ) Disagree Strongly

5. The older a person grows the more respect he should be given.
( ) Agree Strongly   ( ) Agree Somewhat
( ) Disagree Somewhat   ( ) Disagree Strongly

6. The Episcopal Church should resist mergers with other Protestant denominations in the United States.
( ) Agree Strongly   ( ) Agree Somewhat
( ) Disagree Somewhat   ( ) Disagree Strongly

7. What the majority of youth do today is no worse than what their parents and their parent's parents did.
( ) Agree Strongly   ( ) Agree Somewhat
( ) Disagree Somewhat   ( ) Disagree Strongly

8. Life in the city is essentially corrupt and immoral.
( ) Agree Strongly   ( ) Agree Somewhat
( ) Disagree Somewhat   ( ) Disagree Strongly

9. Labor unions generally do more harm than good.
( ) Agree Strongly   ( ) Agree Somewhat
( ) Disagree Somewhat   ( ) Disagree Strongly

10. The religious doctrine of the Episcopal Church today is generally out of touch with the way persons like myself think about life and meaning.
( ) Agree Strongly   ( ) Agree Somewhat
( ) Disagree Somewhat   ( ) Disagree Strongly

11. The government that rules the least is best.
( ) Agree Strongly   ( ) Agree Somewhat
( ) Disagree Somewhat   ( ) Disagree Strongly

12. Businessmen should not be condemned if they sometimes hedge the truth slightly in their business activities.
( ) Agree Strongly ( ) Agree Somewhat
( ) Disagree Somewhat ( ) Disagree Strongly

13. A person should generally consider the needs of his parental family as a whole more important than his own needs.
( ) Agree Strongly ( ) Agree Somewhat
( ) Disagree Somewhat ( ) Disagree Strongly

14. Government is really a voice for the wealthy and those already in power.
( ) Agree Strongly ( ) Agree Somewhat
( ) Disagree Somewhat ( ) Disagree Strongly

15. It often seems as if there's not much point in life.
( ) Agree Strongly ( ) Agree Somewhat
( ) Disagree Somewhat ( ) Disagree Strongly

16. Today's cities have an attractiveness of their own.
( ) Agree Strongly ( ) Agree Somewhat
( ) Disagree Somewhat ( ) Disagree Strongly

17. In general, that which works or does what it is supposed to is good.
( ) Agree Strongly ( ) Agree Somewhat
( ) Disagree Somewhat ( ) Disagree Strongly

18. It usually seems that most things do turn out all right in the end.
( ) Agree Strongly ( ) Agree Somewhat
( ) Disagree Somewhat ( ) Disagree Strongly

19. It seems like life is becoming so confusing that it's hard to know what is right and what is wrong anymore.
( ) Agree Strongly ( ) Agree Somewhat
( ) Disagree Somewhat ( ) Disagree Strongly

242

20. It doesn't matter what church one belongs to, but whether he believes in God or not.

( ) Agree Strongly ( ) Agree Somewhat
( ) Disagree Somewhat ( ) Disagree Strongly

21. Denominational authorities in the Episcopal Church should allow local parishes more freedom to manage their own affairs.

( ) Agree Strongly ( ) Agree Somewhat
( ) Disagree Somewhat ( ) Disagree Strongly

22. Science will some day provide answers to nearly every question man can raise.

( ) Agree Strongly ( ) Agree Somewhat
( ) Disagree Somewhat ( ) Disagree Strongly

PART V

This is the last section of the questionnaire. Here we would like to know about some of the things you do and enjoy aside from religious activities, and to learn something of your personal history.

(53-72) 1. This question concerns the organizations and clubs you belong to. Below are listed various kinds of organizations. In the spaces in front of each kind of organization, *write in the number of organizations like this you belong to*. If none, mark 0.

( ) a. Fraternal Groups, such as Elks, Eagles, Masons, Knights of Columbus, Eastern Stars, the women's auxiliaries to groups like this, etc.

( ) b. Civic Organizations, such as Community Chest.

( ) c. Service Clubs, such as Lions, Rotary, Kiwanis, Jr. Chamber of Commerce, etc.

( ) d. Veterans and Military Groups, such as Military Reserves, the American Legion, VFW, Amvets, etc.

(   ) e.   Political Groups, such as Democratic or Republican clubs, and groups such as voter's leagues, etc.

(   ) f.   Civil Rights Groups, such as Urban League, NAACP, community human relations committee, etc.

(   ) g.   Labor Unions, such as International Typographical Union, Teamsters, etc.

(   ) h.   Sports Groups, such as bowling teams, bridge clubs, or sports sponsoring groups.

(   ) i.   School Service Groups, such as PTA, alumni associations, etc.

(   ) j.   Youth Groups, such as Boy Scouts, Girl Scouts, 4-H, etc. or assistance with such groups.

(   ) k.   Hobby or garden clubs, such as stamp or coin clubs, flower clubs, pet clubs, etc.

(   ) l.   School Fraternities or Sororities, such as Sigma Chi, Delta Gamma, etc.

(   ) m.   Nationality Groups, such as Sons of Norway, Liberian Society, etc.

(   ) n.   Farm Organizations, such as Farmer's Union, Farm Bureau, Grange, etc.

(   ) o.   Literary, Art, Discussion, or Study Clubs, such as book review clubs, theater groups, painting groups, etc.

(   ) p.   Professional Associations and societies, such as the American Dental Association, etc.

(   ) q.   Other Organizations, not listed above (Please write in)

(73-74)   2.   Think of the organization to which you belong which is *most important* to you. In the following space, write the letter of the category in which that organization was classified in the preceding question. (   )

(75)   3.   Not counting church organizations and activities, about how many times a month do you attend a meeting or other activity

connected with organizations to which you belong?

( ) 0 ( ) 1 ( ) 2 ( ) 3 ( ) 4
( ) 5 ( ) 6 ( ) 7 ( ) 8 ( ) 9

(76-80) 4. Have you ever traveled outside the United States?

( ) Yes ( ) No

If "Yes", continue with Question 4A; if "No", skip to Question 5

4a. Please indicate which part(s) of the world you have traveled to.

( ) Canada
( ) Central America
( ) South America
( ) Europe
( ) Africa
( ) Asia

(E27) 5. How many books have you read in the past year?

( ) 0 ( ) 1 ( ) 2 ( ) 3 ( ) 4
( ) 5-10 ( ) 11-20 ( ) More than 20

(28) 6. What kind of books were those mostly? (Check one)

( ) Did not read
( ) Fiction
( ) Biography
( ) Textbooks
( ) Religious
( ) Non-fiction (Other than types mention above)
( ) Poetry
( ) Other (Please Indicate _____

(29-35) 6a. Please indicate whether you have read any books or articles written by any of the following authors. (Check as many as apply)

( ) Paul Tillich
( ) Norman Vincent Peale
( ) Bishop John A. T. Robinson
( ) Reinhold Niebuhr
( ) Billy Graham
( ) Harvey Cox
( ) Dietrich Bonhoeffer

245

7. Which, if any, of the following magazines do you read regularly?
Check each one which you regularly read.

( ) Readers Digest   ( ) Your Diocesan
( ) Saturday Evening   Magazine
     Post   ( ) Cosmopolitan
( ) Ladies Home Journal ( ) The Episcopalian
( ) Time   ( ) National Review
( ) Newsweek   ( ) U.S. News and
( ) Saturday Review of   World Report
     Literature   ( ) Fortune
( ) Life   ( ) Playboy
( ) Look   ( ) Guidepost
( ) American Legion   ( ) Sports Illustrated
     Magazine   ( ) Ebony
( ) New Republic   ( ) Others (Please Indicate)
( ) Esquire

(48) 8. What is your present marital status?
( ) Married
( ) Widowed
( ) Separated
( ) Divorced
( ) Single

8a. If married, has your spouse previously been divorced?
( ) Yes ( ) No

(49) 9. How many children do you have? (   ) (If none, write 0)

(50-53) 10. Using the spaces provided below, indicate the age of each of
your children. Child 1 refers to your oldest child, and so on.
( ) Child 1   ( ) Child 5
( ) Child 2   ( ) Child 6
( ) Child 3   ( ) Child 7
( ) Child 4   ( ) Child 8
Write in additional ages if necessary

(54) 11. Please indicate how much formal education you have had.
(Please check the nearest answer)
( ) Some grade school.

        (   ) Finished grade school.
        (   ) Some high school.
        (   ) Finished high school.
        (   ) Technical, trade, or secretarial school.
        (   ) Some college.
        (   ) Finished college.
        (   ) Attended professional school after college.
        (   ) Attended graduate school after college.

If you attended college, continue with Questions 11a, 11b, and 11c.
If you did not attend college, skip to Question 12.

(55)   11a.   What is the name and location of the undergraduate college which you attended?

_____

(56)   1 b.   Which of the following best describes this college?
        (   ) Church-related
        (   ) Private, non-church related
        (   ) Public (that is, community or state supported)

(57)   11c.   When you were in college, what discipline or field did you major in? (e.g. history, chemistry, etc.)

_____

(58)   12.   Thinking back to the last school year attended (grade school, high school, or college), would you say that your grades tended to be: (Check one)
        (   ) Very good   (   ) Average
        (   ) Below average   (   ) Above average   (   ) Poor

(59)   13.   Were you born in this country? (   ) Yes   (   ) No

(60-61)   If No, then in what country were you born? _____

(62)   14.   In what part of the country were you raised? (If more than one part, check area where you lived the longest)
        (   ) The East or Northeast
        (   ) The South
        (   ) The Middle-West

247

(63-64)

(   ) The South-West

(   ) The West and North-West

(   ) I was not raised in the United States

(63-64) 15.   In column A, below, indicate the size of the community in which you presently reside. In column B, indicate the size of the community in which you were raised? (If raised in more than one place, indicate the one where you lived the longest)

A Present	B Childhood	
( )	( )	Farm
( )	( )	A Town of less than 2,500 persons (not a suburb of a city)
( )	( )	A town of less than 15,000 (not a suburb of a city)
( )	( )	A town of less than 50,000 (not a suburb of a city)
( )	( )	A city of less than 100,000 persons
( )	( )	100,000 to 250,000 persons
( )	( )	250,000 to 1 million persons
( )	( )	A million or more persons
( )	( )	A suburb of a city of 100,000 to one million persons
( )	( )	A suburb of a city of one million or more persons

(65-68) 16.   This question is to learn about your residential history since your 18th birthday. Please write on the first line the name of the community and state in which you now live as well as the year you moved to this community. Then, on the second line, do the same for the community in which you lived prior to your present residence. On the third line, indicate the same information regarding your residence prior to that placed on the second line, and so on until you get to the community and state in which you lived at the time of your 18th birthday. (Omit residences for less than one year) If one or more of these residences was a farm, write "farm" and indicate the state.

	Community	State	Year moved to this Community
Now Reside: _____			
Resided Before			
Present Residence: _____			
Before			
Above: _____			
Before			
Above: _____			
Before			
Above: _____			
Before			
Above: _____			
Before			
Above: _____			

(69)   17. What is your sex?   (   ) Male   (   ) Female

(70)   18. What is your occupational status? (Check one)
   (   ) Employed
   (   ) Was employed, now retired
   (   ) Full-time student
   (   ) Not employed

If employed or retired, please continue with Questions 18a through 18g. NOTE: If you are retired, answer these questions as if you were still employed. If student or not employed, please skip to Question 19.

(71)   18a. What is your occupation? _____

18b. What are the major duties you perform in this occupation?
_____

18c. Are you self-employed or employed by someone else?
   (   ) Self-employed   (   ) Employed by someone else

18d. Which of the following best describes your place of work?
( ) Small Retail Store
( ) Large Retail Store
( ) Small Industrial Shop
( ) Factory Assembly Line
( ) Small Clerical Pool
( ) Large Clerical Pool
( ) Executive or Management Offices in Small Firm or Office
( ) Executive or Management Offices in Large Firm or Office
( ) School
( ) Other Please indicate:

(75) 18e. Do you work at your occupation full-time or part-time?
( ) Full-time ( ) Part-time

(76) 18f. Generally speaking, how much would you say you like your occupation?
( ) I dislike it very much
( ) I dislike it somewhat
( ) I neither like nor dislike my occupation
( ) I like it somewhat
( ) I like it very much

(77-78) 18g. Regardless of whether you like your occupation generally, there are probably some things about it you like more than others. The following are a number of comments that various persons have made regarding the things they like about their occupations. Please indicate the two that best indicate what you like about your occupation. Place a "1" next to the statement which is the closest to what you like about your occupation and a "2" next to the statement which is the second closest.
( ) What I like best is the security of knowing I have a stable job to go to each day
( ) The best part of my job is the opportunity it provides for advancement
( ) The aspect I like best about my occupation is the sense of purpose and meaning in life that my job gives me
( ) The best part of my job is the enjoyment I get from being with my co-workers

250

      (   ) The best aspect of my job is that the work I do is interesting

19. What is your spouse's occupational status? (Check one)

      (   ) Employed
      (   ) Was employed, now retired
      (   ) Full-time student
      (   ) Not employed

If employed or retired, please continue with Questions 19a and 19b. NOTE: If your spouse is retired, please answer these questions as if he or she were still employed. If student or not employed, skip to Question 20.

(28) 19a. What is your spouse's occupation? _____
_____

(29) 19b. What are the major duties your spouse performs in this occupation? _____
_____

(30-32) 20. Were both your father and mother born in this country?
      (   ) Yes (   ) No
If No, in what country were they born?
_____ Father _____ Mother

(33-34) 21. During the time you were growing up, what was the religious affiliation of your parents?
Father's Denomination _____
Mother's Denomination _____

(35-36) 22. While you were growing up, how religious would you say *your parents* were? (If you did not grow up with your parents, think of the male and female adults who raised you.)

Father was:	Mother was:
( ) Very Religious	( ) Very Religious
( ) Fairly Religious	( ) Fairly Religious
( ) Somewhat Religious	( ) Somewhat Religious
( ) Not very Religious	( ) Not very Religious
( ) Not at all Religious	( ) Not at all Religious

251

(37)   23.   When you were of high school age, what was your father's occupation? (If you were not being supported by your father at that time, indicate the occupation of the person who was supporting you.)

_____

_____

(38)   24.   Please indicate how much formal education your father had. Check the nearest answer.
   (   ) Some Grade School
   (   ) Finished Grade School
   (   ) Some High School
   (   ) Technical or trade School
   (   ) Some College
   (   ) Finished College
   (   ) Attended Professional School After College
   (   ) Attended Graduate School After College

(39)   25.   From what countries did your ancestors come? _____

_____

(40-42)   26.   People obtain satisfaction from various aspects of their lives. While most or all of the following probably bring you satisfaction, please mark a "1" next to the aspect which brings you the most satisfaction, a "2" next to the aspect which is second in importance, and a "3" next to the aspect which is third. NOTE: If you are not (or not usually) employed full-time, please check here (   ) and do not consider the first alternative in making your selection.
   (   ) Your career or occupation
   (   ) Your family relationships
   (   ) Your leisure time recreational activities
   (   ) Your religious beliefs or activities
   (   ) Your participation as a citizen in the affairs of your community and /or nation

(43)   27.   What was your age at your *last* birthday?

252

28. By and large, which one of the following social classes do you think you and your family fit into?
( ) Working Class
( ) Upper Class
( ) Lower Class
( ) Middle Class
( ) Upper Middle Class

29. Which of the following social classes do you think your children (or the children you hope to have) will or do fit into as adults?
( ) Working Class
( ) Upper Class
( ) Lower Class
( ) Middle Class
( ) Upper Middle Class
( ) I do not have children nor plan to.

30. Please check the category that comes closest to your present yearly family income.
( ) Less than $3000
( ) $3000 - $4999
( ) $5000 - $7499
( ) $7500 - $9999
( ) $10,000 - $12,499
( ) $12,500 - $14,999
( ) $15,000 - $19,999
( ) $20,000 - $24,999
( ) $25,000 or more

31. What is your race?
( ) White
( ) Negro
( ) Oriental
( ) Other—Please indicate:

32. Do you think of yourself as:
( ) A Liberal Democrat
( ) A Moderate Democrat
( ) A Conservative Democrat
( ) A Moderate Republican

253

(   ) A Conservative Republican
(   ) An Independent (Liberal)
(   ) An Independent (Conservative)
(   ) Other—Please indicate:

(49)   33.   Even if you sometimes vote for candidates of both political parties, which party do you tend most often to support in national elections?
           (   )   Republican
           (   )   Democratic

(50)   34.   What is the name of your parish and in what community and state is it located?
           Name of Parish _____
           Community _____ State _____

This is the end of the questionnaire. Your cooperation and patience are greatly appreciated. If you have any comments to make regarding the questionnaire, we would welcome them. Please remember to print your name on the enclosed post card and to mail it back separately when you return this questionnaire. Again, thank you very much.

Please add any additional comments here.

Notes

Introduction

1. We need not describe at length the history of liberal Protestantism and its long-standing commitments to social justice. Historical accounts are available written by Sydney E. Ahlstrom, *A Religious History of the American People* (New Haven: Yale University Press, 1972); Winthrop S. Hudson, *Religion in America* (New York: Charles Scribner's Sons, 1973); Martin E. Marty, *Righteous Empire: The Protestant Experience in America* (New York: Dial Press, 1970); and Sidney E. Mead, *The Lively Experiment* (New York: Harper & Row, 1963).

2. Actually church attendance, among Protestants and Catholics, dropped steadily from 1958 until about 1970 when it appears to have leveled off. See "Religion in America," *The Gallop Opinion Index*, Report No. 114, 1975. Data from the churches themselves are compiled by the National Council of Churches of Christ in the U.S.A. and presented annually in their *Yearbook of American Churches*. These yearbooks show that membership for the liberal Protestant churches peaked in the mid-sixties and has declined somewhat in the intervening years, especially for Methodists, Episcopalians, and Presbyterians. For an insightful study of the Methodists during this time, see Warren J. Hartman, *Membership Trends: A Study of Decline and Growth in the United Methodist Church 1949–1975* (Nashville: Discipleship Resources, 1976).

3. In addition to the accounts mentioned in Footnote 1, also see interpretations of the social gospel by Henry F. May, *Protestant Churches and Industrial America* (Harper & Brothers, 1949) and Charles H. Hopkins, *The Rise of the Social Gospel in American Protestantism 1865–1915* (New Haven: Yale University Press, 1940).

256

4. Marty, *Righteous Empire*, p. 179.

5. Two of the best accounts of clergy versus lay conflicts are found in Jeffrey K. Hadden, *The Gathering Storm in the Churches* (Garden City: Doubleday, 1969) and Harold E. Quinley, *The Prophetic Clergy: Social Activism Among Protestant Ministers* (New York: John Wiley & Sons, 1974).

6. For a recent empirical study of conflicts among the laity within the Presbyterian Church, see Dean R. Hoge, *Division in the Protestant House* (Philadelphia: The Westminster Press, 1976).

7. This issue is dealt with most forcefully in Dean M. Kelley's recent book, *Why Conservative Churches are Growing* (New York: Harper & Row, 1972).

8. Rodney Stark and Charles Y. Glock, *American Piety: The Nature of Religious Commitment* (Berkeley: University of California Press, 1968), p. 221.

9. Kelley, *Why Conservative Churches Are Growing*.

10. Hoge, *Division in the Protestant House*, pp. 40–46.

11. Will Herberg, *Protestant-Catholic-Jew* (Garden City: Doubleday, 1960).

12. See John Cogley, *Catholic America* (Garden City: Doubleday, 1974) and Andrew M. Greeley, William C. McCready, and Kathleen McCourt, *Catholic Schools in a Declining Church* (Kansas City: Sheed & Ward, 1976).

13. See Nathan Glazer, *American Judaism*, 2d ed. (Chicago: University of Chicago Press, 1972). Also see chapter 57, "Twentieth-Century Judaism", in Ahlstrom, *A Religious History of the American People*.

14. Numerous writers have pointed to the shifting location of mainline religion in contemporary industrial society. See Thomas Luckmann, *The Invisible Religion* (New York: Macmillan, 1967) for a theoretical interpretation; and Martin E. Marty, *A Nation of Behavers* (Chicago: University of Chicago Press, 1976) for a descriptive cultural mapping of religion in contemporary American society.

15. Robert S. Lynd and Helen M. Lynd, *Middletown: A Study in Contemporary American Culture* (New York: Harcourt Brace, 1929); W. Lloyd Warner and Paul S. Lunt, *The Social Life of a Modern Community* (New Haven: Yale University Press, 1941); and Arthur J. Vidich and Joseph Bensman, *Small Town in Mass Society* (Garden City: Doubleday, 1958).

16. This literature is too voluminous to cite extensively here. For a good review of the empirical research in the sixties, see Scott Greer, *The Urbane View* (New York: Oxford University Press, 1972), pp. 68–89. Also see Gerald D. Suttles, *The Social Construction of Communities* (Chicago: University of Chicago Press, 1972) for a recent field study.

17. Benita Luckmann, "The Small Worlds of Modern Man," *Social Research* 37 (Winter 1970): 580–596.

18. Morris Janowitz, *The Community Press in an Urban Setting* (Chicago: University of Chicago Press, 1967).

19. James M. Gustafson, *Treasure in Earthen Vessels* (New York: Harper & Brothers, 1961), pp. 14–28.

20. For discussion of an analytic survey, see Herbert Hyman, *Survey Design and Analysis* (Glencoe: Free Press, 1955), pp. 66–89.

Chapter 1

1. Will Herberg, "Religion in a Secularized Society: Some Aspects of America's Three-Religion Pluralism," *Review of Religious Research* 4 (Fall 1962): 45.

2. Gerhard E. Lenski, *The Religious Factor* (Garden City: Doubleday, 1963). Originally published in 1961.

3. See his early essay, "The Religious Revival in America?" In Jane C. Zahn, ed., *Religion and the Face of America* (Berkeley: University of California Press, 1959), pp. 25–42. Further elaboration of the dimensions is presented in Charles Y. Glock and Rodney Stark, *Religion and Society in Tension* (Chicago: Rand McNally, 1965), chap. 2; and Stark and Glock, *American Piety: The Nature of Religious Commitment* (Berkeley: University of California Press, 1968).

4. Additional studies include Yoshio Fukuyama, "The Major Dimensions of Church Membership," *Review of Religious Research* 2 (Summer 1961): 154–161; Joseph E. Faulkner and Gordon F. DeJong, "Religiosity in 5-D: An Empirical Analysis," *Social Forces* 45 (December 1966): 246–254; Morton B. King and Richard A. Hunt, *Measuring Religious Dimensions* (Dallas: Southern Methodist University Printing Department, 1972); and Gordon F. DeJong, Joseph E. Faulkner and Rex H. Warland, "Dimensions of Religiosity Reconsidered: Evidence from a Cross-Cultural Study," *Social Forces* 54 (June 1976): 866–889. These studies generally argue in favor of multidimensionality. For an alternative argument, see Richard R. Clayton and J.W. Gladden, "The Five Dimensions of Religiosity: Toward Demythologizing a Sacred Artifact," *Journal for the Scientific Study of Religion* 13 (June 1974): 135–144.

5. On factor analysis generally, see Harry H. Harman, *Modern Factor Analysis* (Chicago: University of Chicago Press, 1967). For a critique of factor analytic procedures, see Hubert M. Blalock, Jr. *Causal Inferences in Nonexperimental Research* (Chapel Hill: University of North Carolina Press, 1961), pp. 167–169.

6. For example, Stark and Glock take the position that the erosion of traditional doctrine leads to the decline of institutional participation. They show data suggesting a relationship between degree of orthodoxy and other aspects of religious involvement. See their *American Piety: The Nature of Religious Commitment*, chap. 11. The alternative position, underscoring the primacy of sociocommunal involvement, is taken in Peter Berger's writings. See *The Sacred Canopy* (Garden City: Doubleday, 1967), especially chaps. 5, 6, and 7. A similar position is advanced briefly in Charles H. Anderson, *White Protestant Americans: From National Origins to Religious Group* (Englewood Cliffs: Prentice-Hall, 1970), pp. 135–136.

7. Amazingly little research has been carried out on this problem. But see D.L. Klemmack and J.D. Cardwell, "Interfaith Comparison of Multidimensional Measures of Religiosity," *Pacific Sociological Review* 16 (October 1973): 495–507. They point out differences in the belief structures for Protestants and Catholics,

noting that Protestants in considering beliefs are more inclined to think in terms of their effects on behavior whereas Catholics consider them relative to the rituals of the church. Empirical evidence is provided indicating differing structures of commitment for the two subsamples.

8. His most extensive treatment of these twin aspects of commitment is found in *The Denominational Society* (Glenview, Illinois: Scott, Foresman, 1972).

9. This is a common problem in theory building that takes seriously a data base. See Hubert M. Blalock, Jr., *Theory Construction: From Verbal to Mathematical Formulations* (Englewood Cliffs, N.J.: Prentice-Hall, 1969).

10. *Specification* refers to an analysis of the relationship between an independent and a dependent variable, within categories of a third variable. In this sense it is analagous to statistical interaction, or the joint effects, of two or more independent variables on some dependent variable. For discussion of their similarities, see Blalock, *Theory Construction: From Verbal to Mathematical Formulations*, appendix A.

11. New York: Harper & Row, 1966.

12. Many studies cite an association between orthodoxy and prejudice, although not all actually suggest there is a direct causal linkage. For an excellent review and critique of these studies, see Richard L. Gorsuch and Daniel Aleshire, "Christian Faith and Ethnic Prejudice: A Review and Interpretation of Research," *Journal for the Scientific Study of Religion* 13 (September 1974): 281–307.

13. See Benton Johnson, "Ascetic Protestantism and Political Preference," *Public Opinion Quarterly* 26 (Spring 1962): 35–46; "Ascetic Protestantism and Political Preference in the Deep South," *American Journal of Sociology* 69 (January 1964): 359–366. Johnson's interpretation is challenged by Dean G. Rojek, "The Protestant Ethic and Political Preference," *Social Forces* 52 (1973): 162–177.

14. This position is advanced, for those members whose beliefs are "salient," by Howard M. Bahr, Lois Bartel, and Bruce A. Chadwick, "Orthodoxy, Activism, and the Salience of Religion," *Journal for the Scientific Study of Religion* 10 (Summer 1971): 69–75; and by David R. Gibbs, Samuel A. Mueller, and James R. Wood, "Orthodoxy, Salience, and the Consequential Dimension," *Journal for the Scientific Study of Religion* 12 (March 1973): 33–52.

15. Donald R. Ploch examines the model and lack of attention by Glock and Stark to tests of its basic linkages in "Religion as an Independent Variable: A Critique of Some Major Research," in Allan W. Eister, ed., *Changing Perspectives in the Scientific Study of Religion* (New York: Wiley-Interscience, 1975), pp. 275–294.

16. "Do Christian Beliefs Cause Anti-Semitism?" *American Sociological Review* 38 (February 1973): 33–52.

17. A growing literature focuses upon the civil religion theme. Probably the best known writing is Robert N. Bellah's "Civil Religion in America," *Daedalus* 96 (Winter 1967): 1–23. For a review of relevant literature, see Phillip E. Hammond, "The Sociology of American Civil Religion: A Bibliographic Essay," *Sociological Analysis* 37 (Summer 1976): 169–182.

18. Thomas Luckmann offers the most extensive interpretation of European and

American patterns of secularization. See *The Invisible Religion* (New York: Macmillan, 1967), pp. 28–40. Both references to data and interpretation are provided.

19. Berger, *The Sacred Canopy*, pp. 133–134.
20. Kelley, *Why Conservative Churches Are Growing*, chap. 5.
21. Berger, *The Sacred Canopy*, especially pp. 45–51.
22. See Clifford Geertz, "Religion as a Cultural System," in Michael Banton, ed., *Anthropological Approaches to the Study of Religion* (New York: Praeger, 1966), pp. 1–46; and Robert N. Bellah, "The Sociology of Religion," in David L. Sills, ed., *International Encyclopedia of the Social Sciences* vol. 13 (New York: Macmillan, 1968), pp. 406–413. Many commentators, influenced out of the phenomenological and neophenomenological traditions, approach the study of religion in this way.
23. For reviews of this literature, see Michael Argyle and Benjamin Beithallahmi, *The Social Psychology of Religion* (London: Routledge and Kegan Paul, 1975).
24. A good analysis of age as a factor is found in Charles Y. Glock, Benjamin B. Ringer, and Earl R. Babbie, *To Comfort and to Challenge* (Berkeley: University of California Press, 1967), pp. 38–59. Also, see Argyle and Beithallahmi, *The Social Psychology of Religion*.
25. See Lenski, *The Religious Factor*, pp. 44–56; N.J. Demerath, III, *Social Class in American Protestantism* (Chicago: Rand McNally, 1965); and Erich Goode, "Social Class and Church Participation," *American Journal of Sociology* 72 (July 1966): 102–111.
26. For example, Will Herberg, *Protestant-Catholic-Jew*.
27. Glock, Ringer, Babbie, *To Comfort and to Challenge*.
28. Fukuyama, "The Major Dimensions of Church Membership"; Demerath, *Social Class in American Protestantism*; and Erich Goode, "Social Class and Church Participation."
29. Rodney Stark, "The Economics of Piety: Religious Commitment and Social Class" in Gerald W. Thielbar and Saul D. Feldman, eds., *Issues in Social Inequality* (Boston: Little, Brown, 1972), p. 500.
30. Max Weber, *The Sociology of Religion* (Boston: Beacon Press, 1964), pp. 116–117.

Chapter 2

1. Robert K. Merton, *Social Theory and Social Structure* (Glencoe: Free Press, 1957), p. 393.
2. Stark and Glock, *American Piety*, p. 167.
3. *The Denominational Society*, chap. 5.
4. The theme is common in community studies. For example, see Herbert J. Gans, *The Levittowners* (New York: Vintage Books, 1967). chap. 4, and in Vidich and Bensman, *Small Town in Mass Society*, chap. 9. For survey evidence,

see Serge Carlos, "Religious Participation and the Urban-Suburban Continuum," *American Journal of Sociology* 75 (March 1970): 742–759.

5. See Gerald Thielbar, "Localism-Cosmopolitanism: Social Differentiation in Mass Society" (Ph.D diss., University of Minnesota, 1966).

6. Philip E. Converse, "The Nature of Belief Systems in Mass Publics," in David Apter, ed., *Ideology and Discontent* (New York: Free Press, 1964), pp. 206–262.

7. "The Nature of Belief Systems in Mass Publics," pp. 208-209.

8. Peter L. Berger and Thomas Luckmann, *The Social Construction of Reality* (Garden City: Doubleday, 1966), especially pp. 89–92.

9. Melvin L. Kohn, *Class and Conformity* (Homewood, Illinois: Dorsey Press, 1969), chap. 5.

10. Howard Gabennesch, "Authoritarianism as World View," *American Journal of Sociology* 77 (March 1972): 867–868.

11. These conclusions are based on Stark and Glock's data. The lowest weekly attenders are found among the Congregationalists—15 percent. Methodists are next with 23 percent, followed by Presbyterians with 29 percent and Episcopalians with 31 percent. See their *American Piety*, p. 84.

12. Again, see Stark and Glock, *American Piety*, chaps. 2 and 3. Also, see Hadden, *The Gathering Storm in the Churches*, chap. 2.

13. N.J. Demerath III and Phillip E. Hammond, *Religion in Social Context* (New York: Random House, 1969), p. 172.

14. These findings are reported in an analysis of Gallup data between 1957 and 1968 in Bradley R. Hertel and Hart M. Nelsen, "Are We Entering a Post-Christian Era? Religious Belief and Attendance in America, 1957–1968," *Journal for the Scientific Study of Religion* 13 (December 1974): 409–419.

15. Merton, *Social Theory and Social Structure*, p. 402.

16. See, for example, Georg Simmel's essay, "The Metropolis and Mental Life," in Kurt H. Wolff, ed., *The Sociology of Georg Simmel* (Glencoe: Free Press, 1950); and Louis Wirth, "Urbanism as a Way of Life," *American Journal of Sociology* 44 (July 1938): 3–24.

17. William M. Dobriner, "Local and Cosmopolitan as Contemporary Suburban Character Types," in W.M. Dobriner, ed., *The Suburban Community* (New York: Putnam, 1958), pp. 132–143.

18. See the works of Herbert J. Gans, especially *The Urban Villagers* (New York: Free Press, 1962) and "Urbanism and Suburbanism as Ways of Life: A Re-Evaluation of Definitions," in A.M. Rose, ed., *Human Behavior and Social Processes* (Boston: Houghton Mifflin, 1962).

19. Claude S. Fischer's recent work has stimulated reconceptualization along these lines. See his "Toward a Subcultural Theory of Urbanism," *American Journal of Sociology* 80 (May 1975): 1319–1341, and "Urbanism as a Way of Life: A Review and an Agenda," *Sociological Methods and Research* 1 (November 1972): 187–242.

20. For recent empirical documentation, see Bernard Lazerwitz, "Religious Identification and its Ethnic Correlates," *Social Forces* 52 (December 1973): 204–220.

Earlier, Lenski in *The Religious Factor* had shown that Protestants differed from Jews and Catholics in this respect.

21. For example, Stark and Glock's work is premised on the assumption that theology, or religious belief, is at "the heart of faith" (p. 16, *American Piety*). Chapter 11 of their book makes the theological basis for church commitment more explicit plus offers data in support of this interpretation.

22. The principle of social reinforcement in religious groups is well established. See, for example, studies by Leon Festinger and Henry Riecken, *When Prophecy Fails* (Minneapolis: University of Minnesota Press, 1956); John Lofland, *Doomsday Cult* (Englewood Cliffs: Prentice-Hall, 1956); and John Lofland and Rodney Stark, "Becoming a World-Saver: A Theory of Conversion to a Deviant Perspective," *American Sociological Review* 30 (December 1965): 862–875.

23. "Toward a Theory of Religious Influence," reprinted in Phillip E. Hammond and Benton Johnson, eds., *American Mosaic: Social Patterns of Religion in the United States* (New York: Random House, 1970), p. 19.

24. Quinley, *The Prophetic Clergy*, chap. 7.

25. Harold E. Quinley, "The Dilemma of an Activist Church: Protestant Religion in the Sixties and Seventies," *Journal for the Scientific Study of Religion* 13 (March 1974): 5.

26. Traditionalist and modernist beliefs became elaborated as alternative theologies in the early decades of the twentieth century among Protestants. The key issue in the fundamentalist controversies in the twenties and thirties was the authority of the Bible, and especially its verbal and inerrant inspiration. Fundamentalists insisted on the verbal inspiration of Scripture in every detail whereas modernists sought to accomodate Biblical teachings to a scientific culture. Differences between fundamentalists and modernists were further aggravated by the tendency of Biblical liberals to adopt a "Social Gospel" theology with its emphasis on social reform, brotherhood, and enlightened self-interest. It would be a mistake to assume, however, that fundamentalism was only a religious phenomenon. More broadly, it can best be understood as a *cultural* reaction to the changing conditions of American life brought on by industrialization and urbanization. Fundamentalism was more cultural than religious in orientation, and frequently exhibited, as H. Richard Niebuhr observed, "a greater concern for cultures than for the Lordship of Jesus Christ" (*Christ and Culture* [New York: Harper and Brothers, 1951], p. 102). For historical treatments of the fundamentalist controversies, see Winthrop S. Hudson, *American Protestantism* (Chicago: University of Chicago Press, 1961), pp. 143–153; and Sydney E. Ahlstrom, *A Religious History of the American People*, pp. 805–824.

27. See Gordon W. Allport, *The Individual and His Religion* (New York: Macmillan, 1950) and "The Religious Context of Prejudice," *Journal for the Scientific Study of Religion* 5 (Fall 1966): 447–457. Also, see Gordon W. Allport and J. Michael Ross, "Personal Religious Orientation and Prejudice," *Social Psychology* 5 (April 1967): 432–443.

28. This literature is too extensive to review here. For a good account, see Gorsuch and Aleshire, "Christian Faith and Ethnic Prejudice: A Review and Interpretation of Research."

Chapter 3

1. A brief but thorough review of the typological tradition is found in Charles P. Loomis and John C. McKinney's "Introduction to Ferdinand Töennies," *Community and Society* (New York: Harper & Row, 1963). The local-cosmopolitan typology is one of several discussed.
2. Zimmerman, *The Changing Community* (New York: Harper, 1938).
3. See his "Patterns of Influence: Local and Cosmopolitan Influentials," chap. 10, in *Social Theory and Social Structure*, pp. 387–420.
4. Few systematic statements on localism-cosmopolitanism as general theories of social differentiation can be found. Two unpublished dissertations that attempt to do this are: Gerald Thielbar, "Localism-Cosmopolitanism: Social Differentiation in Mass Society" (University of Minnesota, 1966); and Wade Clark Roof, "Localism-Cosmopolitanism and Social Differentiation: A Theoretical and Empirical Assessment" (University of North Carolina, 1971).
5. One will note similarities between local-cosmopolitan perspectives and George Herbert Mead's distinction between concrete and abstract generalized others. According to Mead, an individual who assumes the attitude of a concrete generalized other identifies and guides his behavior in accordance with the standards of an existing group in direct relations with one another. But in assuming the attitude of an abstract generalized other, one identifies with a collectivity more on the basis of such factors as common identity, common values, and indirect relations. See Mead, *Mind, Self, and Society* (Chicago: University of Chicago Press, 1934), pp. 153–156.
6. Gouldner's major piece on this is in two parts. See "Cosmopolitans and Locals: Toward an Analysis of Latent Social Roles," *Administrative Science Quarterly* 2 (1957–1958): 281–306, 444–448.
7. Gans, *The Levittowners*.
8. Ritchie Lowry, *Who's Running This Town?* (New York: Harper & Row, 1962).
9. Everett C. Ladd, Jr., *Ideology in America* (New York: W.W. Norton, 1972).
10. For a discussion on community formation and the necessity to look at common meanings and values in defining community, see Don Martindale and R. Galen Hanson, *Small Town and the Nation: The Conflict of Local and Translocal Forces* (Westport: Greenwood Publishing Company, 1969), chap. 1.
11. See, for example, Gregory P. Stone and William H. Form, "Instabilities in Status: The Problem of Hierarchy in the Study of Status Arrangements," *American Sociological Review* 17 (April 1953): 149–162. They refer to such differences as a "horizontal" dimension of life-style differentiation.

12. There are numerous studies here but the major ones are Stone and Form, "Instabilities in Status"; William M. Dobriner, "Local and Cosmopolitan as Contemporary Suburban Character Types," and Thielbar, "Localism-Cosmopolitanism: Social Differentiation in Mass Society."

13. Aside from Gouldner's study of college professors, see Peter M. Blau and W. Richard Scott, *Formal Organizations: A Comparative Approach* (San Francisco: Chandler Publishing Company, 1962) and Barney G. Glazer, *Organizational Scientists: Their Professional Careers* (Indianapolis: Bobbs-Merrill, 1964).

14. In addition to Ladd's Hartford study, see Thomas R. Dye, "The Local-Cosmopolitan Dimension and the Study of Urban Politics," *Social Forces* 42 (March 1963): 239–246 and Daniel J. Elazer and Douglas St. Angelo, "Cosmopolitans and Locals in Contemporary Politics," *Proceedings of the Minnesota Academy of Science* 31 (1964): 171–178.

15. See Lowry, *Who's Running this Town?* and Gresham M. Sykes, "The Differential Distribution of Community Knowledge," *Social Forces* 29 (May 1951): 386–382.

16. *Symbolic Crusade* (Urbana: University of Illinois, 1963), p. 140.

17. See *The Community in America* (Chicago: Rand McNally, 1963).

18. The following discussion relies heavily on Thielbar's work. See his "Localism-Cosmopolitanism: Social Differentiation in Mass Society" for a more extended treatment of the methodological complexities.

19. Ibid.

20. In an earlier study I examined several of these items for a sample of Southern Baptists. The patterns were virtually the same as in the Episcopal study. See Wade Clark Roof, "The Local-Cosmopolitan Orientation and Traditional Religious Commitment," *Sociological Analysis* 33 (Spring 1972): 1–15.

21. Cronbach's *alpha* is a coefficient of homogeneity and refers to the ratio of the covariance among items to the total scale variance, in relation to the number of items. As the coefficient approaches 1.0, each item increasingly measures content which all the others measure. See L.J. Cronbach, *Essentials of Psychological Testing* (New York: Harper & Row, 1970). Scale scores are sums of the individual item scores. Where data are missing, integers nearest the mean values are substituted in this and other summated scales.

22. Since acquiescence effects should presumably show up in the pattern of responses to statements positively and negatively worded, I estimated them by comparing responses to the fourth scale item with the other three. The standard deviation for the fourth is slightly less than the average of the others (0.85 and 0.94, respectively); and there are slight differences in prediction, the fourth item being somewhat weaker. The small differences are always in the inverse direction as expected.

23. One may argue of course that measures of religiosity and community orientation are strictly ordinal. To be sure, some error is introduced in treating the scores as interval, but whatever bias results must be weighed against the advantages that accrue to interval analysis, such as more powerful, manipulatable, and interpretable statistics. Sanford Labovitz shows that little error is introduced

by so doing. See his "The Assignment of Numbers to Rank Order Categories," *American Sociological Review* 35 (June 1970): 515–524.

24. Stone and Form, "Instabilities in Status," pp. 149–162. Also see C. Wright Mills's discussion of this in his *White Collar* (New York: Oxford University Press, 1956), p. 48.

25. See Martindale and Hanson, *Small Town and the Nation: The Conflict of Local and Translocal Forces*, p. 71.

26. *Man In Reciprocity: Introductory Lectures on Culture, Society, and Personality* (New York: Praeger, 1956), p. 396.

27. Dobriner, "Local and Cosmopolitan as Contemporary Suburban Character Types."

28. Albert Hunter, *Symbolic Communities: The Persistance and Change of Chicago's Local Communities* (Chicago: University of Chicago Press, 1974) and John D. Kasarda and Morris Janowitz, "Community Attachment in Mass Society," *American Sociological Review* 39 (June 1974): 328–339.

Chapter 4

1. Considerable support can be mustered for this interpretation although the evidence generally is fragmentary and indirect. Studies concerned with the loss of community in an urban context and its religious implications best document this view. See, for example, an older work by H. Paul Douglass, *The Church in the Changing City* (New York: George H. Doran Company, 1927). Also see, for a European study, Emile Pin, "Can the Urban Parish be a Community?" *Social Compass* 8 (1961): 503–534.

2. Compared with church attendance, number of church activities does not usually correlate as well with sex, age, social class, and education. See Yoshio Fukuyama, "The Major Dimensions of Church Membership," and Rodney Stark, "The Economics of Piety."

3. Stark and Glock, *American Piety*, p. 166.

4. William James, *The Varieties of Religious Experience* (New York: Random House [Modern Library], 1937), p. 31.

5. The Gallup polls repeatedly show that 95 to 98 percent of Americans claim to believe in God. See "Religion in America," *The Gallup Opinion Index* (April 1971). For a methodological critique of the questions typically asked in polls about belief in God, see N.J. Demerath III, "Trends and Anti-Trends in Religious Change," in Eleanor B. Sheldon and Wilbert E. Moore, eds., *Indicators of Social Change* (New York: Russell Sage Foundation, 1968), pp. 377–391.

6. King and Hunt, *Measuring Religious Dimensions*, p. 29.

7. The term *indiscriminate proreligious* belongs to Gordon Allport. This describes individuals who agree to both intrinsic and extrinsic religious items. See his discussion in "The Religious Context of Prejudice."

8. Stark and Glock, *American Piety*, p. 114.

9. Luckmann, *The Invisible Religion*, pp. 107–114.

10. The educated classes are more inclined to regard religion as instrumental to their quest for personal identity. For a discussion of "instrumentalization" in religion, see Louis Schneider and Sanford M. Dornbusch, *Popular Religion: Inspirational Books in America* (Chicago: University of Chicago Press, 1958). Basically, they see instrumentalization as a process by which latent functions of religion become manifest.

11. N.J. Demerath, III, *Social Class in American Protestantism*.

12. NORC occupational prestige ratings and Duncan's Socio-Economic Index scores were computed. The predictions were almost all identical. Consequently, only the National Opinion Research Center ratings are used in the analysis reported here. See Albert J. Reiss, Jr. et al., *Occupations and Social Status* (New York: Free Press, 1961).

13. See Claude S. Fischer, "Toward a Subcultural Theory of Urbanism." Also see Alejandro Portes, "The Factorial Structure of Modernity: Empirical Replications and a Critique," *American Journal of Sociology* 79 (July 1973): 15–44, and Alex Inkeles and David H. Smith, *Becoming Modern: Individual Change in Six Developing Countries* (Cambridge: Harvard University Press, 1974), especially chap. 16.

14. See Hart M. Nelsen, Raytha Yokley, and T.W. Madrow, "Rural-Urban Differences in Religiosity," *Rural Sociology* 36 (September 1971): 389–396, and Claude S. Fischer, "The Effect of Urban Life on Traditional Values," *Social Forces* 53 (March 1975): 420–432.

15. In European nations, there are negative associations between city size and church attendance. See Gabriel A. Almond and Sidney Verba, *The Civic Culture* (Boston: Little, Brown, 1963). The North American pattern is attributable to differing modes of secularization. Beliefs have eroded while at the same time cultural norms of church participation have persisted, due in large part to the strong belonging functions religion plays in North America.

16. See Yoshio Fukuyama, "The Major Dimensions of Church Membership," and Rodney Stark, "Age and Faith: A Changing Outlook or an Old Process?" *Sociological Analysis* 29 (Spring 1968): 1–10.

17. See Joseph H. Fichter, "The Profile of Catholic Religious Life," *American Journal of Sociology* 58 (July 1952): 145–149, and Charles Y. Glock et al., *To Comfort and To Challenge*, pp. 38–59.

18. See Howard M. Bahr, "Aging and Religious Disaffiliation," *Social Forces* 49 (September 1970): 59–71.

19. Gerhard Lenski, "Sociology of Religion in the United States," *Social Compass* (1962): 313–334.

Chapter 5

1. Charles W. Estus and Michael A. Overington, "The Meaning and End of Religiosity," *American Journal of Sociology* 75 (March 1970): 776–777.

2. Samuel A. Stouffer, *Communism, Conformity, and Civil Liberties* (New York: Doubleday, 1955).

3. Armand L. Mauss, "Dimensions of Religious Defection," in Charles Y. Glock, ed., *Religion in Sociological Perspective: Essays in the Empirical Study of Religion* (Belmont, California: Wadsworth, 1973), pp. 16–22. For studies on academicians, see Rodney Stark, "On the Incompatibility of Religion and Science: A Survey of American Graduate Students," *Journal for the Scientific Study of Religion* 3 (Fall, 1963): 3–20; Fred Thalheimer, "Continuity and Change in Religiosity: A Study of Academicians," *Pacific Sociological Review* 8 (1965): 101–108; and Edward Lehman and Donald Shriver, "Academic Discipline as Predictive of Faculty Religiosity," *Social Forces* 47 (September 1968): 171–182.

4. In effect, one of the influences operates as a suppressor variable. For further discussion of the statistical implications, see James A. Davis, *Elementary Survey Analysis* (Englewood Cliffs: Prentice-Hall, 1971), pp. 95–98.

5. Fischer, "The Effects of Urban Life on Traditional Values," p. 430.

6. Nelsen, Yokley, and Madrow, "Rural-Urban Differences in Religiosity," and Fischer, "The Effects of Urban Life on Traditional Values."

7. Fischer, "Toward a Subcultural Theory of Urbanism," p. 1337.

8. See Glock et al., *To Comfort and to Challenge*, pp. 45–59. These patterns are also evident in the Gallup polls as shown by Jackson W. Carroll and David A. Roozen, "Religious Participation in American Society—An Analysis of Social and Religious Trends and Their Interaction." Unpublished paper prepared by the Hartford Seminary Foundation, pp. 93–98.

9. This section is adapted, with permission of the publisher, from my article, "Traditional Religion in Contemporary Society: A Theory of Local-Cosmopolitan Plausibility," *American Sociological Review* 41 (April 1976): 195–208.

10. Simple models as these are referred to as *recursive*, indicating that such complexities as feedback effects and reciprocal causation are ruled out by assumption. Hence, they are models for which linear regression procedures are applicable. See Blalock, *Theory Construction* and Otis Dudley Duncan, "Path Analysis: Sociological Examples," *American Journal of Sociology* 72 (July 1966): 1–16.

11. See Charles W. Mueller and Weldon T. Johnson, "Socioeconomic Status and Religious Participation," *American Sociological Review* 40 (December 1975): 785–800 and Greeley et al., *Catholic Schools in a Declining Church*, pp. 170ff.

Chapter 6

1. Stark and Glock, *American Piety*, pp. 16–17.

2. See *American Piety*, chap. 11. An index of ethicalism (consisting of two items: "Doing good for others" and "Loving thy neighbor") was examined as an alternative form of commitment to traditional orthodoxy. See also James D. Davidson, "Religious Belief as an Independent Variable," *Journal for the Scientific Study of Religion*, 11 (March 1972): 65–75. Davidson develops measures of

"vertical" (man-to-God) and "horizontal" (man-to-man) beliefs and shows that the two relate differentially to personal comfort and social challenge functions of religion, respectively. He does not, however, examine horizontal belief as a source of institutional commitment in the same manner as do Stark and Glock.

3. See references in Chapter 1, note 17. For additional writings focusing on nationalism and religion in American life, see W. Lloyd Warner, "An American Sacred Ceremony," from his *American Life* (Chicago: The University of Chicago Press, 1953), pp. 1–26; and Will Herberg, *Protestant-Catholic-Jew*.

4. The literature on social class and religion is of course voluminous. Major works are cited in Chapter 1 of this book. For an empirically based discussion of social class as a context of meaning for church-type religion, see especially Charles W. Estus and Michael A. Overington, "The Meaning and End of Religiosity."

5. See Lenski, *The Religious Factor*, p. 48ff; Demerath, *Social Class in American Protestantism*, pp. 65–66; and Erich Goode, "Social Class and Church Participation." For an opposing argument, see Charles Y. Glock and Rodney Stark, *Religion and Society in Tension*, (Chicago: Rand McNally, 1965), pp. 185–190.

6. See Goode, "Social Class and Church Participation."

7. See Charles W. Mueller and Weldon T. Johnson, "Socioeconomic Status and Religious Participation." Also, James Davidson reports a modest .06 correlation between socioeconomic status and church involvement in an unpublished paper.

8. Rodney Stark, "The Economics of Piety."

9. For a somewhat similar approach to this issue, see Estus and Overington, "The Meaning and End of Religion." They use an "Integration Scale," tapping church members' relations to the local congregation, for specifying the social class patterns.

10. Major studies examining parental religious socialization are Andrew W. Greeley and Peter H. Rossi, *The Education of Catholic Americans* (Garden City: Doubleday, 1966); John L. Thomas, "Religious Training in the Roman Catholic Family," *American Journal of Sociology* 62(1951): 178–183; and Bernard Lazerwitz, "Religious Identification and Its Ethnic Correlates: A Multivariate Model," *Social Forces* 52 (December 1973): 204–220. The latter is not a study in socialization per se, but attempts to establish causal linkages between parental religiousness and various types of religious commitment.

11. John Kotre in a study of graduate students who had attended Catholic schools, found a strong correlation between being "out" of the Catholic church and the existence of religious conflict in the home. Religious conflict, however, presumably resulted from interfaith marriage or one parent being a nonpracticing Catholic, and thus these results do not provide a fair test of parental religiosity effects. See *The View from the Border* (Chicago: Aldine-Atherton, 1971).

12. This is shown, for example, in Lazerwitz, "Religious Identification and Its Ethnic Correlates: A Multivariate Model." His research indicates that parental religious background has more influence on religious belonging than on beliefs and religious meanings.

Chapter 7

1. Lenski was one of the first to argue on the basis of empirical evidence that the various dimensions are not well correlated. Even among the belonging indicators themselves, he reports a measure of association τ of no higher than .03; and among two meaning indicators, orthodoxy and devotionalism, a τ of only .05. These Detroit-based results are discussed in *The Religious Factor*, pp. 22–26. Others emphasizing that belief and attendance in particular are not very well correlated are Gordon W. Allport *Religion in the Developing Personality* (New York: New York University Press, 1960); N.J. Demerath, III, *Social Class in American Protestantism*; and Bradley R. Hertel and Hart M. Nelsen, "Are We Entering a Post-Christian Era? Religious Belief and Attendance in America, 1957–1968," *Journal for the Scientific Study of Religion* (December 1974): 409–419.
2. Stark and Glock, *American Piety*, p. 177; and Morton B. King and Richard A. Hunt, "Religious Dimensions: National Replication," *Journal for the Scientific Study of Religion* 14 (March 1975): 18.
3. Berger, *The Sacred Canopy*.
4. Greeley, *The Denominational Society*, Chapter 5.
5. Arnold Dashefsky, "And the Search Goes on: the Meanings of Religio-Ethnic Identity and Identification," *Sociological Analysis* 33 (Winter): 242.
6. For an excellent discussion of death and religion, see Berger, *The Sacred Canopy*, chap. 3.

Chapter 8

1. Jeffrey K. Hadden found in his research in 1967 that 89 percent of the laity agreed that "the best mark of a person's religiousness is the degree of his concern for others," and 84 percent said that "clergymen have a responsibility to speak out as the moral conscience of this nation." But when Hadden asked about the ways clergymen might exert such leadership, lay approval dropped sharply. Seventy-seven percent agree, for example, that "I would be upset if my minister were to participate in a picket line or demonstration." See *The Gathering Storm in the Churches*, pp. 146–154. Also see Harold E. Quinley's discussion in *The Prophetic Clergy*, pp. 190–191.
2. Thomas C. Campbell and Yoshio Fukuyama, *The Fragmented Layman: An Empirical Study of Lay Attitudes* (Philadelphia: Pilgrim Press, 1970), p. 239.
3. *American Piety*, p. 74. Stark and Glock use two items to construct an "ethicalism" index: the importance placed upon "Doing good for others" and "Loving thy neighbor" for gaining salvation.
4. Quinley breaks the responses down further than Stark and Glock, controlling

for socioeconomic status, church attendance, and orthodoxy. See table 7.2 in *The Prophetic Clergy*, p. 193.

5. Robert Wuthnow, "Religious Commitment and Conservatism: In Search of an Elusive Relationship," in Charles Y. Glock, *Religion in Sociological Perspective: Essays in the Empirical Study of Religion* (Belmont, California: Wadsworth, 1973) pp. 117–132.

6. Hadden, *The Gathering Storm in the Churches*, p. 95.

7. See, for example, Benton Johnson, "Ascetic Protestantism and Political Preference," and "Ascetic Protestantism and Political Preference in the Deep South." Other representative studies include Franklin K. Zimmerman, "Religion: A Conservative Social Force," *Journal of Abnormal and Social Psychology* 28 (January–March 1934): 473–474; Gary M. Maranell, "An Examination of Some Religious and Political Attitude Correlates of Bigotry," *Social Forces* 45 (March 1967): 356–362; and Richard E. Carney, "Some Correlates of Religiosity," *Journal for the Scientific Study of Religion* 1 (October 1969): 143–144.

8. Wuthnow found that all southern studies reported positive relationships between orthodoxy and social conservatism, as did five out of seven between orthodoxy and political and economic conservatism. Outside the South most of the studies do not reveal positive associations. See his "Religious Commitment and Conservatism: In Search of an Elusive Relationship," p. 124.

9. Gordon W. Allport, "Religion and Prejudice," *Crane Review* 2 (1959): 1:1. For an excellent discussion of this, see appendix B on "Paradoxes of Religious Belief" in Milton Rokeach, *Beliefs, Attitudes and Values* (San Francisco: Jossey-Bass, 1972), pp. 189–196.

10. In addition see the related study by Rodney Stark, Bruce D. Foster, Charles Y. Glock, and Harold E. Quinley, *Wayward Shepherds: Prejudice and the Protestant Clergy* (New York: Harper & Row, 1971)

11. See Gorsuch and Aleshire, "Christian Faith and Ethnic Prejudice: A Review and Interpretation of Research."

12. See Appendix B for a description of the indexes.

13. Clifford Geertz, "Religion: Anthropological Study," in David L. Sills, ed., *International Encyclopedia of the Social Sciences*, vol. 13 (New York: Macmillan), p. 406.

14. Hart M. Nelsen arrives at similar conclusions. See his "Sectarianism, World View, and Anomie," *Social Forces* 51 (December 1972): 226–233.

15. Converse, "The Nature of Belief Systems in Mass Publics," pp. 208–209.

16. The basic difference between this and the Stark and Glock model is the causal ordering of variables. Stark and Glock include *particularism* in their model but argue that it is causally dependent upon orthodox belief. On the contrary, the models proposed here assume that a person's world view, or breadth of perspective, is antecedent to religious beliefs.

17. This discussion is taken, with permission from the publisher, from my article "Religious Orthodoxy and Minority Prejudice: Causal Relationship or Reflection

of Localistic World View?" *American Journal of Sociology* 80 (November 1974): 643–664.

18. For similar efforts at unravelling this relationship, see Wallace Dynes, "Education and Tolerance: An Analysis of Intervening Factors," *Social Forces* 46 (September 1967): 22–34.

19. This distinction is suggested by Randall G. Stokes in his "Afrikaner Calvinism and Economic Action: The Weberian Thesis in South Africa," *American Journal of Sociology* 81 (July 1975): 62–81.

Chapter 9

1. See Appendix B for how these indexes are constructed.

2. See Will Herberg, *Protestant-Catholic-Jew*. For empirical studies of the civil religious faith and Americanism, see Michael C. Thomas and Charles C. Flippen, "American Civil Religion: An Empirical Study," *Social Forces* 51 (December 1972): 218–225, and Ronald C. Wimberly et al., "The Civil Religious Dimension: Is It There?" *Social Forces* 54 (June 1976): 890–900.

3. See Nelsen, "Sectarianism, World View, and Anomie."

4. Stark and Glock, *American Piety*, p. 196.

5. On the basis of their California study, they show that Episcopalians increased their proportion by 40 percent at the expense of other denominations. The national data show a comparable figure of 29 percent, still the highest of all Protestant churches. See *American Piety*, chap. 10.

6. Jeffrey K. Hadden, *The Gathering Storm in the Churches*, p. 61.

7. My terms are similar to King and Hunt's *salience-cognition* and *salience-behavior*. See their *Measuring Religious Dimensions*, p. 32.

8. Ibid., p. 29.

9. This is a general conclusion of Allport's extensive work on "intrinsic" versus "extrinsic" orientations in religion. See Gorsuch and Aleshire, "Christian Faith and Ethnic Prejudice: A Review and Interpretation of Research."

10. See Lenski, *The Religious Factor*, p. 329.

11. This approach to conceptualizing how meaning-salience functions in the individual's belief system differs considerably from what is commonly assumed to be the case. Usually the salience factor is seen as *strengthening* the role of orthodox beliefs on conservative ideology. My argument is that it should *weaken* the orthodoxy-conservatism relationship. For arguments along the first line, see Bahr, Bartel, and Chadwick, "Orthodoxy, Activism, and the Salience of Religion," and Gibbs, Mueller, and Wood, "Doctrinal Orthodoxy, Salience, and the Consequential Dimension." For further elaboration of my position, see Wade Clark Roof and Richard B. Perkins, "On Conceptualizing Salience in Religious Commitment," *Journal for the Scientific Study of Religion* 14 (June 1975):111–128. The analysis in the article differs somewhat from that found

here in the book, in that an alternative measure of salience is used and a linear additive rather than an interactive model is discussed.

12. The distinction between church-related and secular consequences is drawn by Gibbs et al. In their research they found an interactive salience effect only in the case of church-related consequences.

13. Robert Wuthnow, "Religious Commitment and Conservatism: In Search of an Elusive Relationship," p. 126.

Chapter 10

1. See my earlier study of Southern Baptists, "The Local-Cosmopolitan Orientation and Traditional Religious Commitment," *Sociological Analysis* 33 (Spring 1972): 1–15.

2. See Marty's *Righteous Empire: The Protestant Experience in America*.

3. Hoge, *Division in the Protestant House*.

4. *Why Conservative Churches are Growing*, p. 44.

5. See Greeley et al., *Catholic Schools in a Declining Church*. They argue that the most serious factor in recent times affecting the decline of Catholicism was the papal encyclical *Humanae Vitae* pertaining to birth control in 1968.

6. See Glazer, *American Judaism*.

7. A number of studies have pointed this out. See Russell R. Dynes, "The Consequences of Sectarianism for Social Participation," *Social Forces* 35 (May 1957): 331–334, and Charles H. Anderson, *White Protestant Americans*, pp. 113–117.

8. Herberg, *Protestant-Catholic-Jew*, p. 234.

9. Anderson, *White Protestant Americans*, p. 139

10. Ibid., pp. 136–138.

11. Peter H. Rossi, "Community Social Indicators," in Angus Campbell and Philip E. Converse, eds., *The Human Meaning of Social Change* (New York: Russell Sage Foundation, 1972), p. 87.

12. This is discussed in its historical context by Winthrop S. Hudson, *American Protestantism* (Chicago: University of Chicago Press, 1961), pp. 149–153. Also see Franklin H. Littell, *From State Church to Pluralism: A Protestant Interpretation of Religion in American History* (New York: Doubleday, 1962.)

13. The phrase describes religious movements spawned within Christendom in the latter Middle Ages. See Williston Walker, *A History of the Christian Church* (New York: Charles Scribner's Sons, 1959), pp. 225–242.

Index